Women in New Asia
Changing Social Roles

Women in New Asia
Changing Social Roles

M P Kumar

MD Publications Pvt Ltd
New Delhi
www.mdppl.com

Published by :

MD Publications Pvt Ltd
"MD House", 11, Darya Ganj,
New Delhi - 110 002
Phone : +91-11- 45355555
E-mail : contact@mdppl.com
Website: www.mdppl.com

ISBN : 978-81-7533-347-5

Published and Printed by Mr. Pranav Gupta on behalf of **MD Publications Pvt Ltd** at Repro India Limited.

Preface

Gender issues in South Asia represent a complex challenge. There has been a greater recognition of the problem across the region. In most countries women have experienced improved access to services and credit markets. However, despite the recent economic growth and changing social norms, dramatic gender inequities persist in South Asia. Addressing the inequities will require greater voice of women in the political decision-making of communities and states.

Women have been making great strides in society and the workplace. More and more young women are going to college and pursuing careers. Also be aware that in some cultures, Western women are considered "easy" and immoral. This notion was most likely created by the media portrayals that make it over to Asia.

The United Nations International Development Fund for Women (UNIFEM) noted in the year 2000 that women accounted for more than half of the work force in Asia, but their careers remain concentrated in social areas (14 percent), legal (9 percent), economics (4.1 percent), political affairs (3.4 percent) and executive (3.9 percent). Only 13 percent of women are in managerial and administrative posts, although experts recognize this as a significant increase in the past 20 years.

In spite of strong traditional views still held by many Asian societies, the advancement of women continues but these women are multi-tasking often logging very long working hours, bringing work home and even working on weekends and public holidays. After all, it is still a man's world with many men desperately holding onto traditional views of what a woman's role in society and the home should be. Also, many women continue to rank themselves third in importance, behind the husband and children. Women in Hong Kong still put in 63.3 hours a week of office work, (men 66.1 hrs), not including looking after the children, relatives and housework.

But success often comes at a price - young, educated Asian women are now finding it more difficult to get married or are marrying later and having fewer children. With better education come higher aspirations and many successful women refuse to marry down. Men, on the other hand, often are afraid of marrying a woman who is smarter, better educated, has more earning power, who talks back and most important of all, is not keen on motherhood.

As a result, many educated women opt out of the marriage game, to stay single and live either with their parents or in their own apartment. But with all the freedom and choice - marriage to a person of their choice, able to go to college and find high paying jobs - come new worries - health, life after retirement and how to continue to play an active role in society.

I am very grateful to Mr. Pranav Gupta, Director of MD Publications Pvt Ltd, New Delhi, for his kind cooperation and support for this book.

M P Kumar

Contents

1

Women and Change in Understanding Social Roles in New Asia

Today, the model minority myth and asexual media representations have emphasized the feminized Asian-American male. Yet, no empirical study has examined how Asian-American men construct their own masculinities. Toward this end, this study sought to examine: (a) how college-age Asian-American and white men express their masculinities, (b) how Asian-American and white women perceive Asian-American masculinities, and (c) how Asian-American men negotiate their gender expectations. Through quantitative analysis of surveys, we found that U.S.-born and immigrant Asian men view their masculinity as distinct from white hegemonic masculinity. Unlike white men, Asian-American men did not view their masculinity in opposition to their femininity.

Some Asian-American men, especially the U.S.-born, appeared to be creating a new, more flexible masculinity—one free from male dominance. U.S.-born Asian men linked their masculinity with certain caring characteristics and were the only men's group willing to do domestic tasks. Women viewed Asian-American men as having more traditional gender roles and being more nurturing, in contrast to their views of white men, which matched American norms of masculinity. Overall, these results contribute to the masculinity literature by showing how Asian-American men negotiate their contradictory positions as members of a privileged gender group and subordinate racial groups.

Changes in Asian-American heterosexual masculinity are of great interest within the Asian-American communities and to the general public. Historically, this racialized masculinity was both hyper-masculinized and desexualized as a way to limit economic and racial opportunities in the United States. While these dichotomous ideas about Asian-American masculinities are still pervasive, new articulations of what it means to be male, straight, and Asian American are affecting different Asian-American communities and interpersonal relationships at home and in workplaces. Issues of Asian-American masculinities are brought up in relation to interracial dating and marriage, expectations about supporting the family and community, sexual violence within the home and sexual harassment in public spaces, racial violence stemming from economic scapegoat and white supremacist ideology, mass media portrayals of Asian-American men, and complexities about ethnic identity and politics.

The present quantitative study uses survey data to examine, from a social psychological perspective, how college-age Asian-American and white men express their masculinities and how Asian-American and white women perceive Asian-American and white masculinities. This study also explores how Asian-American men conceive and negotiate their expectations about gender relations. This study contributes to our understanding of newer expressions of racial-ethnic masculinities by focusing on contemporary youth to expand the limited theoretical literature on Asian-American masculinity and by providing empirical evidence. There has been exciting fictional and artistic expressions of Asian-American masculinities but little quantitative analysis of these issues. Furthermore, this study enhances our understanding of racial-ethnic masculinities by focusing on changes in racial and gender power relations and expectations.

Masculinity is an important component in the social construction of gender relations. Gender refers to the material and ideological relations and consequences based on social distinction made from female and male physical differences. Gender expectation refers to a normative conception of appropriate attitudes and activities for a particular racialized and gendered group. Gender embodies relations of power. This distinction functions to create and maintain unequal power relations between people of different biological sexes and results in the domination and exploitation of women as a group. It is not biology but patriarchal social institutions, interactions, and practices that limit each sex to those characteristics and activities defined as feminine and masculine.

The ideas of what constitute masculinity and femininity are contingent on a given society and historical moment even though individuals are capable of the full range of abilities and emotions. No innate and universal gender qualities automatically accompany physical sex differences. In contrast, some believe gender qualities are strongly related to biological sex differences. These arguments rest on notions of racial and sexual superiorities. For instance, eugenicists like Rushton (1996) argue that Asians are more intelligent and less sexual than whites, who in turn are brighter and less sexual than blacks. They link race and masculinity to genetics, which we view as faulty arguments. This study is based on the former notion that gender embodies power. Sexist attitudes and actions valorize masculinity and accord men power and privileges. But if masculinities are socially constructed by and for each generation of men growing up rather then genetically inherited, then masculinities can change, and sexism in principle can be eradicated.

While masculinity is gendered, socially constituted, and intrinsically connected to power relations, it is also differentiated in its production, reproduction, and negotiation by everyone in society at the level of both group interactions and institutional practices. Masculinity is not one way of being for men; rather it takes a variety of forms. It is different for the working class and the upper class; for heterosexuals, gay men, and bisexuals; for blacks in Panama and in South Africa; and for the young and the elderly. Male masculinities are bound up with the complex weaving of race, sexuality, class, and other social distinctions used for domination and exploitation. Moreover, male masculinities also relate to the ways some men have power over other men.

White men used rape as a means of controlling and terrorizing black women during slavery, and the myth of the black male rapist was created to justify the lynching of black men. These events of rape and racism resulted in the social regulation of both black masculinity and femininity. However, these sexualized and racialized images never completely took hold, because when possible black men and women fought back against these images and acts of physical violence. These active struggles for control over their sexualized bodies offered possibilities to change gender relations.

For Asian-American men, the masculinity issue is about who one is and how one relates to family and relatives, loved ones, emotional partners, close friends, and acquaintances. It is also related to the ways one presents oneself to the world at the workplace, at school, in leisure situations, and other public gatherings. It is in these ways Asian-American men reproduce and negotiate gender relations with women and other men in their lives. In this section, we discuss the historical context shaping their masculinities attending to issues of power relations. Here we focus on heterosexual masculinities given the scope of this study. Historically, racialized immigration policies, labor practices, and media images helped shape and regulate previous Asian-American masculinities and affect present forms of these masculinities.

One set of practices involved the tension between recruitment and exclusion of Asian male laborers from 1850s to 1930s. On the one hand, these workers were recruited as a source of cheap labor to work in plantations, canneries, mines, and agricultural fields. On the other hand, hostility, race riots, and anti-Asian sentiments created an atmosphere of racial hatred against all Asians and resulted in the passage of race-based immigration laws and exclusionary policies. Moreover, the exclusionary policies were gendered by allowing a sizable number of Asian male laborers to enter, while restricting the entrance of Asian women, thus producing highly skewed sex ratios. Further, images of Asian people as members of inferior races, depraved heathens, opium addicts, and Yellow Peril invaders perpetuated popular media during this period. Not only did these images serve to heighten hostility against Asians in the U.S. and fuel the movement for their exclusion, these images also create lasting racialized Western narratives of the East and serve as one key justification for U.S. imperialist expansion into "foreign" lands.

These policies, practices, and images shape and regulate early Asian-American masculinities in several ways (Bulosan, 1946/1973; Espiritu, 1997; Okada, 1957/1976). The dominant society made these men to be perpetual outsiders, foreigners, different. Whites saw Asian-American men as treacherous, dirty, and criminals. They were viewed as sex-starved gangs of men lusting over white women, as potential rapists, and as hypersexualized invaders ready to produce Asian children in the U.S. if given the opportunity. They needed to be constantly monitored by employers, groups of white men, and the police to keep them docile and submissive.

IN TOURISM

The Government of Kerala has taken a policy decision to develop tourism. The tourism programme has grown very rapidly, as the figures for tourist arrivals in the state indicate. The growth has covered both inbound and outbound international tourism as well as the arrival of domestic tourists to Kerala. The Department of Tourism at the State level has also taken up Central Government projects and following from the National Action Plan, Kerala was the first state to identify a special tourism area, Bekal, to be developed with foreign investment into a big mass tourism project, to help India achieve its 5 million arrivals and access higher returns in foreign exchange. None of these developments have involved discussion and debate at the state or local level. These have been administrative decisions, and when the secretary, tourism was questioned on the undemocratic manner in which tourism decisions were taken, he saw the issue of tourism as beyond the comprehension of local people.

On the other hand, foreign experts were invited to suggest how and what kind of tourism should be developed in Kerala, which had very little exposure since the Kovalam Beach Resort never realised the potential of international arrivals, being overshadowed by Goa. Today, the tourism policy of the government visualises many new products and new players in the sphere of tourism. These include new beach resorts, hill and wildlife as the basis for adventure tourism, special tourism areas for intensive development, backwater cruising and festivals that package the culture and craft of Kerala for the benefit of the tourist. Every district now has a privately sponsored tourism festival, which often contravenes the Coastal Zone Regulation as it promotes tourism awareness.

The second aspect of the tourism policy is the dependence on the private sector to develop the infrastructure and the superstructure for tourism and its related activity. Today, the Kerala Government, Tatas and the Casino Group are the major players in tourism development and they have an understanding of tourism that does not look beyond the commercial aspect of tourism development. There is also the desire to invite foreign investment for large-scale development to increase the number of arrivals from abroad to enhance foreign exchange earnings. An intervention-in policy making by office bearers of local self government bodies who can function in the interest of local people is essential. This can be effective only when they have an enlightened awareness on the developmental options that the government offers to the people of the state.

When EQUATIONS began to acquaint itself with the Bekal development plan, it was surprising for us to learn that not a single panchayat opposed tourism development because the thrust of the government's propaganda was that tourism generated income and employment. Several studies relating to tourism development in Kerala indicate that the socio-cultural impacts of tourism have been very negative, particularly, relating to the issue of drugs and prostitution. Tourism projects have also displaced local people and affected their traditional occupations. The environmental impacts of tourism have also been negative particularly in the coastal zone and in the hills. Tourism needs regulation rather than promotion. Not only regulation, but the issue of tourism needs to be debated so that there are people-centered objectives rather than growth-centered objectives. Unless the people of Kerala arrive at some consensus on the kind of tourism they want to develop to achieve economic objectives, the control of outsiders, multinationals, international agencies and the monopoly houses in India will not end.

One area that needs to be focussed on is the issue of gender and tourism. Women panchayat members, being leaders of their communities, have the added task of familiarising themselves with the gender issues that emerge in the developmental debate, since most planners are male and most models are male dominated. India is a gendered society, which means that human relations in economic, social and cultural life, as well as in the political framework are determined and mediated by gendered perceptions. To clarify further, gender does not mean only the difference between men and women biologically but on their human relations being based on the status of women in society and therefore the perceptions of their social role and function. Tourism and the industry that supports it, as well as the administration that encourages its development, growth and expansion, is an interpersonal activity which is influenced by and in turn influences local and global gender perceptions. There is a list of global perceptions that have been researched, to develop a gender framework, for analysing developmental activity particularly tourism.

TOURISM AS A PART OF MODERN CONSUMERISM

Consumerism embodies social practices as well as signifies social change. As leisure time and wealth increase, tourism consumption also increases. As expansion reaches the remotest corners of the world, the marketing and consumption models between guests and hosts have indicated several possibilities for gender analysis. Power, control and equality in tourism are articulated through race, class and gender in the practice of tourism. Men and women through interconnected economic, political, cultural, social and environmental dimension., are involved in different ways in the construction and consumption of tourism. It is the recognition of these differing realities that shape tourism marketing, tourist motivation, and resident action. This process may be called the creation of stereotypes. For example, in all Asian societies where traditional society is intersecting with global economic systems, we have seen that the major public role of women in the tourism industry is in sex tourism. The faster the process of liberalisation and globalisation, the greater the spread of sex tourism.

TOURISM AS AN AID TO DEVELOPMENT

Women activists have always seen the statistical approach to tourism as apolitical. If tourism is seen as an activity that depends on leisure time and disposable income, then the enabling conditions are hierarchical and influenced by class and global economic strengths. In tourism advertising women are seen as passive, available and dependent. Women are thus sexual and exotic markers in the tourism brochure. Destinations reinforce this stereotype not only of the resident community as a whole (poor and ready to serve) but also of the women as inferior or as objects of gratification or as playthings.

TOURISM AND DIVISION OF LABOUR

Tourism, like other activities, perpetuates the international and domestic division of labour. This means that there are gendered employment activities (cooking, cleaning, serving, handicraft etc.) as well as control of waged work. There is also no computation of unpaid labour by women. The question that tourism raises is that women do not have leisure from certain types of work, and this compulsory, unpaid labour is extended to their working life as well as economic opportunity. Tourism encourages classifications like women's work.

TOURISM DEVELOPMENT AND ITS INFLUENCE ON CHANGING VALUE SYSTEMS

Tourism is an essentially modern activity that promotes 'tradition' as a unique and authentic product. In this process of commodification, not only is it important to define the other, but to define the gendered other. These changes are reflected in identification with tourist behaviour, changes in family systems age and sex hierarchies in the struggle for economic power as well as changes in the social and political status of different sexes in different classes and different production systems.

TOURISM AND ENVIRONMENT

What is our relationship to the environment, how do we use these resources, how can we regulate the consumption driven nature of tourism and how can traditional practices be documented and compared with the approach of providers of tourism services, is now being looked at. For example, it is suggested that as agriculture becomes less productive, tourism (rural, farm, beach or resort) becomes a valuable alternative because it allows a combination of domestic responsibilities of women (which are nurturing as well as reproductive), with tourism work, which is seen as an income source that can support small scale farming and thus conserve the countryside. Such an approach suggests that there is a need to change (through an external intervention) women's relationship with nature, the environment and their place in the ecological system.

Our perspective must include certain issues. For instance, the division between one who enters the business and earns an income from it and one who is displaced. The latter has to move away, adapt to a new location and find new survival strategies on how to access new resources. For example, tobacco, coconut harvesting, fish sorting and processing are women-dominated activities in Bekal. Tourism is a loss of income for them and does not use their traditional expertise. Neither does it provide them compensation or retraining or reemployment. Then there is the time element in tourism benefits trickling down. The deterioration of traditional communities and their activities is faster and the upward mobility slower.

This is because tourism is established for the high spenders and in the organised sector, rather than in the informal sector. Similarly, in the handicrafts production industry, market forces demand mechanisation, which results in the retrenchment of women workers, who are then shifted to finishing, which is lower paid. Soon this process is also mechanised and women have to look elsewhere for jobs. At the social level, tourism has forced middle class families to send their girls (aged 9-12 years) away from Kovalam, so that they are known as the Kovalam girls whom no one wishes to marry since the reputation of the beach resort for prostitution brings dishonour to the whole community. Honour of the family and the community in gendered societies rests in the chastity of the women of the household, the village or the township. Domestic tourism is also predominantly single male tourism, which encourages prostitution. Indian women are not encouraged to travel on their own.

Tourist behaviour is seen to be unsafe for women who are the repositories of the family's honour and the tourism process may bring dishonour. This need for safety and security is not met for women in Indian society although it is seen as the duty of the men in the family. The changes that tourism introduces benefit those sections that are a part of the new land use pattern. This is generally the educated, urban middle class. Since the middle class owns land, it recognises and promotes money as an indicator of status, aspiration etc. However, the landless, the poor and the small peasants are also looking for an opportunity, therefore they look at the panchayat plan and the for such openings. Rural women, though educated do not find the time or the money to attend courses or find employment in the travel trade.

They have to await the establishment of the services in the organised sector and then find employment at the lowest level. The policy and the People's Plan look at basic needs like roads, drinking water and have now included tourism, but there is no support in the policy for the informal sector in tourism. Similarly, when a district, like Wynad, is declared a tourism district by doing an audit of its resources for tourism, does the developer and the planner focus on the needs of the tribal, the migrant, the agriculturist, the plantation owner or the women who need an income supplement? Or is the focus on the tourist and the industry? What happens to the demands and needs of women and their role in development?

It is upon these questions that we need to focus on, bring in support for women's organisations and see that the tourism issue is put on their agenda and that we adopt their understanding on women's issues in our agenda. There is need, therefore, to build a data base and alliances with different sections of the government, the industry and social activists and concerned citizen groups to study the issue of tourism and debate the model being implemented in Kerala. Information and awareness is not only to be based on the motivations of the tourists and their need for services and products. It is to be based on the needs of the people and their perceptions of how tourism is to be developed and what benefits are to be derived.

We must also be made aware of the negative consequences of tourism. Finally, there is the issue of income generation as the only measure of development. Income, particularly in the case of tourism, is not stable, not under the control of the hosts, but manipulated by the trade. Secondly, income alone need not indicate growth or mobility because income is only one relation in the production-consumption process, and its impact on interconnected social issues need not be productive or liberating.

As far as the issue of foreign exchange earnings is concerned, one must examine how global economy and lifestyle affects the individual and the community. In what way does it to bring women more power, influence and prosperity? In what way does it bring freedom to them? Does income or foreign exchange change the gendered perceptions of society to transform the social position of women? Attempting to answer these questions and issues will be the first step in the direction of empowering panchayat women as they plan not only for today but also for the future because once the engines of tourism have been set in motion, it will be difficult to stop them.

IN FISHERIES

Women play significant roles in all aspects of fisheries—both in the artisanal, small-scale sector and in the commercial sector—roles that remain unarticulated and unrecognized. Importantly, women's roles span reproduction and production. Women's reproductive roles are essential for nurturing and sustaining families and communities, and ensuring food security through fishing, food foraging, farming and related activities. The productive roles of women in fishing—collecting seaweed and other aquatic resources, processing and marketing the fish catch, making and repairing nets and gears, baiting longlines, helping in the preparation for fishing trips and in unloading and sorting the fish—contribute significantly to household incomes and local economies. With the monetization of the fishing sector, the productive role of women has, in some cases, been extended to include new activities, previously forbidden by gender norms.

For instance, in some regions more women go fishing with their husbands or with other groups of women. In several countries of the North women are part of the commercial fishing sector, working as crew or skippers on industrial or family-owned vessels. Women also form a significant proportion of the workforce in industrial fish processing within the organized and unorganized sector, working for wages to sort, clean and process fish. The accompanying increase in work and incomes has not always resulted in increase in women's status within families and communities. Often, in keeping with prevailing patriarchal norms, the control of resources remains vested in men. In many cases, diversification and increase in roles has only meant an increase in women's labour.

The papers in this section provide descriptive, detailed and in cases, ethnographic information on the work women do in fisheries, and the impact of changes within the sector on women's work and roles in the fisheries. Governments in developing countries are increasingly involved in outsourcing: contracting out to a third party the provision of goods or services which could otherwise be provided by the client organisation. We can characterise two quite different models used, each of which has some potential shortcomings. Some governments use what we might call "workfare outsourcing": employment schemes for poor citizens often paid on a daily basis and focused on public works projects. Examples include the Employment Guarantee Scheme used in India's Maharashtra state and Argentina's Trabajar programme.

These have undoubtedly delivered important poverty alleviation benefits. The shortcomings of this approach, though, may include problems of sustainability, difficulty of application to urban poverty (schemes have tended to be rural and seasonal, focused on the agricultural "lean period"), and the failure to create any institutional basis for enterprise and independent income-generation. There are also accusations corrupt diversion of funds, and of creating public works assets that are ultimately damaging rather than beneficial to the poor.

At the other extreme is what we might call "commercial outsourcing": competitive contracting out of internal and external services to private sector firms. Examples include outsourcing of information technology (IT) services by the Barbados government and outsourcing of solid waste management by Kampala City government. The shortcomings of this approach may include the subjugation of public service values and goals to profit-seeking, and a loss of public sector control and accountability. Outsourcing has also been politically unpopular with public sector trade unions.

One may see workfare outsourcing as driven by a developmental and poverty reduction agenda seeking to deliver equity goals. One may see commercial outsourcing as driven by a neo-liberal and new public management agenda seeking to deliver efficiency and effectiveness goals. Both can, of course, also be seen to be driven by a political agenda and political goals, claimed to run from vote-banking to union-bashing to corruption to career enhancement. Partly because of the problems associated with both workfare and commercial outsourcing, governments are showing an increasing interest in a hybrid form – "social outsourcing": contracting out the provision of goods or services to a social enterprise.

In the UK, a number of local governments have outsourced activities such as leisure centre management, care services, and community transportation to social enterprises. There are also examples of social outsourcing by private sector firms, such as the "social offshoring" of IT services to firms like Digital Divide Data in Cambodia. And there are examples of social outsourcing by NGOs, such as use by international NGOs of social enterprises for printing or mailing activities.

RESEARCH QUESTION, METHOD AND FRAMEWORK

But is this aspiration met in reality? In particular can social outsourcing by government deliver the development benefits that other forms of outsourcing sometimes struggle to provide? In order to answer this question, we undertook a case study of the Kudumbashree initiative set up in India by the Kerala State Poverty Eradication Mission (SPEM). Kudumbashree began formally in 1999. It initially focused on the assisted formation of a series of women's self-help groups around the state, based on two successful pilots run during the 1990s; first in Alappuzha municipality, and then in Malappuram district.

These self-help groups were initially seen as performing a social development role but this was soon expanded to encompass savings/credit functions. They were then seen as the potential nucleus for economic activity. Building from this, the self-help groups have been used to stimulate the formation of more than 50,000 micro-enterprises since 1999: both rural and urban, both group and individual. Within this overall picture, the focus here is on group enterprises in urban areas of which there were 1,345 by 2006 set up through support from the central government's Development of Women and Children in Urban Areas scheme. These are seen as social enterprises because they fulfil the three criteria for a social enterprise: they are enterprise-oriented; they have social as well as business aims (such as encouraging savings, alleviating poverty and addressing female unemployment); and they are socially-owned in the sense that they are co-operatively owned by women from poor communities.

These 1,345 social enterprises cover a wide range of activities such as clothing production, food processing and direct marketing. Our particular focus was on the 234 IT sector enterprises that have been set up. This focus came partly because the average annual double-digit growth of the IT sector worldwide provides significant general opportunities in this sector; partly because IT outsourcing from governments is a multi-billion-dollar activity annually, thus providing a specific business opportunity for IT enterprises. Field research was undertaken in collaboration with a local partner, Planet Kerala. It began with pilot interviews and enterprise "case sketches" in January 2005 and then proceeded to a broader set of data gathering activities that was completed in January 2006:

- Group interviews with the women members of 32 IT social enterprises, used mainly to build up detailed case studies of each enterprise;
- Structured interviews conducted with 133 individual women working in IT enterprises, focused particularly on the livelihood impacts of their work;
- Unstructured life-story sessions completed by six women from the IT enterprises, used as a source of broader background and contextual factors; and
- Four semi-structured interviews with SPEM officials.

In addition, observational data and documentary evidence (such as annual audit figures) was gathered during visits to the IT enterprises and, in September 2005, a set of feedback sessions and visits was organised. In order to answer our main question about the development benefits of social outsourcing, a natural point of departure was poverty. Of late, discussions on poverty have moved on from understanding this merely in terms of income, to understanding the *multidimensionality* of poverty. Perhaps the most well-known conceptual model drawing from the new perspective of multidimensionality is the Sustainable Livelihoods (SL) framework (DFID 1999).

For the work reported here, we chose to focus on a subset of components within the SL model, taking an assets–vulnerability approach of the type that has been used previously for work on women and anti-poverty initiatives. This approach starts with an identification of what the poor have (in terms of a multidimensional view of assets which can be deployed to reduce poverty and vulnerability) rather than what they do not have (such as baseline monetary indicators) and so it "contributes to the development of analytical tools to facilitate those interventions which promote opportunities, as well as removing key obstacles". It incorporates the notion of vulnerability as a dynamic, contextual concept which captures change processes and which can be linked to the ability of the poor to own and manage assets to promote livelihoods.

Assets are thought of not simply in tangible terms, such as physical tools but also in terms of intangible items such as social relations. Our pilot work suggested that four of the five main SL framework classes of assets would be relevant:

- *Human capital* represents the skills, knowledge, ability to labour and good health that together enable women to pursue different livelihood strategies and achieve their livelihood objectives.
- *Financial capital* denotes the financial resources that women use to achieve their livelihood including available stocks which can be held in several forms such as cash, bank deposits, liquid assets like livestock and jewellery, or resources obtained through credit-providing institutions;

and regular inflows of money, including earned income, pensions, other transfers from the state, and remittances.

- *Physical capital* comprises the basic infrastructure and producer goods needed to support livelihoods.
- *Social capital* is the genre of social resources which women draw upon in pursuit of their livelihood objectives; mainly conceived as networks and relationships based on trust, reciprocity and exchanges.

Although we did ask questions about the fifth asset - *natural capital* - it did not emerge as a factor directly associated with work in an IT sector enterprise. On the other hand, the issue of empowerment - what one might in broad terms define as *political capital* - was a frequent theme of interviewees, and we therefore substituted this for natural capital.

SOCIAL OUTSOURCING OF IT SERVICES IN KERALA

Social outsourcing, like any outsourcing, requires a conjunction of demand and supply. Demand was provided in Kerala as a result of the state's IT strategy which, in part, has sought to promote computerisation of government activities, to develop the IT sector in Kerala, and to increase the IT skills base of the state through training. Demand and opportunity have been assisted by specific decisions, such as a 1999 court ruling that mandated some computerisation within local councils (*panchayats*). Like most governments worldwide, that in Kerala faced an internal supply constraint; both a lack of staff with IT skills capable of supporting the planned computerisation and training programmes, and a retention problem - that staff who gained IT skills were tempted to leave for the private sector.

External outsourcing has been seen as a solution to such supply problems, and there were private sector IT services firms operating in Kerala that could have been called upon. However, officials in SPEM decided to adopt a different approach, answering the demand via the creation of IT-oriented social enterprises under the Kudumbashree initiative. Starting with just one or two pilot enterprises in 1999, this approach fairly quickly developed a standard business model. Support is provided to bring together a group of (typically ten) unemployed women from below-poverty-line households. They are nominated or occasionally invited from the self-help groups; sometimes from a single group, sometimes from two or three neighbouring groups.

They must each be able to invest US$30, something – at least during initial days of uncertainty about the viability of IT enterprises – that excluded some of the poorest or more risk-averse participants. Government then supplies a grant of ten times the total amount of the group's investment, and helps secure a matching amount as a bank loan. The women thus typically register their cooperative enterprise with starting capital of roughly US$6,000 of which half must be repaid.

As noted above 234 of these IT social enterprises have been created since 1999, and they operate in three main areas:

- IT training: 151 of the enterprises work mainly on IT training. Almost all are attached to a state secondary school, with their computer equipment in a classroom, and most of their work involves the paid training of school children, with some after-hours/vacation-time training of others such as local community members.
- Data entry and digitisation: 80 of the enterprises do data entry work that mainly supports computerisation of government; for example, digitising the state's voter records or entering and helping process the results of a state-wide poverty survey.
- PC assembly and maintenance: an activity of just three of the women's enterprises, who build PCs from parts, sell them (mainly to public sector organisations) and arrange annual maintenance.

The digitisation enterprises operate largely on the most straightforward outsourcing basis. Tenders are issued by government departments for the data entry and processing work they need to undertake. Bids are received from the social enterprises and from competing private sector providers, and a contract is issued to the winning bidder. Similarly, there is open competition for the supply of PCs. The IT training units work on a rather different basis. Discussions are held with individual secondary schools to see if they wish to have a training enterprise attached to their school; typically if they lack either the human or IT resources necessary to undertake IT training. If they agree, an enterprise is assigned to the school and training work is outsourced but there is no open tender for this business.

THE LIVELIHOODS IMPACT OF SOCIAL OUTSOURCING

Having provided the background, we can now turn to the originally-posed question and outline findings on the impact for women enterprise members of involvement in this social outsourcing project. It should be noted that this analysis relates only to the core women members of each IT cooperative, of whom there were roughly 1,500. However, these IT enterprises also significantly affect other poor women and men indirectly: those employed for additional work (an estimated 2,500 women); those whose good and services are purchased through the earned income of the core women members; and members of the core-group households and wider families.

Financial Capital: almost every enterprise was achieving the goal of providing its members with an income of at least US$1 per day. Although a relatively limited sum, this was seen to have made a significant difference to the lives of the women surveyed. In just over half of cases, this income represented 50% or more of total household income and, in a few cases, it was the sole source of household income (for example, single women living with elderly parents).

Some of the money was spent on everyday household expenditure but the value of the income was more often reported in relation to exceptional items: purchase of healthcare when family members had been ill; funding of educational expenses; paying for land purchase or house construction; redeeming loans or items such as gold jewellery that had been pawned; paying for the marriages of family members. In the case of almost every woman interviewed, it was this income that was seen to have been the main benefit delivered by social outsourcing and the main factor in reducing the vulnerabilities they had previously suffered. The presence of an income had allowed some women to join savings schemes or to take out individual loans. In addition, 75 per cent of the enterprises studied had paid off their initial loan, some within two or three years of start up despite it being originally offered as a five-year loan, and some had taken further loans to update or expand their IT infrastructure.

Income from the enterprises may be the main source of vulnerability reduction but it does bring its own vulnerabilities that stem from the source of this income: outsourcing from public sector organisations. One issue – listed by every surveyed enterprise group as one of its main challenges – is the irregularity and delay in payments received. Enterprises sometimes had to wait three, six, even twelve months to receive payment for services or goods provided. The cash flow problems created were such that some women had resorted to pawning gold items in order to ensure that loan repayments were made on time. A second issue, discussed further below, is the sustainability of this income source over time.

Human Capital

The Keralan population has higher levels of education than found in areas with equivalent income levels thanks to its particular institutional history, even though there are limited opportunities for the employment of the competencies thereby created. Hence, the women working in the IT enterprises typically had up to ten years of education prior to joining; many had basic typing skills as well. Despite this comparatively high starting level of human capital, work in the IT enterprises had enabled the women to strengthen this asset yet further. This has happened most clearly in relation to technical skills: all had built up computer operational skills but many had specialisms around computer troubleshooting or networking.

Particular roles within the group - leader, deputy leader, secretary - were rotated to allow a spread of managerial and supervisory skill development. Entrepreneurship skills were rather harder to pin down: about half of those questioned did not feel they had built up such skills but others did recognise the way in which they now had a much better understanding of basic enterprise issues: balance sheets, cash flow, customer relations, etc.

Physical Capital

Investment in physical capital varied but a typical pattern has been for an initial IT investment of around US$5,000 for five computers, a printer and software that was subsequently doubled, after two-three years, to ten computers. These assets are cooperatively-owned but they mean that each woman has a work-related asset worth the equivalent of something like two years' income. This can therefore form useful collateral for additional loans. However, the pace of technical change quickly erodes this value since all IT assets, whether hardware or software, depreciate to near zero worth within about five years. Mirroring this, there must be continuous investment to replenish these assets.

Social Capital

Because of its intangibility, changes in social capital did not seem to be particularly well recognised by the women surveyed. The majority of individuals did not identify significant changes to any of the three main relations that women in business may forge: business linkages to suppliers and customers; social and community linkages; and other institutional linkages such as those to supporting or regulatory institutions. However, when asked directly and collectively about such changes, many more did become apparent. All the interviewed groups identified important new linkages they had forged to public officials; particularly those in the State Poverty Eradication Mission and in local government offices.

These were typically a combination of business and institutional linkages since SPEM itself often acted as an intermediary between the IT enterprises and both their suppliers (of hardware, software, training and even some loans) and their public sector customers (though in other cases the women were in direct contact with their customers). Dominance of the public sector was reflected by the relative lack of private sector contacts which most women felt they had built up. There was little recognition of changes to social and community linkages except for the key linkages women had forged with the other core members of their own enterprise.

Political Capital/Empowerment

Women described their empowerment in terms of changing self-identity and status. They talked constantly about their new confidence - in tackling problems, in approaching institutions, in dealing with other people. They talked too about respect, recognition and acceptance in their communities - not simply because of having a job but because of having an IT-related job: something associated with modernity and progress. Change in gender relations was less clear. These women were taking on traditionally male (e.g. management) roles; some were hiring and managing men as employees; some were breaking away from traditional female goals of security and stasis to push for growth in their enterprises.

However, men still filled the pivotal roles in the State Poverty Eradication Mission and as local government customers. There remained a degree of deference to fathers or husbands as ultimate decision makers in the household. And women's triple role - wife/mother, worker, community member - constantly came to the surface as women described their own aspirations and the expectations of others around them.

Sustainability

Several of these social enterprises have been running for more than six years, and the great majority for more than four - longer than the average lifespan of an IT small enterprise. However, questions still arise about the sustainability of this social outsourcing initiative around three main aspects:

- *Membership*: the average number of core members in the surveyed enterprises was seven: less than ten because women drop out due to marriage or taking a new job. In only one or two cases, though, has this loss of members seemed to jeopardise the enterprise: most groups simply replace lost members with other employees.
- *Support*: development of these social enterprises has required a significant degree of institutional support from government departments, banks, other financial intermediaries, and other local organisations. The social enterprises may find it difficult to sustain themselves without ongoing intervention and support. Having said this, they have moved beyond the start-up phase and there is a solid network of different small enterprise support institutions that could be called upon to provide finance, training, etc. if any individual institution stopped providing support.
- *Markets*: the intervention of a single institution - SPEM - has been critical in providing access to markets and it remains a key intermediary in the location of and interaction with public sector customers for many enterprises. Action taken on disintermediation of SPEM includes more direct response to tenders by IT enterprises, the taking on of private sector customers, and the planned creation of a separate body that could provide marketing and support services for the enterprises. There are also concerns about loss of market. Some IT enterprises, for example, are diversifying into call centre and data analysis work in case the pace of digitisation work slackens.

In all, there are some concerns about sustainability but they are not yet an overriding issue and they must be balanced against a recognition of the outcomes that any unsustainability cannot take away. Even in the inconceivable event that all these IT social enterprises were to cease operations, this could not remove the household assets already purchased: land, housing, gold, education for children, healthcare for family members, marriage; etc. In addition, there are assets that the women can take forward into future employment.

When asked about this, they mentioned the more obvious and tangible items: their computers and software and, even more "time-proofed", their computing knowledge and skills. Almost all mentioned two other factors: their "team spirit", with a widespread assumption that their cooperative group would continue to work together as a social enterprise in any new venture and, most frequently mentioned, aspects of empowerment, particularly the self-esteem and self-confidence that are central to the success of new business ventures.

This is an initiative that demonstrates social outsourcing can be used to bring direct benefits to members of poor communities in developing countries. These are not the most excluded or the absolute poorest of the poor and they have received an education but there is no sleight of hand here: these are women who had no job, who came from below-poverty-line households, most of which were scraping by on US$1 per day or less. Through social outsourcing they have undergone an experience of change that is centrally about empowerment. In part this has been the empowerment of accessing new assets: new skills, new income, new physical assets, new contacts. But just as much this has been a story of psycho-social empowerment: new attitudes, new confidence, new status, new roles and new identity.

Of course, the Kudumbashree project comes with caveats: ongoing vulnerabilities, introduced vulnerabilities, questions of sustainability, uncertainties about comparative benefits of alternative livelihood pathways. But these should be seen as question marks rather than fatal flaws. This is not a study in perfection but it does demonstrate that social outsourcing can touch and improve the lives of the poor over a sustained period of several years. In looking to broader conclusions, some care must be taken because of the importance of context.

Kerala is characterised by a particular institutional history of government, civil society and culture; the women involved were poor and jobless but educated; a strong public sector market for digitisation and training created a window of opportunity for this type of activity; there was a political will to allow outsourcing to be shaped by developmental goals; and individuals - notably TK Jose, the Executive Director of Kudumbashree - have been pivotal to creating and sustaining the initiative. Nonetheless, social outsourcing has delivered sufficient benefits to warrant greater attention by other governments.

We have described here its developmental benefits. But government departments report positive feedback on achieving their IT goals at low cost. And the initiative's political credentials have ensured its survival despite changes of government in Kerala in 2001 and 2006. Overall, social outsourcing shows how business and development can be brought together. Poverty reduction and empowerment are being achieved through social outsourcing not by rejecting business but by embracing it: by creating new enterprises; by seeking to create new entrepreneurs; and by demonstrating how small business can deliver development goals.

2

Patterns of Social Change in a Burmese Family

There have been remarkable increases and demographic shifts in the Burmese populations along the Thai-Burma border region over the past several years, which appear to have accelerated since 1995-96. While refugee populations in the established camps have remained relatively stable these populations are now a minority of those in need of health services, food security, and protection from rights abuses. The larger and growing populations include Burmese migrant workers to Thailand in factory and agricultural sectors, newly arrived refugees without formal refugee status, internally displaced persons (IDPs) inside Burma, Burmese sex workers, and Burmese urban residents in Thai cities and towns, including Mae Sot in Thailand's Tak Province and surrounding areas.

The Thai Ministry of the Interior admitted that there were roughly 1 to 1.2 million Burmese migrants in Thailand by 1998, although official estimates are lower, and registered Burmese migrant workers number less than 250,000. In the Mae Sot area alone the non-governmental agency World Vision has documented 72 known factories with an estimated population of 50,000 workers, many of whom have families with them. Agricultural migrants are the most difficult to quantify, but include at least 100,000 Shans in upper northern Thailand, and another 100,000 Burmese further south, according to the Burma Border Consortium. The estimate of

IDPs in the Thai-Burma zone on the Burmese side is 400,000 persons according to several non-governmental organizations (NGOs) working along the border. Urban residents and those working in service jobs and as domestics are another large population difficult to assess and will not be addressed in this report.

While the numbers of both internally displaced persons and migrants to Thailand has grown, the demographic shifts have been perhaps more marked than the absolute numbers. Populations crossing to Thailand now include many more whole families with the elderly and children than in the past, and more of the migrants are not from areas of ethnic insurgency (such as the Karen or Shan areas); they are urban and rural Burmese from areas including Moulmein and Thaton in Mon State, the Irrawaddy Divisions, Bassein, and from as far as Arakan. These populations are overwhelmingly civilians, and many have fled from Burma since 1995, and significantly, since 1997.

These new migrants have placed tremendous burdens on the health care system along the border, which was established primarily to provide services to the generation of students who fled after the 1988 uprising and ethnic insurgents and their families. The earlier model was field-based care for young people involved in armed struggle. The needs now are much more centered on maternal and child health, family planning services, care of the old and chronically ill, and provision of health services to impoverished families employed or partially employed in the Thai agricultural and manufacturing sectors.

The internally displaced population in this same period has expanded to an estimated 400,000 persons in the Thai-Burma zone, and an unknown number in widely dispersed areas including the Naga Hills, the Chin States, Arakan, and central Burma. What little is known concerning IDPs is best understood in the Shan and Karen areas, and this is due, at least in part, to the information and organizational capability provided by non-cease-fire groups. The health and humanitarian challenges for these populations are staggering, and the unmet health needs diverse and changing.

The constraints under which such services must currently be provided are also many and varied. Virtually all the groups in Thailand are vulnerable to local security concerns; providing services to IDPs in the context of the Burmese civil conflict is fraught with security and operational challenges; and Burmese program staff in either setting face security concerns similar to the people they serve. Harassment, fines, and detention by Thai authorities continue to complicate the lives and work of all concerned with providing services to these groups.

BORDER AREA POPULATIONS

FACTORY WORKERS

In the Mae Sot area of Tak Province there has been extensive development of factories and light manufacturing shops based on the availability of cheap Burmese labor. According to World Vision, which is operating an HIV education program in the factories, Mae Sot district now has 72 known factories and sweatshops employing an estimated 50,000 workers. Sectors include garments, canning, light manufacturing, and parts assembly. Most factories are closed to inspection and maintain on-site housing for Burmese illegal workers. The evaluation team visited several large sweatshops in this industrial zone to assess the health and humanitarian status of workers.

The first was a large Thai-owned canning complex with approximately 2,000 workers and their families. Management stated that 20% of the workers were Thai and the remainder Burmese. Of the 30 or family members the team met, all were Burmese (ethnic Burman or Mon) from urban/rural areas in southern Burma. All of the Burmese came to Thailand illegally, are fearful of arrest, and thus live on site. Workers were living in four barn-like structures and a number of bamboo and tin shacks. This housing was intensely overcrowded, with families living in cardboard or plywood divisions within the barns, each roughly 8 by 10 foot square. Lighting, ventilation, cooking space, sewage, and water were grossly inadequate, with open sewage running through the lower slope barns. About 500 families were living in each barn. Workers earn between 40-50 baht per day and are required to work overtime when necessary. Overtime pay is five baht per hour, about 15 US cents.

A mother of five whose husband worked in the factory (a Burmese family from Tavoy) said these wages allowed her to buy meat about twice a month. The family survived on rice and vegetables (bought from the owner) and was unable to save. The team was not permitted to visit the factory working areas, but did visit an on-site school. This was built by the Thai owner and was free for the Thai children—the workers' families had to contribute to pay for a Burmese teacher, which they were doing. Only elementary education was available. Nearly all children over 12 years were out of school and working. Major health problems were associated with the lack of access to care.

Burmese workers fear arrest and fines if they leave the compound and are thus afraid to visit local health facilities. Typical fines are 3,000 baht to avoid a month's jail time, or about 75 days' pay. None of the persons interviewed could speak any Thai, further limiting access to Thai facilities. Drug and treatment costs were another barrier. Health problems included childhood illnesses, respiratory and diarrheal diseases, and complications of unsafe abortions—an outcome of lack of access to family planning. Younger women described fear of rape and sexual harassment from male management and senior staff; sexual advances many cannot refuse for fear of losing employment. Indeed, many of the Burmese "sex workers" identified at local clinics are women in factories, and they make up a significant component of the recent, steep rise in septic abortion cases presenting at Mae Tao Hospital.

The owner of this complex reportedly had extensive canning factories in other areas in Thailand but has moved all operations to Mae Sot in the past several years due to the availability of so much cheap and compliant Burmese labor. The second site visited was a large complex of garment sweatshops on the Thai side of the Moei River. This was a Taiwanese-owned complex which had been built as a condominium development. The ground levels were converted to sweatshops, with upper levels housing ten workers per room. There were approximately 3000 workers in the complex. In contrast to the closed canning factory, this complex housed largely young single Burmese workers, about 75% of whom were women.

Virtually all workers interviewed were ethnic Burmans. Salaries were in the 40-60 baht per day range, depending on experience. While this population was considerably healthier, and reported adequate salaries for single people to survive and send small remittances to families in Burma, the same issues of fear of arrest, inability to speak Thai, and sexual abuse by management prevailed. The complex had a brothel on-site where local men could access the workers. Women reported essentially no ability to refuse sexual favors to management, and abortion is a common form of pregnancy prevention. A smuggling dock was within walking distance of the complex, so these workers could, and did, visit family in Burma when able. The clothes are manufactured for the "Old Navy" brand sold in the US.

There is apparently considerable local Thai antagonism toward this complex because the revenues and tax income leave the country and the complex generates few jobs for local residents. Thai authorities resent the health burdens placed upon them by the large population of workers. in both settings voiced consistent reasons for coming to Thailand, including the burden of forced labor for SPDC [State Peace and Development Council] that has made life economically non-viable for Burmese in numerous areas; fear of forced conscription into the SPDC military among young men and their families; burdens of corrupt officials and local military commanders and their demands for money and/or labor;

confiscation or theft of food, livestock, and lands by local military. Few reported histories of any political involvement as reasons for fleeing; however these persons tended to be the most harassed. Virtually all of them told accounts of arrest, imprisonment, torture, and beatings.

AGRICULTURAL MIGRANTS

This is a very large, widely dispersed, mobile and difficult-to-reach population. In the northern area the great majority of farm laborers are Shans, estimated by the Shan Human Rights Foundation at over 100,000. The majority live in huts or converted barns on farmland in small hidden settlements. Their living is much more seasonal and uncertain than that of and their security issues are much more acute. The health problems of this huge population include malaria, particularly among men; pesticide exposures; vaccine preventable childhood illnesses; and diarrheal diseases. About 75% of admissions for severe malaria at Mae Sot Hospital are male migrant farm laborers. Demographic patterns among these migrants have significantly changed.

Before 1996-97, the majority was single adults or young couples. Recent migrants (1997-99) are generally multi-generational families with dependents. In contrast to seasonal migrants in the past, these new migrants generally cannot, and do not, return to Burma in the off-season. Among the Shans, many reported having lost their homes, land and livestock through the SPDC forced resettlement policies of the past four years. In the Shan areas there are essentially no health services for the majority of migrants. The team visited two migrant settlements in the agricultural belt of southern Tak Province. The first was a series of shacks and one converted barn hidden off a dirt track on a large Thai orchard estate. This was home to about 300 families, a mixed Burman and Mon community, mostly from Moulmein, Bassein, and Pegu.

The housing was cardboard and rice sacks stretched over bamboo frames, there was no electricity or running water, and the compound was extraordinarily over-crowded. Again, this was a settlement almost entirely of whole families, with grandparents doing childcare while older children and other adults worked in the fields. Income varied from 30-50 baht per day, depending on the laborer and the availability of work. These were survival wages only, allowing no opportunity to save. Malnutrition was less of an issue however, than among children in the factories, as these families can forage in forest tracts and gather some wild foods in these areas. We interviewed two older adults recently released from prison in Burma. The first was an National League for Democracy township activist in his sixties from lower Burma who had escaped with his entire family after release from his third jail term.

He reported repeated beatings, torture, and chronic malnutrition in prison, and the total impoverishment of his family for his political activities. He was unable to work and was supported by grown children working on the farm. The second was a Mon grandmother from Moulmein, who had fled two months before with two grown daughters, both of whom had also served prison sentences. This woman, and both daughters, had been jailed for two years and fled shortly after their releases. She was also the mother of two sons, both of whom were active in the 1988 uprising and had then joined the armed resistance. One was killed in battle in 1992 against SLORC [State Law and Order Restoration Council] forces.

The second, an ABSDF [exile student organization] member, returned to Burma in 1995 under a promised amnesty, but was immediately pursued by SLORC. The junta arrested his mother and sisters, detained them for two years, and released them only after the son's capture and death in detention. The mother reported frequent beatings and verbal abuse during her incarceration. Her elderly husband, who required care for chronic illness, died during her detention, as did a grandchild. The family lost their home and land during the detention. The surviving family was now living in a cardboard shack. The mother appeared to have a severe case of Post-Traumatic Stress Disorder.

The second settlement visited was a community of 120 families living on a rice and orchard plantation. This community was 18 months old, and composed of two groups of Mon, one from Moulmein and one from Thaton, who had fled since 1997. Again, burdens of forced labor and corrupt officials had led to their impoverishment in Burma. Many reported that they had lost their land and livelihood since the Mon cease-fire and could no longer survive in their home areas. Due to a compassionate Thai owner, this group was living in marginally better conditions, with access to running water, adequate food, and some degree of protection from local authorities while on site.

INTERNALLY DISPLACED PERSONS

The Burmese civil conflict and the policies of the SPDC toward ethnic peoples, most notably the forced relocation and forced resettlement of many populations in the ethnic Shan, Karen, and Karenni areas, have led to large numbers of internally displaced persons within Burma. Little is known about IDPs in other areas distant from the Thai border, although there are recent reports from India of Naga IDPs there. Many of the Thai-Burma region IDPs are villagers who have fled or been driven out of their home communities and survive in hiding, living in forest or hill tracts to avoid detection. They live without security, regular food, or access to medical services, and many are in heavily land-mined areas. These are arguably the neediest and most difficult-to-access populations in the current Burmese Diaspora.

An indigenous program to provide services to these groups has been under development since 1995, using a mobile medical team approach. These teams, with several medics, were eventually found to be too large, and had difficulty reaching many isolated IDP areas. To respond to these needs, local medical groups, in collaboration with several ethnic organizations, developed a new model and program based on backpack health workers. There are currently 50 such backpack health workers serving IDPs, with a target service population of 100,000 persons. Training for 60 more such workers will begin this year. Fourteen people participated in an evaluation of the Backpack Program, including the management team and seven backpack health workers. Several constraints were voiced by the group. These included:

- Security of IDPs and health workers

This is the major challenge. Threats include the Burmese military, landmines, bandits active in IDP areas, and security concerns while moving within Thailand. Among the 50 workers in the first group to work inside Burma this year, one backpack worker was killed by a landmine while assisting the IDP community he was serving to flee from an SPDC attack. A second was arrested by SPDC authorities while trying to reach a Karen IDP site. His fate is currently unknown.

- Disease rates and severity

Several workers brought up issues related to the very high disease and injury rates among the IDPs, including malaria, diarrheal diseases, obstetric emergencies, and landmine and other war-related injuries. In addition to high disease rates, severity, often due to lack of early or appropriate care, is a further challenge.

- Community participation and support

The backpack teams must rely on community participation and support to identify cases, transport patients, provide space for treatment, and bring members together for health promotion and education sessions. In areas where strong ethnic, youth, or women's organizations exist and function, these relationships appear active and effective. However, where they do not exist, backpack workers have had to do considerable grassroots organizing to mobilize communities.

- IDPs in jungle/forest areas

Several workers discussed the grave difficulties of providing services to displaced villagers hiding in forest areas. These groups appear to be in the most severe health situations, with widespread malnutrition and under-nutrition, chronic insecurity, and high exposure to forest illnesses, including malaria and other infectious diseases. Most survive on bamboo shoots and other forest foods markedly lacking in protein.

These groups are generally villagers who have been targeted for forced relocation programs but do not want to leave their lands. They move into hiding in forest tracks, generally near their home villages, and attempt to evade SPDC patrols. In several Karen areas Democratic Karen Buddhist Army (DKBA) irregulars working with SPDC are a significant threat. In both Shan and Karen areas bandit gangs looting abandoned villages are also a major security threat. All three groups, SPDC, DKBA, and bandit gangs, regularly target grain stores and livestock for their supply needs in forest areas, further impoverishing these IDPs.

Morbidity and mortality are extremely high. With the exception of indigenous healers, the backpack teams are currently the only health care providers available to these populations. SPDC health services have little or no penetration in most areas and are widely feared by locals. In a few cases IDP areas do have SPDC supported health workers, however, they appear to have no supplies or medications and have, on several occasions, come to the backpack teams requesting essential drugs. The team visited one large IDP settlement. This was a community of about 5,200 people drawn from three Karen villages.

The three source communities had been attacked and burnt down by Burmese-backed troops in a January-February 1999 systematic campaign. Community members and village headmen were unable to say whether this was done by SPDC alone or by SPDC with DKBA support. They had no explanations for these attacks and village burnings. Community members maintained some links to their home villages, and men were visiting their homes with some regularity to collect food. The area between their new settlement and their home villages was heavily land mined early this year, presumably to prevent their return.

At the time of our visit, one man had just been killed by a mine after tending to his cattle. Security for this community was provided by Karen National Union(KNU) troops active in the area. Villagers were adamant that they did not want to leave their land or livestock and move to Thailand as refugees. Food security is the major concern, as the community is unable to grow enough food for the existing population, and about 100 persons a month were continuing to arrive from SPDC attacked areas. Malaria is the other principal health threat. This settlement was a forest area seven months before and is heavily malarial.

POLICY OPTIONS

The past three to four years have seen an increase in the number of internally displaced persons in Burma, increasing migration to Thailand, and a dramatic shift in the demographics of migrants from young adults to multi-generational families. These changes appear to be the result of cumulative effects of the political, humanitarian, and economic crisis in Burma. In ethnic areas including the Shan and Karen regions, forced population transfers, village burnings, and military assaults on ethnic communities have driven hundreds of thousands of minority people from their homes. Another large and growing migrant population appears to be urban and rural Burmese from southern areas, particularly Mons and Burmans from the southern and coastal regions. These groups have been forced to flee largely due to the additive effects of demands for forced labor, heavy corruption, taxation, impoverishment, and theft or confiscation of property, livestock and land.

Paired recurring themes among migrants from all areas are the impossibility of survival for their families under the current regime in Burma and the intense desire to go home, if and when this is possible. For those in Thailand, the fear and real threat of arrest and harassment by Thai authorities make their lives ones of constant insecurity. For IDPs, the struggle to survive in zones of political, military, and criminal insecurity is constant and precarious. It is clear that Burmese migrants and the availability of the very cheap and controllable labor they provide is driving the creation of a new economy in the border region. This has, to some extent, allowed for the survival of these migrants. However, given the current situation, these workers are bound to a system of poverty, debt, and very limited educational opportunity or hope for their children and the future.

Clearly, the long-term principal policy option for addressing this wide array of social problems is political change in Burma. As long as current policies prevail, and Burmese families continue to find life impossible in their home communities, these populations will continue to flee. This is true in non-cease-fire ethnic areas, in cease-fire areas such as Mon State, and in Burman areas impoverished by SPDC policies. Similarly for IDPs, short-term solutions including increased food or health aid, or fleeing to Thailand as refugees, will not resolve the fundamental issue of villagers forced off their lands. Greater and urgent pressure must be brought to bear on SPDC and its proxies to cease ethnic cleansing in minority areas.

POLICY OPTIONS

Support for IDPs through SPDC-sanctioned programs, including those of UN agencies, are highly unlikely to reach IDPs in jungle areas for several reasons:

- SPDC health programs do not now reach these populations. In the few communities backpack workers encountered that do have government health programs, these staff have no supplies.
- Any agency appearing with SPDC security (and some security will be essential, given the levels of banditry and social chaos in the forests) will cause IDPs to flee.
- IDPs are in the forests and hills to avoid leaving their homes and living in forced resettlement areas. Program which provide support for IDPs are likely to do so not in jungles, but in resettlement sites. Thus support for IDPs could easily be perceived as a program of outside support for ethnic cleansing—as only IDPs who accepted the loss of their homes might receive aid.

The argument could be made that those areas with active resistance movements are targeted by SPDC for forced relocations as part of counter-insurgency activities, and that these policies could be addressed by cease-fires. However, many recent migrants are now coming from cease-fires areas, including Mon State, where there is little or no active insurgent activity. The situation of the Mon now coming in large numbers to Thailand suggests that the end of insurgency would have little or effect on the status of communities now targeted by SPDC. Thailand and other regional business investors are profiting significantly from Burmese migrant labor.

The harassment of Burmese in Thailand for fines and short imprisonment, however, benefits only the Thai police and security agencies. These policies have clearly had little or no effect on migration rates, but have served to restrict access to health care, education, and decency of life for countless Burmese. Thai authorities should be urged to address the widespread abuse and bribe taking by Thai authorities of the vulnerable Burmese in their country. Sexual assaults against Burmese women and girls in detention and in factories must be addressed to the full extent of Thai law.

Burmese migrant workers to Thailand and their families, both in agricultural and factory/sweatshop settings, are a rapidly growing population with considerable needs. Currently, many of these people remain undocumented, in hiding, and subject to a wide range of abuses and health threats. Health and food security programs for these populations are an urgent priority, but are currently sharply curtailed by Thai policy. Aid programs targeting Burmese migrant workers and their families are an emerging priority. These populations, however, are more difficult to reach and support than those in formal refugee settings, and current programs are inhibited by Thai policy. Aid to these populations must be increased, and this aid must be delivered in a context acceptable to Thailand and in cooperation with Thai authorities.

Finally, indigenous organizations have managed to provide some services cross-border to IDPs, and indeed, these are the only services that can currently reach these hidden and isolated communities. These efforts should be supported by aid agencies interested in assisting these populations. There are essentially three approaches to assisting the Burmese communities in this crisis: aid inside Burma, working through or with SPDC; aid in Thai refugee settings; or cross-border indigenous programs. Given the realities of the current situation, only cross-border interventions by trained indigenous staff appear to have any hope of reaching needy IDP populations. These programs should be supported, expanded, and allowed to operate without harassment in Thailand.

Because of the country's context, operating in Burma is extremely complex. Aside from the usual problems with infrastructure, limited capacity stemming from isolation, ethnic diversity and all the tension involved in that, as well as limited material and financial resources, Burma is also complicated by multiple stakeholders who do not agree on the long-term objectives for the country. They don't even acknowledge the legitimacy of the others' existence. There is also intense scrutiny of every action, and politicization of every activity, particularly, in my experience, humanitarian assistance. For the UN operating in Burma, it is further complicated by its own organizational liabilities and challenges. The success or failure of the UN to date has been deeply influenced by internal as well as external factors and constraints.

In spite of this, I believe a solid foundation has been established. With understanding and a strategic policy position, it is very possible for the UN to play a significant and constructive role in the long-term development of Burma. I believe the role of the UN in Burma should be quite straightforward. The role should be: to facilitate the development of the human potential of the entire nation within a reasonable time frame. The how and whys of achieving this noble objective however, are more complex, especially in Burma. Typically the UN seeks to achieve its developmental objectives in a given country by: doing no harm; promoting mutual understanding; fostering cooperation and coordination;

formulating and articulating shared long-term strategic goals; assisting in the establishment or expansion of the necessary infrastructure, institutions, capacities, and operational framework; as well as providing resources and input necessary to achieve those shared long-term strategic goals.

This is my definition of what the UN tries to do, somewhat idealized perhaps, but I think it's appropriate. In most countries, the UN works towards its objectives through the existing systems, structures, and mechanisms, most of which are, or are at least part of, government structures. But in Burma, this traditional UN approach is knocked off its track. In a Governing Council resolution passed in 1992 the United Nations Development Programme [UNDP] was required to change its mode of operation. It was told to work outside of the existing government institutions and work directly with people's groups. As you can imagine this resolution placed a number of constraints on UNDP, while at the same time creating some interesting opportunities.

Being the largest agency in the UN family, the UNDP resident representative is often the resident coordinator of the UN agencies operating in a given country. That is true in Burma. Because of the Governing Council resolution, however, the UNDP is now required to operate in a way that is not required of the other agencies. The unique requirements placed on the UNDP complicated the relationships between the UNDP and the other UN agencies operating inside the country. It also caused the de facto military government to examine, with even greater vigor, the actions and operations of the UNDP and other UN agencies. And, it gave the military government a way to treat the UNDP and the other agencies differently. The UNDP responded to the Governing Council resolution with a comprehensive, integrative, development program called the Human Development Initiative, or HDI.

This program, ingenious and appropriate, is bureaucratically quite complicated. It is a program that essentially seeks to facilitate grassroots development by providing a range of programs in a participatory, bottom-up way. To bring in the requisite expertise quickly, the UNDP in effect subcontracted out the sectoral components of its program to other UN agencies for implementation. So the HDI project officers who are employed to administer components of the HDI, officially are employed by the UN agency they call their head agency, but they must implement their projects according to the rules of another UN agency, the UNDP. This bureaucracy alone makes implementation very difficult.

In addition, HDI project officers face other variables, including stringent accountability requirements and an unforgiving work environment. To ensure compliance with the comprehensive Governing Council requirements, a great many time-consuming accountability requirements were added. These include intensive yearly reviews, along with the normal regular progress reports, and rigorous approval requirements for any action taken. So they are scrutinized every step of the way, and that slows things down. There is also the unforgiving work environment. The de facto military government was upset, of course, that the mode of operation of the UNDP was changed; the UNDP was treating them differently from any other country in the world, even though their status in the UN was unchanged. The fact that there was also less access to the cash flow required to administer the UNDP projects further strained relations.

The Governing Council resolution may well have been the right step to take. However, it is important to recognize the level of complexity it introduced to program implementation for the HDI, as well as for all the UN agencies:

- Due to the Governing Council Resolution of 1992, the UNDP team in Burma is required to implement programs outside of the existing government structures and institutions, even though they are present in the country at the invitation of this de facto military government.
- They are required to use operational approaches outside of their traditional mode of operating. They must establish programs that work directly with local communities and

these programs should be responsive to the needs of the community, participatory, independent, and ultimately self-sustaining.

- They are required to use existing UN agencies, systems, procedures, and personnel to implement these extraordinary programs. And they are required to involve international NGOs in this process.

I'm a big fan of the concept of the UN. One person said to me a couple years ago, "If the UN didn't exist you would have to invent it." That probably is true. But there are limits. The UN is a large bureaucratic structure. Like any organization it has its internal politics. Add this to the picture of multiple stakeholders, both within as well as outside the UN-donors for example [who] all have a wide range of opinions and perspectives-and you can see that the pressure placed on the UNDP team is amazing.

Burma has a de facto military government that is very suspicious of outside influence and an opposition group that is extremely concerned about the secondary impact of humanitarian assistance and how it might affect the prospects for political change. The scrutiny and attention Burma attracts for the comparatively small UN program it supports, is brutal. Understanding the inherent complexities of implementing UN programs in Burma, explains why sometimes things don't function as well as they might. But the UN is accomplishing many things in Burma. This I will readily and happily acknowledge; I do not believe, however, that the UN is achieving anywhere near its potential. This crystallized for me recently when a diplomat asked me why the UN is not achieving its potential in Burma. That question stopped me in my tracks. It's not because people aren't capable or they aren't trying.

It's not because the situation is impossible, although I believe it's very, very difficult. The reason the UN has not lived up to its potential is because the UN asked its normal personnel to use its normal budgetary processes and its normal systems and procedures, to implement extraordinary programs designed to achieve extraordinary results. I think we've asked a lot of the UN, and that I think we need to acknowledge. It's easy to engage in UN-bashing, but I think we ought to be aware of the situation in which they've been placed. So I would not give up on the UN, and I certainly would not give up on Burma. I believe there are important roles for the UN to play in Burma, and I believe there are important roles for the international community to play. Humanitarian assistance can add to the capacities of social infrastructure that are necessary to achieve the kind of long-term repercussions that we all desire and welcome for the people of Burma. It's the people of Burma that this is all about.

As long as certain caveats and guidelines are followed, I firmly believe that humanitarian assistance can and should be delivered in Burma at this time. Burma is not the only country in the world with a restrictive and highly challenging working environment. Furthermore, the UN is not the only agency that works in these countries. There are other agencies tackling the same challenging contexts. Among these agencies is a wide range of non-governmental organizations or NGOs, operating with a wide range of modalities. I would say that these organizations are most successful when they study the country context, seek to understand the inherent strengths and constraints, determine which methods and modalities are likely to be most effective to achieve their stated goals and objectives, and then develop an operational strategy accordingly.

Over the past 50 years, NGOs have developed a reputation for having the ability to inexpensively implement relief and development programs at the grassroots level, directly with people's groups. When done well, these programs prove to be participatory, independent, responsive to the needs of the people, dynamic, and lead to sustainability. Many NGOs have developed a strong track record for solid performance and for serving multiple stakeholders. All accomplished while continuing to be people-focused and community-focused. Keep in mind there is a natural shake-out. Those NGOs that consistently do not perform well do not get funded.

Peter Drucker, the management guru, argues that NGOs

have much to share with businesses in regards to the management of a complex product-process mix. Perhaps NGOs have much to share with the UN as well. I would like to believe that this is at least part of the reason that the donor community insisted that the UNDP/HDI program be implemented with the involvement of NGOs.

There have been several deterrents, however, to the effective involvement of NGOs in the recent UNDP/HDI-funded projects:

- Mixed, and perhaps, unreasonable performance expectations for the UNDP and other UN agencies.
- Unclear roles and expectations of the NGOs.
- A funding time lag. It has taken as long as 12 months to be funded by the UN, and this is when you have an 18-month time limit to implement your program.
- And of course, government anger.

One of the issues that we NGOs anticipated was that the de facto military government would be angry that the UNDP was not operating in its usual manner. We asked the UNDP and the UNDCP [United Nations Drug Control Programme] to earmark a portion of their funds specifically for NGO use. This was not done. When the government reacted, many NGOs found that they had become a political football, caught between the military government and the UNDP. At first, working with UNDP funds seemed like a wonderful option to add to the extremely limited funding mix available to NGOs. After a while the UN funds became more of a curse. But I believe that amidst this complex and difficult situation, the UN and the NGOs have accomplished a great deal.

Much more is needed however, and much more can be done. I propose the following recommendations:

- Continue and expand the coordination and cooperation role of the UN. This is important. UNDP is well positioned to play an important umbrella role in Burma, for the whole UN aid system. This includes setting an operational tone and setting standards for all agencies working in the country. If the UNDP plays this role of cooperation and coordination, it would begin to resolve the inter-agency rift that the military government is using as a wedge.

- Establish and use coordination and cooperation mechanisms with NGOs. There is a great desire and need for the UNDP to play an active role in this regard.
- Earmark funds that are intended for implementation by NGOs only. These funds would not be for use by the UNDP itself and would not be [dispersed] through existing government structures and institutions; they'd be earmarked only for NGOs.
- HIV/AIDS is a major problem and needs a concentrated effort. Use the enormous HIV/AIDS problem as a focal point for humanitarian assistance. Earmark more funds to address this pressing need that cannot be, and in good conscience should not be, postponed.
- UNDP should continue its liaison role with the NLD and Aung San Suu Kyi. This is an important role the UN can play because of its status in the international community. Furthermore, communication between NGOs and the NLD has been called for by the NLD and many human rights groups. The pressure on NGOs to communicate with the opposition groups is increasing. As part of its "umbrella function, the UN system should consider developing an informal mechanism for communications between the NGO community residing in Burma and the NLD.

Communication cannot be done formally, but it can be done informally. If the UN fulfills this need, then the process remains somewhat apolitical. If an embassy facilitates this process for NGOs there is a danger of the entire effort being politicized to the point that it is destructive to the very objectives we all seek to achieve, that is, to help the people of Burma. I would ask that the UN bear that burden, and try to play that role as part of the umbrella function for helping NGOs working in the country.

3

The Life of Ceylon Women

Since the outbreak of war in 1983, Sri Lanka has been the site of one of the world's longest running civil conflicts, which has wreaked devastation upon the tropical island and its population for almost two centuries. Whether the result of ancient hostilities between Sinhala and Tamil civilizations, or a conflict borne of divisive colonial , opposing nationalisms and territorial disputes over 'homeland' have led to this ongoing armed conflict between the Sri Lankan government and the Liberation Tigers of Tamil Eelam (LTTE). In general, the Sri Lankan civil war has been characterized by long-term military engagement, political terrorism, communal violence, large-scale internal displacement, wide-spread physical destruction, declining economic conditions, and extraordinary human loss.

Since 1983, Sri Lanka has witnessed repeated and massive civilian displacements, numbering over one million in total. Roughly 80% of all those displaced are Sri Lankan Tamils from the Jaffna Peninsula, the Vanni region and the eastern provinces. While the vast majority of people have been displaced internally, others have fled across the Palk Straight to refugee camps in India, or have sought asylum within growing Tamil diaspora communities in Western Europe, North America and Australia. In general, vicious cycles of internal displacement have ebbed and flowed according to communal rioting, military offensives, guerrilla attacks and shattered cease-fires.

Most internally displaced persons (IDPs) have been displaced multiple times, and for varying lengths of time, fleeing from their homes to temporary welfare centres, to the homes of friends and relatives, or to the jungle. After ten years of broken ceasefires and abbreviated repatriation schemes, however, February 2002 witnessed the cessation of hostilities between the Sri Lankan government and the LTTE, and the beginning of peace negotiations brokered by a Norwegian diplomatic initiative. Since then, the Ministry of Rehabilitation, Resettlement and Refugees and the Office of United Nations High Commissioner for Refugees (UNHCR) have been working to facilitate permanent repatriation of displaced Sri Lankans, both from within the country and from abroad.

By the spring of 2002, an estimated 260,000 displaced Sri Lankans had returned to their homes, and rates of return are continuing at a similar pace at present. With much activity in Sri Lanka on the international level, and a well-established NGO community, island-wide efforts have begun in order to encourage sustained, longer-term development and rehabilitation projects for retuning IDPs. In the preliminary stages of my research with IDPs in Sri Lanka, I was encouraged by thought that the "present anthropological moment" was ripe for intensive investigation of migration, due to growing recognition "that people are increasingly moving targets... and the shifting of [anthropology's] lens of enquiry to examine peripheries, boundaries, borderlands, migrants, and the processes of apparent flux and disorder".

Such an intellectual climate, I believed, would provide me with a prime opportunity to reconsider conventional debates on both internal displacement and return migration. Now, almost a year-and-a-half later, however, as I begin trying to turn my scrawled field notes into a master narrative for academic scrutiny, I am troubled by the disconcerting, slowly-acquired knowledge that while migration may indeed be breaching anthropological consciousness, its' fundamental cause - violence - still remains at the margins of disciplinary imagination. As several anthropologists have suggested, "the practice of socio-cultural anthropology... is particularly well suited to understanding the subjective, experiential, meaningful dimension of social conflict".

And yet, as Green notes, anthropologists have until recently approached the study of conflict from a distance, examining societal manifestations of violence in often abstract terms, divorced from the harsh historical realities and lived experiences of human beings (1994: 228). Indeed, as Chambers writes, "[I]n the aseptic and sterilized accounts of history, sociology and anthropology, the 'pain of violence' is written out of narratives and forgotten". Thus, despite the alarming rise in political repression, state terrorism and internecine warfare in recent decades, such topics have yet to capture "anthropological imagination".

Recognizing early-on that violence would become the meta-narrative of my research with resettled Sri Lankan women, I believe the various methodologies which governed this research were reflective of my own attempt to conduct both politically and socially relevant ethnography. To this end, the time I spent with resettled women provided me with ample opportunity to both document and reflect upon their testimonies of displacement and resettlement, inquiring into the "insidious and pervasive effects and mechanisms" of physical, social and political violence, and exploring how they functioned simultaneously on the level of lived experience. Through both formal interviews and casual conversations, women's words took on a wide variety of overlapping narrative genres, and thus I found myself at different times playing the differing roles of ethnographer, oral historian, life historian and witness.

Though historically, the canon has had little room for unwritten oral narratives, recent interest from across the social sciences has emerged as a result of wider social, cultural and political developments since 1945, namely the radical protest and liberation movements in Europe, the USA, the former Soviet Union, Latin America and other former colonies. Due to growing interest in radical narrative genres such as *testimonio*, oral narratives have been increasingly recognized as particularly useful in understanding the significance of violence in individual lives, and exploring "both personal trauma as viewed within a social context and society as reflected in an individual's life".

Indeed, throughout the course of my research, I came to realize the power and potential richness of oral sources, not simply to record facts or events, per se, but to provide insight into their subjective, personal meanings instead. I believe oral narratives were a means through which resettled Sri Lankan women alternatively made sense of, interpreted, or commented upon their experiences of violence and displacement, and thus, they provide great insight into the ways in which relationships between public and private, personal and political are continually negotiated within a turbulent social context. This chapter is about stories and story-telling. Therefore, writing them down, submitting them to academic analysis, "committing them to paper surely violates them in a way that retelling them does not".

Creating a written narrative from oral sources has thus been a troubling process, for as Singer notes, oral narratives "are intended to be communicated by word of mouth. They are designed to be transient, changing with each retelling. Recording them fixes them in time like a written text", which they are not. And yet, spurred on by the stinging commentary of anthropologists such as Nancy Scheper-Hughes, I have come to realize that not to do so, constitutes an "act of indifference," a "hostile act." For as Scheper-Hughes argues, monographs may become "'sites of resistance,' 'acts of solidarity,' or a way to 'write against terror,' and anthropology itself employed as an agent of social change'".

This chapter draws on oral narratives collected over the course of nine months that I spent doing research with IDPs in the northern provinces of Sri Lanka. While my research was conducted within Sinhala, Tamil and Muslim communities, the oral narratives which form the basis for this chapter come exclusively from Tamil women from Vavuniya and Mannar who were resettled back into their villages after being displaced. Though I spoke with women of all ages, most were younger than forty, and had several children. Indeed, the narratives reproduced here come from a range of individuals with differing backgrounds and histories of displacement, and thus this study is not meant to be a scientific survey based upon a representative sample, but is one which relies upon the stories of those among whom I lived.

Gathering and documenting narratives through interviews and conversations was a particularly challenging process given the tumultuous social and political timing of my research, and it clearly had a pronounced effect on both the content and form of many narratives. Despite the declaration of a cease-fire and rumor of peace talks during my fieldwork, many women were cautious and guarded in their verbal communications, and there was therefore much less spontaneous discussion of violence and displacement than I had expected. While many women's narratives emerged during formal interviews conducted inside their houses, others surfaced during more casual conversations throughout a wider variety of contexts: while fetching water from the well, buying bread from the store, or preparing lunch in the kitchen.

There are a number of both methodological and ethical issues which demand attention when conducting this sort of ethnographic fieldwork, though unfortunately, it is not within the scope of this chapter to address them all here. With regards to the content of the narratives, I believe they were often influenced by other family members or villagers who were present during the interviews, in front of whom women's narratives were constructed and shaped in certain ways, with certain silences interwoven. Furthermore, it is important to note that a translator was used for many of the interviews, and even where it was possible for me to communicate in Sinhala with some women, for none was it their first language.

As is now commonly recognized, oral material can hardly escape being shifted throughout the processes of transcription and translation, and should thus be regarded critically. Finally, deeply complex issues such as power, authority, agency and authorship have attended this study at every stage of research and writing. In an attempt to locate myself within my own field research and the resulting text, it is important to note that the oral narratives presented here are far from unmediated, and instead reflect interactive, reflexive processes of mutual collaboration and agency through which both researcher and informant co-produce, or create a source and text together, though rarely through an entirely equal relationship.

Indeed, while honoring ethical obligations such as acquiring informed consent, ensuring confidentiality, accurately documenting interviews, making interview material accessible, and so forth, my privileged position as a Western researcher ultimately allows me the unmistakable power to interpret women's words, and adopt their insights to support my own. In the end, while consciously striving for 'a shared authority' throughout my research, it has been continually informed by the humbling recognition that I, among others, have yet to create an ideal methodology which negates such inequalities and power imbalances between researcher and informant, or adequately addresses the "politics of representation".

THEORETICAL CONTEXT

Within the fields of both migration and refugee studies, out migration has traditionally been of far more interest to scholars and the international community than return migration. Such is evident in the way that the fields of migration and refugee studies have been shaped and considered, or perhaps more precisely, in the ways they have not yet been considered. In general, immigration and refugee influxes have been widely studied, in part due to the perceived impact of large-scale population movements on the global order.

Indeed, as a result of increasing immigration, the birth of the international refugee regime, the UN Refugee Convention and the previously-favored practice of refugee resettlement, scholarly inquiry and international attention have come to rest firmly in out migration. To this end, the impact of migrants on their resettlement societies and vice versa, and related processes such as integration, adaptation and acculturation have been central points of inquiry for academics, practitioners and policy makers alike. Such issues have been taken up by numerous scholars from around the world, and have inspired both research institutions and social service providers to place significant emphasis on understanding the meaning of out migration at the national, communal and individual levels. Until recently, however, return migration has been relatively neglected by scholars and the international community.

As Zetter wrote, "a vacuum in our research becomes apparent... a research void dramatically exposed", when compared with the volumes of research that exist on immigration and refugee resettlement. Until the late 1980s, when refugee repatriation was considered at international gatherings for the first time since the end of the Second World War, there was an enormous scarcity in both theory and data on return migration. Over the past decade, however, return migration has become an increasingly urgent phenomenon, due primarily to the changing nature of conflict and patterns of displacement around the world, and resulting revolutions within the international refugee regime.

Indeed, rapidly increasing numbers of refugees and asylum-seekers world-wide, economic recession in the early 1980s, the growing reluctance of states to grant asylum, and profound changes within international politics (namely, the end of the Cold War,) have resulted in a shift in international refugee policy, making voluntary repatriation, rather than resettlement, the preferred 'durable solution' to the global refugee crisis, and UNHCR's organizational goal. Since the San Remo Round Table on Voluntary Repatriation in 1985, voluntary repatriation has been pursued in most refugee situations, and has been the primary response to refugee influxes in recent years.

Despite this shift, however, and its weighty implications for international order, refugee repatriation and other forms of return migration have been poorly documented beyond internal agency and government reports, and have been slow to attract international attention. As a result, the myriad of processes and consequences which follow the actual physical return 'home' remain cloaked in relative obscurity. Literature on return migration has remained comparatively sparse and limited in scope, determined largely by international political and financial considerations, and restricted in analysis to three main themes: international law, political motivations and practical logistics.

As Sepulveda notes, there is a tendency to perceive return migration as "a unified, monolithic experience in policy, practice and research" (1995: 84), and thus few scholars have explored the experiences of returnees themselves, creating an ever greater research gap around repatriated populations and the processes of reintegration which take place after return. One can only muse over the variety of reasons for such neglect - namely, the perceived greater burden of immigration on states and national communities, and perhaps the additional assumption that once migrants have returned home (often to the developing world), they are less relevant to the international global order. As Koser notes of the political construction of the 'refugee problem', "return takes people out of the scope of international concern and assistance".

The most common assumption stifling inquiry into return migration, however, and the one I will deal with most explicitly throughout the course of this chapter, is the implicit assumption that because return migrants are resettling back into their own 'homes,' there exist less dynamic or extreme processes of adjustment and integration than for refugees or immigrants entering a foreign society. Due to the relative scarcity of research considering the complex relationship between repatriation and reintegration, the assumption persists that the return 'home,' involves a transition process much less problematic and multifaceted than that of immigration. The privileged status of refugee repatriation compounded with a conspicuous lack of inquiry into return migration more generally betrays a further set of assumptions often taken for granted within the international community.

A whole host of assumptions – about fixed, static, and pre-existing relationships between people and place, and about 'natural' processes of returning home – support the image of voluntary repatriation as a positive process and optimal solution, and explain well the general absence of inquiry into return migration in general. Within the dominant international discourse, the return 'home' is conceived of as the reverse of displacement, or 'refugeeness,' signaling the end of the migration cycle, and offering the cure to discontinuity and disconnection.

Underlying this approach are territorialized notions of home which suggest that by returning, migrants go home to the place where they belong, and what necessarily follows are the natural processes of reconnection and reintegration of people to place. Several scholars have recently begun to question such notions of home, implicitly criticizing the founding assumptions on which both migration theory and international policy are built – that "a singular and immutable bond exists between a people and a particular space"; that there is a mathematical equation or "a one-to-one correspondence" between the two; that people possess "static and sedentary identities"; and, that "flight and exile [imply] a rupture in the symbolic representation of this bond which links people with land, repatriation [being] the sole means through which to heal this severed bond".

Indeed, as the language of repatriation suggests – its operational vocabulary riddled with terms such as 'reintegration' and 'rehabilitation' – scholars and policy-makers alike assume that return 'home' reverses the negative experience of displacement, naturally reestablishing roots, repairing lives to their 'normal,' pre-displacement status, and offering up a "therapeutic intervention" which terminates displacement and restores people to a familiar environment. To this end, displaced people "are seen as the product of crisis; their situation is abnormal; repatriation will resolve the crisis and restore normality".

Furthermore, the presumption of familiarity which words such as 'reintegration' reflect, betray an obliviousness to time and an institutional neglect of important historical and socio-political processes and changes which are continually taking place in both displaced populations and their homes. Assumed to be the "end point of a refugee's trajectory from flight to return", return is thus conceived of throughout international imagination as a timeless process by which people naturally resume their lives, as though returning to a "negative" or empty physical space, void of history and socio-political realities. As Warner notes, institutional conceptualization of return "denies the temporal reality of our lives" (1994: 169) and in doing so, fails to attend to the changing personal, historical, social and political contexts through which 'home' is continually redefined, particularly upon return.

INTERNALLY DISPLACED PERSONS

And yet, there remains a further gap in the literature of return migration. In general, migration has been traditionally conceived of within academia and by the international community as primarily an *international* phenomenon. As recent large population movements within national borders have demonstrated, however, *internal migration* is an increasingly relevant phenomenon, with Internally Displaced Persons (IDPs) constituting the largest numbers of internal migrants. Despite composing the vast majority of the world's displaced population, IDPs have been relatively ignored throughout migration studies, and by the international community.

Though Francis Deng, the Representative of the UN Secretary General on Internally Displaced Persons, has succeeded in bringing the plight of IDPs to international attention in recent years, they remain today a contested people, inspiring debate within the UN and other international organizations over the role of the international community in protecting and assisting IDPs. Contentious issues such as state sovereignty and international responsibility have impeded the development of international support for IDPs, and partially account for the traditional absence of scholarly research and concern. Despite the fact that numbers of IDPs have grown substantially in the past decade, reaching 20 to 25 million displaced due to conflict alone - twice the number of refugees - only two definitive texts have been written on the subject, both by Roberta Cohen and Francis Deng at the Brookings Institution.

UNHCR and other international relief organizations have also begun documenting their work with IDPs, though most studies are limited to annual surveys, agency and government reports. While the global crisis of internal displacement seems slowly to be breaching the consciousness of international, humanitarian and academic communities, however, the vast majority of attention has been focused around issues of state versus international responsibility, institutional mandates, and humanitarian concerns. As a result, few efforts have been made to understand how IDPs themselves perceive, experience, and respond to displacement, or subsequently, to the return home. Indeed, if studies of return have been slow to develop with regards to international migration, then scholarly focus upon resettled IDPs has been virtually non-existent.

That repatriated IDPs have not only returned 'home', but never even left their countries of origin seems to serve as legitimate justification for the neglect of such issues by the international community, and thus assumptions about home and return are uncritically accepted to constitute the prevailing framework for research on, and humanitarian assistance for, IDPs as well as refugees. As the Global IDP Project confirms, [I]nformation on return is little documented… The return of IDPs is given little attention by governments and members of the international community, who do not necessarily give a high priority to care programmes for IDPs in the post- conflict reconstruction and economic development of the country.

Once returned, IDPs are often merely subsumed into larger categories of vulnerable, impoverished populations, and are therefore redefined and no longer considered separately, stifling specific attention on returned IDPs as a distinct population (Norwegian Refugee Council 2002). Thus, what little focus there *is* on internal displacement almost completely neglects the issue of resettlement, and the reintegration processes through which returnees attempt to reestablish themselves economically, politically, socially and emotionally in their homes.

AGENCY INTERVENTIONS

According to UNHCR, the goal of repatriation is reintegration, a concept vaguely defined as "a process which enables formerly displaced people and other members of their community to enjoy a progressively greater degree of physical, social, legal and material security". Thus, recent debates around return migration consist of attempts to define and measure different aspects of the reintegration process - economic, social, psychological, political, and legal. As growing research on NGO policy reveals, however, most current approaches to reintegration attribute primary, if not absolute importance to economic factors, and assume that economic rehabilitation will necessarily lead to social, psychological and political reintegration.

As Rogge notes, "all too often, the fact that there may be problems of social reintegration... may be discounted or even repudiated". In privileging economic determinants, discourse surrounding reintegration assumes that the true challenges facing return migrants are economic ones, and that once these have been met, complete rehabilitation will naturally follow. Though such notions are beginning to be challenged by a handful of scholars who have recently begun to consider more complex realities of reintegration, and by social scientists from diverse disciplines - law, political science, anthropology, geography, and psychology - an urgent need Despite this emphasis, states rarely monitor returnees after their physical repatriation, and thus the lack of investigation into returnees' experiences further reinforces the predominant discourse which believes repatriation to be the best solution for displaced persons.

Still exists for more sophisticated analyses and holistic understandings of the reintegration process. Within the context of internal displacement, agency interventions remain largely unconcerned with resettlement and reintegration. Indeed, the only two comprehensive texts assessing agency responses to

IDP crises focus little attention on IDPs after resettlement, concentrating primarily on factors causing internal displacement, national and international responses, human rights and humanitarian concerns. While acknowledging that successful reintegration of IDP populations is crucial to the reconstruction and reconciliation processes of any war-torn society, their almost exclusive focus on economic aspects of reintegration, generally fails to address the pressing social, political and psychological issues which determine resettlement processes.

Thus, current approaches to IDP reintegration often repeat the biases found in agency responses to refugee repatriation, and betray devotion to a similar, over-simplified discourse on the meaning of 'home' and return for displaced populations. According to Cohen and Deng, "successful reintegration depends on development aid to increase the absorptive capacity of return areas". As described, however, this entails improving economic conditions, rebuilding physical infrastructure, providing local opportunities for education, training and income-generating activities, and generally integrating other developments projects into relief programmes.

Similarly, the few other authors who assess IDP resettlement also restrict their attentions to the material, structural hardships of return, wholly neglecting consideration of the complex personal, social and political experiences which influence reintegration and rehabilitation processes. Lamenting the lack of donor and development agencies recognition, will and funding for sustainable implementation of reintegration schemes and post-conflict reconstruction, Cohen and Deng explain that the main priority of most NGOs working with IDPs is emergency assistance - providing food and health services, water, sanitation and shelter - and that few NGOs persist in the provision of services after IDPs have been resettled (1998a: 192).

Even international standards for resettlement as established by the *Guiding Principles on Internal Displacement* are primarily concerned with ensuring voluntary and safe return, and recovery of or compensation for lost property, rather than promoting sustainable reintegration and rehabilitation (UNHCR 1998). Since current NGO debates revolve principally around issues of protection, emergency assistance and institutional mandates, issues of IDP resettlement are largely overlooked during agency interventions, and thus academic disregard of the complexities involved in return migration are largely mirrored by NGO practice.

NARRATIVES OF RETURN

Throughout this chapter, I will argue that both discourse and practice surrounding return migration reveal a general lack of understanding of the popular experience and processes of resettlement for returnees themselves. Insofar as the varying meanings and experiences of resettlement have been consistently neglected, it is only when one ventures outside traditional migration literature "that one begins to see the enormity of issues involved in exile and return to home". Drawing upon my own research with resettled Sri Lankan women, I contend that IDPs' own experiences and perceptions of resettlement reveal dangerous myths within international conceptualizations of home and return, thus compelling us to question the multitude of assumptions which underlie both institutional treatment of, and agency responses to, return migration.

As I will argue, failure to adequately consider resettlement and reintegration has led to the erroneous conclusion that physical repatriation equals a return home to the familiar, an end to displacement, and the beginning of natural processes of reconnection of people with place. To the contrary, I suggest that the concept of return involves much more than the simple physical relocation of formerly displaced persons, and that given the tumultuous experiences of violence and displacement, and the dynamic nature of both society and the individual, IDPs return to 'home' may in fact be just as complex an experience as that of refugee resettlement or immigration to a foreign country.

Indeed, research with resettled Sri Lankan women suggests that "the conventional image of displacement, return and resettlement as linear processes, proceeding from loss to recovery and development" is flawed both in its perception of return and reintegration as linear, predictable, natural processes, and in its static, territorialized notions of home. Instead, I will argue that the resettlement process is a dynamic and multi-dimensional one, involving profound economic, social, psychological, cultural, political, legal, personal and communal change which transforms locations of return into sites of struggle and contention.

Furthermore, I contend that socio-political factors are of extreme importance in shaping women's resettlement experiences. That is, in addition to material and physical dispossession, there are also profound forms of social and psychological dispossession which continue to have a marginalizing effect even after resettlement and economic rehabilitation. In an attempt to understand the complexities of resettlement, this study asks the following questions: What are key factors influencing the process of resettlement for Sri Lankan women? How does the narrative process reflect their responses to such pressures? Specifically, it explores return through an investigation of two key themes which were central to women's narratives of their resettlement experiences: *identity reconstruction* and *memory negotiation*.

While such themes are indeed common throughout literature on immigration and refugee resettlement as well, I suggest that they gain particular importance for those returning to their very own 'homes'. Indeed, a detailed exploration of women's narratives suggests that there are both acute events and prevailing conditions which occur as a direct result of violence and displacement which can render 'home' a strange and unfamiliar place, or which require great struggles of readjustment upon return. As I will argue, both the social construction of identity and the political weight of memory exert powerful influences over the processes of return and reintegration, and make issues of gender and violence, and relations of power, history and memory, key factors in the struggle toward 'home'.

Certainly, for many resettled Sri Lankan women, return to their villages has meant transforming a series of social, political, historical and psychological spaces into home all over again, and recreating or reinventing both a self and a future through processes in which the locations of return are re-inscribed with meaning as the result of a intricate blend of historical, political, economic, social, psychological experiences.

IDENTITY RECONSTRUCTION

What is at stake in an ethnic conflict and ethnicide in Sri Lanka is more than the mortality of bodies, more than the destruction of life and the demise of security. Rather, what is at stake, especially for those whose bodies have been spared the destruction of death, is a death of a way of being-in-the-world, the death of that which constitutes their identity, honor, and dignity".

Over the past thirty years, literature regarding identity politics among resettled refugees and immigrants has grown to abundance. Indeed, as Zetter argues, identity is one of the key points of analysis in refugee life and mechanisms of refugee control (1991). Malkki confirms this, writing, "identity is a highly mouldable, dynamic key-element in the creation of peoples' (self-) images, especially when it comes to refugeeness" (1992: 308). As is well- documented, refugees and immigrants commonly grapple with changing identities in strange, foreign contexts, often in unknown languages, among unknown people, amidst an unknown land.

Indeed, their professed alienation and identity confusion is easily understood, given the social and cultural transformations that occur upon entry, and thus, scholars of migration studies have often investigated international migration with respect to its resulting reconfigurations and ambiguities of personal and social identity. In contrast, there is a dearth of literature regarding identity in the context of return migration. As noted previously, prevailing assumptions maintain that returnees return home to the familiar, thus commencing natural processes of reconnection in which displacement is terminated, and lives are repaired to their pre-displacement status. Such a discourse is founded upon what Malkki describes as sedentarist beliefs about the inseparability of identity from place, and implicitly suggests that when natural ties to land are severed, so too are individual identities, and thus repatriation is a process of reestablishing these ties, and the association between identity and a familiar land.

To this end, identity is assumed to be solved when located back into place. As I contend, however, as war-torn societies shift themselves into place in the aftermath, new lines are drawn and differentiations made as a direct result of violence which often necessitate IDPs' identity reconstruction despite returning home to the very people and places from which they came. In such cases, the condition of displacement may persist, disallowing the resolution of identity and prohibiting reintegration despite the return home. Furthermore, processes of identity alteration may even render 'home' a bewildering, unfriendly, and unfamiliar place, thus challenging the assumption that individual identity and notions of home depend solely on a territorial connection with place, instead suggesting that they rely heavily on the relationship with community.

CASE STUDY: SRI LANKAN TAMIL WAR WIDOWS

Such is the case for many Sri Lankan Tamil war widows. Since the outbreak of war in 1983, the population of Tamil widows has risen dramatically due to repeated massacres of entire male populations of Tamil villages, and particularized killings. As a result, thousands of Tamil women have been left displaced and widowed. Crucial to any discussion of Tamil war widows, of course, is a brief consideration of gender. As Schrijvers notes, gender is fundamental to the process of identity construction, especially in situations of conflict, war and displacement (1999: 308). While in 'normal' circumstances, gender heavily influences people's lives, in war-time it is "renegotiated afresh, gaining new weight, meaning and expression". Located at the very heart of human identity and dignity, gender "has far-ranging consequences for the overall positioning of women... and it determines to a great extent the way in which people experience their lives".

Insofar as it refers to "relations of power, privilege and prestige," gender constitutes a key force in Tamil widows' lives.

While Tamil war widows face a multitude of difficulties upon resettlement to their homes, the vast majority of humanitarian assistance focuses on their economic vulnerability. In many families, the husband was the sole breadwinner, and thus widows are suddenly responsible both for providing for the families daily needs and running the household. Many women have had no previous experience with income-generating activities and thus experience great difficulty finding employment, earning a suitable income, and raising children alone.

Additionally, many widows' rights to their husbands' land and property are often violated by the husband's family or even their own sons. In an atmosphere of hostilities, security is another very real concern for many widows. Without husbands for physical protection, many are vulnerable to rape or sexual abuse from the surrounding armed forces, men in the community, or even male kin. Furthermore, many widows are extremely emotionally vulnerable due to sadness and grief at the loss of their husbands, worry for the future, and memories of violence and displacement. Often, they had no time to mourn their husbands' deaths in the chaos of displacement, but had to immediately begin providing for their families, despite heavy emotional stress.

Upon resettlement, many women simultaneously face extreme social discrimination as a result of their new identity and social position as widows. As their stories revealed, the personal loss of identity as a result of violence is an already traumatic experience then further exacerbated by reduced social status within their native villages. Throughout Sri Lanka, Tamil war widows commonly remain at the mercy of religio-cultural traditions which yield power over their personal identities and material lives due to conservative discourses on gender. According to still powerful images of Tamil womanhood, women are conceptualized through their relations with men, and are thus recognized as wives, mothers, and daughters, but rarely persons in their own right.

Being a wife is therefore a position of both power and powerlessness, as it represents the core of womanhood and lends women their dignity, respect, social status and identity, and yet is contingent upon the living presence of the husband. According to ancient Hindu proscription, once widowed, women are robbed of their ordained functions as wives, and thus the root of their identity is stripped from them, as is their source of respect and authority within the community. As Chakravarti explains, widowhood constitutes state of social death, as they effectively depart from social life (1998). Widowhood often connotes the exclusion of women from the functioning social unit of the family and community, as the woman ceases to be both wife and person, and has neither social nor religious existence outside of her husband.

Institutionalizing widows' marginality, Brahmanical patriarchy reduces widows to "a liminal state between being physically alive and socially dead... [The widow has] ceased to belong and [has] been expelled from normal participation within the community... She is the object of divine and social disfavour". Brahmanical ideology, as expressed in the Hindu *Dharma,* deprives widows of personhood, sexuality and social status, imposing upon them a code of renunciation and demanding a celibate, pious and ascetic lifestyle.

Cessation of the widow as a social entity and rejection of her personhood are often symbolically expressed through ritualized patterns during funeral procedures which enact the disfigurement of the widow: the removal of the *pottu* (a sacred mark on the forehead, symbolic of auspiciousness and good fortune), the *tali* (wedding necklace), cosmetics, jewels and ornaments, adornment in plain, white clothes, and often, shaving of the head. Such rituals and symbols used to mark or define widowhood constitute important instruments of the community's power over a widow, and mark her transition from the central place in the family and community to its margins.

Necessarily implying self-negation and patriarchal subordination, widows are seen as the opposite of *sumangali* (auspicious woman), since good fortune and prosperity are virtues bestowed upon women through marriage. As stated in an ancient Brahmanical text, just as the body, bereft of life, in that moment, becomes impure, so the woman bereft of her husband, is always impure... Of all inauspicious things, the widow is the most inauspicious. There can never be any success after seeing a widow. The wise man should even avoid her blessing... for it is devoid of auspiciousness, like the poison of a snake."

While conservative Hindu ideologies have never played as dominant a role in Sri Lankan Tamil society as in India, widows are indeed regarded as bad omens, and are said to bring misfortune. As a result, they are relegated even further into the domestic domain, are unwelcome in public, and are the site of much social stigmatization and humiliation. While in discourse and in practice, ideologies regarding gender relations have loosened in recent years, violence and displacement have also "fed a strikingly conservative discourse... The new conservativism is a reaction to real changes, brought about by war", such as thousands living in refugee camps and thousands more fleeing to the West. Indeed, displacement has created a very real fear about the complete collapse of family values among IDPs and the Tamil diaspora.

As Schrijvers notes, images of the liberated woman, intensified by real social transformations in the context of civil war have created wide-spread fear regarding perceived chaos in gender relations due to increased movement and collapse of traditional gender hierarchies, thus allowing the reemergence of patriarchal, Brahmanic discourses on Tamil womanhood (1999: 328). To this end, attempts to deal with extreme loss, sorrow and fear by clinging to familiar cultural patterns have increased restrictions on widows in recent years.

WIDOWS' NARRATIVES

Indeed, social violence and discrimination emerged as the foremost concern of most widows I spoke with, and appeared to most profoundly affect their self-perception, relationships to 'home', and resettlement experiences. As their narratives revealed, even a once familiar home may be made strange by violent ruptures to personal identity and social life, leaving the individual a stranger in her own society, continuing displacement, and inhibiting the anticipated 'homecoming'. Throughout my research, countless stories indicated that for many widows, their husbands' deaths were conceptualized not only as a crisis of individual identity, but also of social meaning. Themes of social death and estrangement, the severing of social bonds, of being forgotten and rejected were common among widows' stories.

Neglected and ostracized by the community, excluded from social life, and subject to strict dress and behavior codes, many widows were forced to renegotiate their identities and relationships to 'home' anew. To this end, even return "involved multiple losses", and thus many narratives revealed the ongoing struggle to recover continuity and control within the social space of return. As Gardner suggests, "[N]arratives prove powerful tools in indicating the diverse elements which constitute identity, and the ways in which identities shift and are contested within the same individual". In addition to revealing the challenging process of identity reconstruction, the reformulation of meaning and the "reconstitution of self-hood", however, widow's narratives also took on an activist role "that… not only report[ed] on, but actively participate[d] in the process of identity construction".

Primarily involved in processes of self-recognition and preservation within a place of extreme disruption and loss, many widows' narratives reflect an effort to come to terms with the changed social space of 'home', accept their new identity within it, and make "highly ambivalent experiences and emotions whole or complete". As Knudsen notes, "[T]o secure a positive feeling of self (who I am) through identity management, the individual often tries to negotiate on the basis of past, now lost, positions (who I was) rather than present conditions (who I have become). Central to these processes of negotiation… is the strategic presentation of life histories…" (1995: 25). Indeed, for widows, "who I have become" presents a great threat to the concept of self. As I will suggest, however, widows negotiate the past in order to explain present conditions (who I have become), and present life histories in order to both chronicle this painful transformation and chart their futures.

SOCIAL DISPLACEMENT

Commonly, widows' narratives began by describing the painful reality of their continuing displacement, despite return to their native villages. To this end, many narratives were constructed to establish the vast discrepancies between social life before and after widowhood, thus continually turned around their husbands' deaths as the fundamental point of departure from past into present. Many widows' sought to establish a secure and reliable past through detailed descriptions of life before displacement and widowhood, representing economic prosperity, individual happiness and prominent social status – all things denied them in the present.

As Bhavani said, before my husband died, we had a nice life... this was a good home, and we were a good family then. I was a fine wife, and we had a good place within the community – we helped to develop this village! My husband earned well – we weren't very rich, of course, but we could provide for our children. They were happy, they ate well, and my son got good marks in school. As Peteet notes of such reminiscences, "Narratives of the past evoke a nostalgic longing for something irretrievable and confirm a contemporary reality that is painful and alienating" (1995: 180). That widows may have essentialized the past using a 'selectively reconstituted memory,' however, highlights further the intensity of their dismay at conditions after resettlement.

After securing a picture of the past in which their personal identities as wives were central to social well-being, many widows' narratives then explained the sudden alteration of this identity – from wife to widow – as the source of their present state of social displacement. Their stories of flight and return were repeatedly punctuated by mention of their husbands' deaths, and many referred to events in time not by date, but as "before my husband died," or "after my husband died." In this way, their stories turned around the husband's death as a rupture point in life, identity and in the narration of life, first interrupting life and identity in reality, and then serving as a 'temporal marker' in narrative, signifying the loss of status and protection in economic, social and personal terms. That widows' life stories so often hinged on the death of their husbands suggests that this trauma was not an isolated event in life, but a continuous injury which "played a decisive role in their perceptions of life afterwards, and in their interpretations of subsequent events".

Explaining the condition of widowhood, Suriya said, everything changed after my husband died. There are so many difficulties for us now... it is hard to tell them all. We have so little income, it is difficult to educate our children. We need assistance, but we're reluctant to take loans, because if we can't pay them back, we'll be branded as defaulters and get a bad name. These days, I make Rs. 50 each day doing fishing labor - how can I raise my family on this? Now all our lives are restricted because our husbands were killed. Young widows who go out and talk to men in the town, they develop bad talk around them - there is suspicion and they are shunned. A few women are supportive and kind to the widows, but generally, we are not recognized.

We aren't allowed to go to village functions because people think we're bad omens. They have reservations to talk to us. Now we cannot move freely in public, and we can't mix at village celebrations because of this state we're in! We're asked to leave funerals and weddings, or to come late, when everyone else has gone. Most widows are still very young, but people think we're inauspicious, bad luck. The villagers discriminate against fatherless children and look down on them! Since my husband has died, my life is lonely, I am only in this house. And of course, I cannot remarry.

Who would marry a widow? Women here won't dare try to marry again, then they will have no respect. We know the attitudes of the villagers, they all think in this way. It is our society. Often, the contemporary reality of widowhood was framed in terms of a past that had come to an abrupt and violent end, leaving only an uncertain future. For many widows, all their fears and apprehensions regarding the future were constructed as a result of their changed social identities, and poverty, alienation and insecurity were explained as an effect not only of a physical reality (the death of the husband), but also as a combined result of the induced social condition (widowhood), making survival in the village suddenly very tenuous. For many widows, the return home brought merely an end to physical displacement, while enacting new forms of social displacement, and continued disconnection and discontinuity from their past lives.

Indeed, for a Tamil widow, whose husband lent her a "way of being-in-the-world," his death signified the burial of her own "identity, honor and dignity". Thus, despite efforts to cope with traumatic experiences upon return, resettlement constituted a painful return to a world of distorted connections and disassociations. Many widows struggled to come to terms with the knowledge that it was their own community which stifled attempts to recover social position and self-esteem, instead forcing the adoption of a brand new identity, with neither honor nor dignity. Indeed, as Karthi said, even my neighbors who knew me as a young girl, even they are shy to speak with me now! To, them, I am only a widow these days. They think I am bad luck. Even my own sisters, my own family is different now... Now I am just the widow, Karthi. So this will be a lonely life for me. Clearly, fellow community members often prove most effective in undermining self-identity and making one's past irrelevant.

As Knudsen notes, "When an individual is no longer able to gain the necessary support from close relatives and friends, and when even the family has proved incapable of living up to its expected therapeutic potential... the individual is alone in a new and heightened sense" (1995: 27). Certainly, for many widows, the quest for familiar structures fails when they are no longer respected as wives or even mothers, and with their ultimate role and function in life gone, they must occupy a new social space within Tamil culture, and spend their lives defined by an absence. Once revered within Hinduism and the Tamil community, it is these very same structures which then relegate them in widowhood to the social, economic, and legal margins, provoking bitter disappointment upon resettlement, and prohibiting social reintegration. Insofar as discrimination and ostracization also had a profound impact widows' personal sense of themselves, their narratives simultaneously attempted to negotiate widowhood's implications for their own personhood. For many widows, the death of their husbands immediately signified not only the violent smashing of a familiar social structure, but the shattering of family life and the fracturing of personal identity. A "disconcerting sensation of disjuncture" was evident in many widows' narrations, reflective of a pervasive sense of loss and the abrupt alteration of selfhood. Indeed, many narratives reflected widows' personal sense of themselves was now as "someone else," or "someone other" than who they once were.

As Padmini recalled, When they told me he was killed, I got a great shock. From that day, I knew nothing would be the same for me and my children. I thought my life was over. I felt like I died too. My whole life was gone, and now I had to start all over again… Now, without my husband, I feel like a different person.

See, I have grown very thin – I am not the young girl I once was. Now I'm old after just a few years… As Kotre reminds us, autobiographical memory often divides life into two categories, separated by "[p]ersonal landmarks that come to the forefront of remembrance [marking] occasions in which we stepped into a new role and became a new person… As a new self emerge[s], the old one recede[s] into the past". Clearly, widowhood was one such landmark, significantly impacting self-perception, inducing feelings of "'broken' or 'splintered' personhood" (Zur 1999: 54), and confirming the power of both physical and social violence to dismantle identity, "hindering attempts to integrate the 'self' of the past with the 'self' of the present".

Re-imagining History, Society and the Self

In many cases, widowhood and its resulting social marginalization interfered with women's efforts to both recognize and reintegrate into their villages, thus making resettlement an often profoundly painful process. Amidst narrations of return, many widows described their difficulty coping with the hostile, alien atmosphere they found awaiting them in their villages, citing widowhood as that which had rendered their villages strange or unfamiliar. Clearly, for many widows, homelessness is not exclusively a physical condition, and thus return does not necessarily indicate 'homecoming.'

To the contrary, widows' narratives were testimony to the potential of violence to dramatically alter personal identity, creating new social outcastes, and rendering 'home' an unfamiliar, unwelcoming location of return. Estranged from the community and forced to abandon the old kinship structures and social networks which once constituted 'home,' resettlement merely represented return to a physical location for many Tamil widows, as many were still far from 'home'. Faced with the impossibility of reintegration, or return to life as they had once known it, many widows' narratives reflected creative processes of innovation and imagination through which they negotiated a new place for themselves within history, and formed new relationships to society and the self.

Through such reinterpretations, many widows' narratives attempted to forge an integrated version of 'home,' while simultaneously rectifying personal disunity by establishing continuity from past to present, and confirming a coherent identity through which to renegotiate a vision of the future. Widows' narratives reflected patterns of innovation which sought to establish continuity on multiple levels – through historical tradition, society, and self-perception. For example, many widows turned to religio-cultural traditions in order to explain their social demise and re-imagine their place in history. Indeed, establishing a historical tradition to legitimize their suffering and placing their individual experiences within a larger historical context appeared to help assuage feelings of isolation and alienation, and made possible an understanding of their new relationships with society.

As Sangeetha explained, My mother and grandmother were also made widows at a very young age. It is the same for all of us. This is what was meant for the women in my family –

actually, this is how it's always been. It has always happened to widows, even long ago - it is our *karma*. At least we do not suffer like Sita. Similarly, many widows' narratives aimed to establish societal continuity through repeated discussions of the common suffering of Tamil widows throughout Sri Lanka as a result of civil war. As Padmini said, "[W]e are a great tragedy of this war - there are so many women left alone after their husbands were killed. All the widows in the country are suffering."

Sangeetha's reference to Sita refers to the heroine of the Hindu epic, *The Ramayana*, who is immolated on her husband's funeral pyre after his death. This practice, called *sati*, was historically prevalent throughout India, and still occurs on occasion today, though it was formally outlawed by the British in 1829.

Drawing strength from historical and communal continuity, many widows clearly relied on this sense of shared identity to give meaning to the hardships they faced upon the return to home. Maintaining continuity in one's personal identity was also central to widows' resettlement struggles. As Daniel and Knudsen argue, since self-identity is anchored firmly the past, it is thus "the foundation upon which a meaningful world may be rebuilt" (1995: 5). Indeed, many widows' stories strove to maintain meaning in their own personhood and womanhood through connecting both past and present. As Bhavani said, I was a good wife to him, and I will still care for my children well. I was a good wife, and I will be a good widow. I know how people will talk if I meet men in the streets... I do not want to get a bad name - I am still a good woman. I won't ever remarry, of course. It would look bad to the villagers, and I am still my husband's wife.

There are his children to raise, so I must make a good home for them again. Clearly, locating personal identity within newly invented perceptions of history, society and the self helped many widows find continuity and order amidst violent, profound social transformation. Furthermore, many women suggested that their affiliations with other widows offered them much needed companionship, and that integration within the work force allowed them to participate in a new, meaningful sphere of society. Thus, through creative processes of remembering the past and imagining the future, many widows redefined their identities, social affiliations, and economic participation as part of the process of returning 'home'.

DISCOURSE AND POLICY IMPLICATIONS

Refugee status is considered the "perilous territory of not belonging", with the refugee "hover[ing] at the edges of her adopted society, an alien body". As the case of Tamil war widows indicates, however, such is also the plight of many return migrants, for whom violence has transformed 'home' into an unfamiliar site of continuing disconnection and displacement. For as widows' narratives suggest, the return 'home' is largely the return to a community, and thus, insofar as widows' new identities enforce their social estrangement, home - as a place of belonging and affinity - is no more.

Far from reestablishing lives to their pre-displacement status, or initiating the natural reconnection between people and place, resettlement for many widows meant the return to a whole new world of challenges and struggles, profound transformations conditioned by the social realities of violence and gender, and a new relationship to the social space of home. Clearly, widows' testimonies have grave implications for contemporary rehabilitation assistance schemes, most of which focus largely on returnees' economic reintegration. Indeed, the harsh social realities of widows' lives complicate this approach, presenting yet another formidable challenge upon resettlement.

As we have seen, economic and social factors are in constant and dynamic interaction, since while many widows are excluded from economic opportunity due to their social status, others are aided in their social lives when allowed to participate in the economic sphere. Instead of existing in isolation from one another, economic and social realms constitute a reflexive relationship within the widow's life, and should thus be treated in collusion with one another. Dynamically influencing each another, economic and social aspects of return must be approached through holistic strategies which integrate the two so as to deny neither the social constraints upon economic rehabilitation nor the economic implications of social status.

MEMORY NEGOTIATION

As a result of increased multidisciplinary inquiry into refugee resettlement, refugees' psychological adaptation has recently come to the fore in both academic literature and organizational agendas. Indeed, it is now generally understood that refugees who have lived through violent experiences such as war or torture may suffer profound psychological distress during resettlement, given that traumatic events are rarely isolated incidents, but rather violent processes which persist in destroying the psyche long after their actual occurrence, even when far distant from danger.

Permanent resettlement and its founding principle of *non-refoulement*, however, may afford refugees some degree of psychological assurance by implying that they should never again have to face their perpetrators or the scene of violence, and thus they may cope with their memories and experiences of violence in a setting vastly removed from that in which the trauma occurred. On the other hand, the myriad of psychosocial issues that accompany returned migration have rarely been addressed by researchers or the NGO community.

As Farwell notes, "[R]epatriation programmes typically emphasize infrastructural assistance and material aid rather than psychosocial support during reintegration" (2001: 44). As mentioned previously, predominant approaches to repatriation stifle sophisticated investigation into psychological dimensions of return given that psychological rehabilitation is generally assumed to follow naturally after successful economic reintegration. Thus denying the historical, political and psychological contexts in which 'home' is continually situated, conventional wisdom regarding repatriation implicitly suggests that return involves a natural process of reconnection between people and place, and posits a fixed, static, relationship between the two which excludes troubling historical and socio-political realities so often embodied in a physical place.

As I will argue, many returnees are also involved in similar processes of psychological adjustment, though they must negotiate traumatic memories and experiences of violence amidst the very physical, historical and political contexts which produced them. It is this very return - to the physical site of violence, the political site of repression, and the emotional site of memory - which creates great challenges for many resettled IDPs, and renders the process of psychological adaptation a formidable one in its own right, not necessarily following the physical return 'home'.

As research among resettled Sri Lankan women revealed, unresolved memories of violence can render resettlement a highly troublesome process, particularly when 'home' is a place replete with traumatic historical events, continued political repression and forbidden memories. Far from natural processes of reintegration, returnees must often negotiate anew the meaning and place of their memories within the physical, historical and political spaces of home, and are thus engaged in continuous struggles to reconcile their haunted reflections of the past with visions for a future, despite the violence and silence still alive within their villages.

CASE STUDY: SRI LANKA - VIOLENCE AND SILENCE

Such is the case for thousands of resettled Sri Lankan IDPs. Since the outbreak of war in 1983, violence has become endemic within Sri Lankan society in general, and has largely shaped collective memory within the Tamil community in particular. Throughout the north and east, repeated attacks on Tamil civilians and repressive state military control have produced a 'culture of terror' in which fear is omnipresent and the pervasive threat of violence has become a reality of life for all. Rather than an acute reaction, fear is a chronic condition instilled throughout the Tamil population as a result of decades of direct military attacks, civilian massacres, murders, torture, disappearances, systematic harassment, round-ups, detention, imprisonment, interrogation, searches, threats, ubiquitous military presence and surveillance, checkpoints, garrisons, patrols, and various other forms of state violence and repression.

Violence has been the "motor of oppression" used by the Sri Lankan state against its Tamil citizenry, and combined with internecine warfare, was so central to the lived experiences of IDPs, that its memory formed the core of my interviews with most resettled women. As Pohlandt-McCormick argues, however, beyond the experience of actual physical violence lies an insidious form of discursive, rhetorical violence, and thus, if the first casualties of physical violence are human lives, "then the first casualties of the discursive violence that follow[s] are the stories of what [people] had experienced and seen" (2000: 27).

As with many repressive governments, violence manifested itself in Sri Lanka in the way evidence was destroyed, concealed, or manipulated in order to deliberately distort the historical record and change what is known, written, and remembered about the past. As Pohlandt-McCormick notes, though the state cannot change what has happened, it may compound the physical violence done by violent attempts to hide the evidence thereof, thereby changing the official meaning of events, and altering the process of historical memory (2000: 29).

Similarly, Manz argues that the primary objective of a government involved in terror is to create an official version of the facts - an official story or memory - which "ignores crucial aspects of reality, distorts others, and even falsifies or invents still others" (1995: 158). As many women I spoke with testified, beyond the physical violence which they had experienced or witnessed, was a silence enforced through fear and official practices of deceit and disguise which were, in themselves, violent attacks on the dignity of victims, survivors and witnesses.

According to Zur, official denial of violent events constitutes a 'historical amnesia' which acts as a means of social and ideological control through its power to "obliterate, silence and negate" (1999: 49) the lived realities of a people.

As Gittins reminds us, "silence has long shadowed violence" (1998: 61), and is woven into the very fabric of historical evidence, texts and memory, making history a potentially destructive force due to its capacity to distort the truth and invent mythical pasts (1998: 61).

While this is not the place for a full discussion of power and the production of history, I believe that an exploration of the relationship between violence, memory and silence is crucial for an understanding of the complex psychological dimensions of IDP resettlement processes. For within the Sri Lankan context, violence and silence have acted in collusion with one another, "and can be read as a war against memory, a... falsification of memory and negation of reality [and an]... attempt to deny people access to the truth", thus rendering 'home' the site of much historical and emotional contention.

WOMEN'S NARRATIVES

Despite the pronounced cessation of warfare during my fieldwork, only a fragile, "eerie calm" reigned throughout the north and east, and a fearful uneasiness lay just below the surface of daily life, permeating and tearing at the social fabric through a "low-intensity panic [that] remain[ed] in the shadow of waking consciousness". Indeed, violence experienced at the hands of the state remained a central element of both individual and collective memory, and rather than fading amidst a climate of political reconciliation, continued to violate everyday life, disrupting peoples' ability to find continuity and meaning upon the return 'home'.

Far from erasing memories of violence, the silences enforced upon victims and survivors alike have created individual memories that remain "torn with pain, anger, distrust and unanswered questions", thus making many IDPs' return 'home' an often volatile journey. In spite of continued peace talks and resettlement back to their villages, violence was still an intimate, integral part of everyday life, and fear and suspicion still penetrated the social memory of many communities, increasing the hesitancy with which I proceeded in my research, and governing the time, place, and overall nature of my interviews. Indeed, the sites for discussing memories of violence were carefully restricted, and women were constantly guarded and alert for informers.

Due to the continued military presence in many Tamil villages, most conversations took place in whispers, and were punctuated by instructions to turn off my tape recorder, or move out into the fields. Despite some initial reluctance, most women gradually warmed to my presence in their villages, and subsequently allowed their narratives to emerge. The nature of their recollections varied greatly: while some women spoke for the first time about their experiences, others unleashed a flow of seasoned, often-told stories.

Through close examination of one woman's narrative, I will explore memories of violence in an attempt to capture a sense of the challenges that permeate Tamil women's lives upon return to a 'home' engulfed in hideous memories, ongoing militarization, and chronic fear. Due to growing literature on trauma, memory and narrative, it is currently understood that traumatic memories often constitute the core of life stories narrated by those who have survived. That such stories are often told and retold reveals the "central importance of narration to remembering and recovery" and the individual's purpose to bestow past experience with meaning: "a meaning which will contribute to the meaning of the present".

Additionally, however, I will argue that uncovering and narrating memories is vital not only for integrating violence into one's own personal life, but for understanding its significance within the larger historical and political contexts, thus reaffirming hidden memories within the location of return, despite continued violence, silence and fear.

Geetha's Tale

I knew Geetha for a long time before finally learning the troubling circumstances of her husband's death, and the violent events which had preceded her flight from home. Though she spoke of her husband often, and continually alluded to his death, it was months before an appropriate moment came for me to ask her how he had died. When

Geetha began the vivid tale of her husband's death, her initial words betrayed the difficulties of finding a language to recover a memory hidden in fear, or to articulate a pain and suffering which have been denied and covered up. Her uncertainty about how to tell me of an event whose reality was dangerous and painful reflected the difficulties of "fixing fear and terror in words", and she was immediately aware of her own limitations and those imposed upon her by language: How did my husband die? You want to hear this story? I do not even know how to tell this story... I don't know where to start.

That time was a very bad time for me, and I cannot speak of his death. I do not know what are the right words for this story - that time was all sadness for me. How can I explain this sadness? It is always with me, and this fright. I have not spoken of it for so long... Despite the halting, haunted beginning of her narrative, her insecurities about whether she was telling her story "right," and her self-professed difficulties in finding the correct words, often causing her to back up and begin again, Geetha's narrative quickly became dynamic and charismatic, replete with detailed descriptions, spirited recollections and forceful movement.

Reconstructing for me in compelling whispers the scene which she had watched unfold before her own eyes - how her husband had been coming home from work during an army attack on the village, how an army truck had brutally run him down on a road nearby their house, as she stood watching from the cross-roads - Geetha's words were evoked in a torrent of speech. She described the ensuing army attack, and those that followed throughout the week, during which time the villagers fled their homes into the jungle. In the shelling and bombardment that accompanied their flight, Geetha's twelve year-old son was also killed, shot as they were climbing a wall to escape.

Once safe, Geetha then lived with her youngest son in a welfare center for three years before returning to her village in 2000. Like Geetha, many women I spoke with had been victims of, or witnesses to, hideous violence at the hands of the Sri Lankan Army. In addition to bearing witness to the physical violence which had unfolded in their villages, however, many narratives also provided eloquent testimony to the silences which had long enshrouded these memories. As Geetha explained, It is not wise to trust these people - that is why we must speak out here [in the garden], like animals. Everyone - the government, the LTTE. But they [the Army] know I saw, so they are also afraid... They say they took him to the hospital, but I don't know where they took him, I don't know if he ever went there... They took his body, and they wouldn't release it to me. For a long time, they wouldn't give me his body - they said if I wanted it, I must sign some papers saying that the accident was done by the LTTE, that the LTTE ran him over.

They didn't want to get into trouble - they found out my husband wasn't in the LTTE, and they were afraid of getting trouble. Through her account of the Army's deceit and the lies it forced her to tell and retell, Geetha's narrative reflects the damage done to individuals when those who have committed physical violence erase the history of their victims, and deny their own culpability. Such silencing constitutes a "violence within", woven as it is throughout the texture of everyday life, on individual, family, communal, and national levels. Many women I spoke with admitted that though they had longed to return home while living in the welfare centers, the actual resettlement process had been an excruciatingly painful one due to their sudden confrontation with, and habitation in, various sites of violence and horrific memories.

Indeed, upon her return home after three years, Geetha's efforts to come to terms with the violent legacy which haunted her village were persistently frustrated by the lies surrounding her memories, and the powers which tried to nullify and distort them. Geetha's words reflect the realization that not only had violence shattered her personal dignity and family life, but that the denial of violence had destroyed her home, severing the affective affiliations and feelings of security which she once knew there.

As she reflected, This village has become a very sad place for me, since we went away. When we were in the camps, I wanted to come home – I thought it would be better here. But everything has changed here – this village has only bad things for me, so many places are sad to remember. It is not a good place to live now, our own homes are filled with so much blood… The Army is still here, so people are afraid, and still, I cannot speak freely in my own house! Clearly, for Geetha and others like her, resettlement meant the return home not to an empty, or 'negative' space, but to a land pregnant with unresolved memories, silences and traumatic historical and political events which have yet to be accounted for, and laid to rest. Indeed, 'home' for Geetha was a place which harbored secret, raw wounds, scraped open afresh by their daily public negation.

Memory, History and Home

Far from describing natural processes of reintegration, Geetha's narrative reflected her struggle to both resurrect memory from its silent grave, and negotiate its place within the historical space of her home. As I will argue, where silence and speechlessness have clearly been the insidious, pervasive results of violence, private memory such as Geetha's provides a way to excavate these silences, and testify to past injustices which are otherwise impossible to articulate. Indeed, the rapid excitement with which Geetha recounted the events of her husband's death both vigorously enacted the retrieval of suppressed memories, and betrayed a desperate attempt to make a lost moment of history real through its retelling. As Geetha told me, I watched him die, you know.

They say it was an accident, and I signed to say it was the LTTE, but we all know. I saw the Army kill him, so did the other women. We all ran into the street when we heard them coming, and there was shouting, and we all ran, ran into the street, but then we got afraid, so we hid behind the stalls. So I was watching from behind, we were all just watching people running and there was so much noise… I saw when they crashed down on him and I was screaming… That truck had very big wheels, and they never slowed down, that Army truck. Their papers say it was the LTTE, so it was, but it wasn't! Rogers et al. claim that "[W]here there is silence, where there are no witnesses, it may seem as if an event has not occurred" (1999: 11).

And yet, as Geetha's narrative repeatedly implores, "I saw." This struggle to bear witness, to resurrect a hidden truth, to reassert the veracity or reality of an officially denied event is clear through Geetha's insistence that while on one level (that of official documents and history) "it was" the LTTE who killed her husband, on another level (that of individual memory and personal truth) "it wasn't!" In her persistence to speak, to struggle with memory, to get the story "right," Geetha was consciously combating "the in authenticating effect of living behind a lie (the official truth)" establishing the truth as she knew it, and creating an engagement between narrative and history. Thus through her political act of remembering, by joining memory to language, Geetha became the "testimonial bridge which, mediating between narrative and history, guarantees their correspondence and adherence to each other," and establishes memory as a means through which to resist both violence and silence.

For as Geetha recalled, "I know what I saw... Yes, I signed those papers, but I still know what happened." Clearly, a crucial aspect of Geetha's struggle to cope with her memories amidst a context of fear included contesting official versions of the violent events she had witnessed, thus actively locating herself within the historical space of home. While silent due to fear, Geetha's insistence upon the truth within her own memories, and her refusal to forget, or accept the official version of her husband's death, immediately confronted the military agenda, turning private thoughts into political ones, "reinterpreting the political domain and challenging the 'natural order of things'", as put forth by those in power.

In this way, witnessing and remembering were not passive functions, but acts of personal resistance in which the individual, lone act of memory, however small, indicated an active engagement with officially sanctioned versions of history, "acting into these spaces and contesting their hold". Thus, by maintaining these secret, unofficial memories, Geetha and other women like her sought to establish authority over the historical spaces of their homes, lending them personal meaning and historical significance despite the unforgiving silence.

Memory in Space, Time and National Politics

Furthermore, Geetha's narrative denied the existence of a fixed, static relationship between people and place, instead reflecting a continuing struggle to re-cultivate an affiliation with home by carving out a place for memory within the physical space, time, and politics of her village. For Geetha, resettlement demanded not only return to the site of memory, but to that memory denied, thus inspiring in her a concerted effort to make sense of her memories amidst a context which had both produced and obliterated them. One day, weeks after she had told me the story of her husband's death, Geetha asked me to accompany her to the town center.

Choosing a different route than we had walked before, she stopped alongside a dirt road just west of her house. Pointing, she said, Even now I do not like to return to this place. These days, when I go to the store, I take the long way through that woman's garden so that I do not pass by. Look at the road – it looks as though nothing has happened here... It has not even left marks on this road. Earlier, there must have been marks – they must have cleared them away. But I know this is the place. See over there? I know it's here because of that jack tree.

Combined with the detailed physical and geographical descriptions that emerged throughout her narrative, Geetha's desire to show me the site of her husband's death suggests "[T]he need to penetrate... silences, to know where somebody was killed, what exactly happened... [and] reflects a need to locate a person or an event in history, to find a place or a site in which memory can orient itself, create boundaries and spatial dimensions...". By revisiting the site of her husband's death, I believe Geetha was reclaiming a memory obscured by the lies of the state (and those she herself had committed,) transforming it into one with tangible, physical characteristics through which she could locate and affirm a site of personal mourning and loss.

Wresting power from the Army, Geetha sought to re-inscribe physical space with meaning, truth and personal memory, thereby recreating a relationship with physical land in the aftermath of violence. Similarly, Geetha's stories continually reconnected the memory of her husband's death to other temporal markers, 'real' and publicly known events whose reality could not be negotiated or denied, such as her son's birthday, and the day the villagers had fled. Thereby affixing the violence she had witnessed to a dependable time, Geetha was able to locate her memories within the chronology of her own life and that of the village.

As she recalled, Since we returned, it seems to be a different place, different from the home we left. How can it ever be like our old home? This used to be a beautiful village–there was plenty of fruit on the trees, though now it is dry and we cannot grow well... When I was a young girl, this was a prosperous village. I was very happy and we earned well. There was food to eat, and I studied well in school. Now that all this has happened, our lives will never be the same here... Thus, in her attempts to understand the effects of violence on the life of her village, and come to terms with the violent legacy of her home, Geetha's words both sought to imbue time with personal truth, and establish a relationship to her village that encompassed personal memory, despite its official non-existence.

Finally, in her efforts to imagine a future in which her violent memories of the past could be reconciled, Geetha's words reflected sophisticated recognition of the political changes taking place around her, suspicion of their authenticity, and an attempt to lend political significance to her memories, fitting them into a larger political context in the hopes of reconciliation. As she mused, Now there is talk that the war has ended, that the Army will leave here and there will be peace talks. But how can there be peace when such things have happened to so many of us?

Longing for the end of violent conflict to bring redemption to memory, Geetha's hopes indicate a yearning for political reconciliation with her home and its history, and a recognition that not to account for violence serves as "a perpetration of its tyranny". To this end, her words betray the still "foaming, eddying presence of the past", and that the death of her husband is an event which is not yet over. By imagining the future of national politics as an opportunity to reformulate an attachment to home and restore a semblance of dignity, Geetha's words reflect a multi-faceted struggle to resolve the painful process of 'homecoming'.

Discourse and Policy Implications

Turner contends that if a refugee has faced intense traumas in his home, this compounds the experience of alienation and may inhibit successful integration into the asylum country. As Geetha's narrative demonstrates, however, the return *back* to one's very own home may constitute a similarly challenging process of *re*integration for the precise reason that the return home is a return to the site of this trauma. Thus, home is not a 'negative' or empty space into which people naturally reintegrate, but a physical, historical and political place in which people must struggle to carve out a place for their memories of the past and visions of the future while subjected to violent historical legacies and ongoing political repression.

To the extent that such forces have the potential to alienate people from their native lands, the attachment of people to place is not a natural given, but an affiliation that must be cultivated and re-cultivated through complex psychological and political processes. Furthermore, insofar as the resettlement process is one of coming to terms with violence, silence and the painful memories embodied in home, I believe that psychological adaptation is unlikely to be a natural corollary of economic reintegration. To this end, rehabilitation assistance must approach the processes of psychological adaptation as real and vital ones in their own right, and while they must not be pursued in isolation, psychological well-being must be conceived of as an end in itself, and not merely a benefit of economic reintegration. If the psychological needs of returnees go unattended, deep, pervading wounds to the psyche may persist in damaging the entire individual, thus undermining even the goals of economic rehabilitation. Indeed, the processes of reestablishing trust and affective ties to a land haunted by warfare depend on much more than simply improvement of living conditions.

Unfortunately, despite recent political developments towards peace in Sri Lanka, a "veil of official secrecy" continues to shroud the past in ambiguity, impeding a necessary reassessment of the state's role in violence against the Tamil population. Recently, we have begun to hear calls from Sri Lanka to 'overcome' a violent legacy and 'move on' toward a peaceful future. While national reconciliation is an admirable goal, it is also a fragile, potentially dangerous process in that it "risks abandoning those individuals and communities who have suffered trauma, with no public recognition of, or accounting for, the causes and impacts of their loss".

As Dawson notes, Where the language of reconciliation speaks of forgetting the past... this amounts to a denial of the psychic and political realities of those communities. In such a situation - where violent conflict has only recently ended, it remains fresh in living memory, and is liable to break out again... The psychic and political legacies of history are not overcome quite so readily: they remain a source of profound tension within and between the warring communities. That which the language of reconciliation would smooth over and erase, the language of trauma insists upon: it names the realities... as traumatic, and points to the necessity of remembering in order to go forward to any viable alternative future".

Indeed, I believe that remembering - forcing individual memories of pain and suffering into the public domain where they may be heard, and their burden shared - is a prerequisite for genuine reconciliation. Without such acts of public witnessing, the buried past may remain a raw and open wound, slow to heal and continually re-emergent, exerting "a malign influence in a range of morbid symptoms, silences and emotional reactions". Therefore, it is essential to create both social and political spaces in which death, destruction and personal losses can be recognized, and their traumatic effects acknowledged.

Clearly, public and official acknowledgement about the truth of atrocities committed is central to the distribution of responsibility, and is needed for both "social reparation", and for "repairing the damage wreaked within the inner world of the psyche". Such acknowledgement is one way of recognizing the dignity and worth of both victims and their survivors, and thus beginning the process of both individual and collective healing and recovery. As Jelin notes, Truth telling is said to address the social need for knowledge to become acknowledgement.

It is said to bring victims back into the fold of society, by recognizing their suffering, providing a form of distributive or social justice, and giving out non-conventional resources such as social awareness, collective memory, solidarity... Truth has also been seen as a form of 'justice as recognition,' acknowledgement or admission. It can further be seen as a form of compensatory justice, in that it restores a sense of justice that had been broken down" (1994: 25). To this end, pursuing accountability and combating "social amnesia" or denial supports social rehabilitation, "allow[ing] individuals to acknowledge and reconcile the past openly, to acknowledge at last the culpability for the death of their loved ones and to lay them to rest".

For as we have seen in the case of Sri Lanka, painful aspects of the past live on "whether as private nightmares or public conflicts", and thus remain to pollute the present. Thus, in an effort to counter the vast silence and isolation of victims and survivors, societies must attempt to "heal the great divide between the personal and the political". And yet, while memory is vital to such a process, as Manz notes, "personal liberation cannot be fully realized while the social conditions remain in a state of oppression and distress. Real liberation and trust cannot be cultivated and sustained separate from the society that binds individuals".

Clearly, for many returnees, the concepts of both home and return often mean something vastly different than the meanings attributed by academic literature and international policy. While the predominant discourse on repatriation uncritically accepts and continually reaffirms territorialized notions of home, resettled Sri Lankan women's narratives repeatedly imply that the concept of home suggests something much more than merely a territorial space or their physical, geographical place of origin. To the contrary, home for many women was made up of a series of interconnected social, political, historical and psychological spaces, the return to which involves processes of struggle and contention.

Similarly, many narratives consistently portrayed return not as a natural process of reconnection and reintegration between people and place, but as a challenging process of transforming these various spaces into home all over again, through dynamic, contested, and often painful processes of power and inequality. For many women, their struggles during return hinged on the fact of violence, the physical, social and political forms of which governed their everyday lives, constituting an integral, intimate part of their memories and identities, and obstructing their efforts to return *'home'*.

To this end, while resettlement to their native villages may have signified an end to physical displacement, the return to violence simultaneously enacted the beginning of other forms of social, political and psychological disarticulation, ensuring the profound impossibility of return at all, and instead requiring creative processes of reconstruction, reinvention and re-imagination. Indeed, women's narratives suggested a far more creative concept of home, one which acquires meaning through complex processes of remembering and narrating the past, and imagining a future in the location of return. In fact, women's narratives imply that the existence of, or connection to, home cannot be taken for granted, but is rather something worthy of explanation.

As Warner argues, disciplinary assumptions about return and home "assume a world of order and symmetry" which over-simplifies the relationship between individual, society, state and territory (1994: 160). As Warner notes of refugees, The situation of the refugee is the physical incarnation of the rift in being; it is the physical incarnation of the denial of symmetries, alignments and equations... It is in this sense that the refugee shows us the rifts in ourselves that we wish to deny. The refugee's return to home, and our desire to prioritize that return, is all our desires to return to a world of alignments and symmetries.

Refugees and non-refugees wish to be in a world of equations and alignments, a world that... never was (1994: 168) Sri Lankan women's words deny the existence of such equations and symmetries, bearing witness to the divergence between both discourse and policy on repatriation, and the actual, lived experiences of returnees themselves, and effectively highlighting a dangerous gap between official images of home and return for policy-makers, and the harsh realties of post-conflict resettlement. Such images are the result of a theoretical framework that has yet to truly comprehend the complexity of experiences involved in return and reintegration, and therefore dangerously neglects certain crucial needs of return migrants, while simultaneously failing to recognize the harsh realities of social change in the aftermath of war and displacement.

To this end, oral narratives must not be seen merely as research methodologies, but as a means through which to reevaluate the humanitarian community's impact on returnees. Clearly, reintegration programmes must strive for a more holistic approach to development for assistance to be at all relevant, successful and sustainable on an individual level. Insofar as women's narratives encourage a more complex understanding of personal, social and political life after resettlement, they challenge organizations to develop multi-faceted approaches to rehabilitation which will effectively address the profound effects of violence and loss on the return home.

We are in dire need of both a new theoretical discourse and practical strategy which incorporate returnees' own meanings, perceptions and experiences of home and return into their fold, thereby altering the ways in which we conceive of return migration. Such an institutional shift must acknowledge the ways in which personal, social, historical, psychological and political experiences influence notions of home and identity in the location of return. Furthermore, insofar as repatriation presents returnees with new challenges and opportunities upon return, their responses point us toward a new course for both policy makers and academics, translating the vocabulary of return - reintegration, reconstruction, and rehabilitation - into one of "construction, creativity, innovation and improvisation."

One could observe that today all the world over there is a discussion on the place and role of Muslim women. From Saudi Arabia to England and from France to China we come across this debate. It is equally focused in both the Middle Eastern countries and the other countries where there is today a substantial presence of Muslims. Understandably the position of Muslim women in Western societies has drawn much attention. It is pertinent to see how this has become the focus of attention in such a widespread manner covering the different countries and cultures. The manifest reason is perhaps the exclusiveness Muslim women exhibit or adopt in terms of the attire which covers out of their religious needs.

This exclusiveness in terms of attire and public behaviour raises a great deal of interest in their exclusiveness especially in the context of in the process of secularization which had prompted and encouraged avoidance of religion in civil life. It is important to hear these considerations which in their own way create an interest in a study of the place and role of Muslim women in the society within which they live. Any analysis relating to the place and/or role of any particular group of people in their societies should inquire into the functional roles they have within that society and the place assigned to them in terms of the organization of the social group.

This is quite a fundamental aspect in the analysis of the social roles of individuals and groups for instance a study of the youth problem would reveal that the nature and the characteristics of that problem would vary from society to society depending on the vital question as to how the youth are viewed within that society and the place they have in the family unit and so on. More important is a knowledge relating to the culture within which these people live. It is a well known fact that all "living beings" whether human or animal, even the plants live within known "cultural" background. Environment plays an important role.

When it comes to the human society, equally important are the faiths the values, and attitudes. Looked at this way culture is the sum total of the environment, the gender, the modes of productions, available in the societies, the social relationships, which arise out of the production relations. Religion constituting the areas of faith and of a world - view, values which arise out of socio-economic and religious interactions along with habits and modes of behaviour fall within culture. The discipline of sociology and anthropology demand us to take such all encompassing, at the same time synoptic view of culture. Thus an inquiry into the social role of women would imply an analysis of the cultural norms of the society within which they live.

Hence an analysis of the place and role of the Muslim women would entail an analysis of the Muslim society, the norms it has relating to women. However we should exercise some caution in our understanding of the term culture especially when we relate religion to culture. Thus societies which have the same religion would have different cultural traditions; for instance Christianity in Western society and in Indian and Sri Lankan society. An equally forceful example would be the differences in the Hindu societies living in North India and South India.

A book of North Indian Hindu society would reveal the system of the PARDAH, associated with the Muslims, in not confined to the Muslim alone. Thus we could see that even within one religion these are social variations based on regional and historical factors. Viewed in these terms an analysis of the

Muslim society would have to be viewed at two levels. The first one is that of the religious social norms that Islam stipulates. The second would be the social changes arising out of modernization technolisation etc. which enable an overall global conformity in human interactions. Regarding the first Islam stands out as a religion very different from the other religious in terms of the norms of rules and behaviour it stipulates.

A look at the Islamic society would show that irrespective of geographical spread of the religion, there is a stipulation in terms of the organization of units of social evidence within an Islamic society. Islam provides a guide line for the organisation and functioning for each of the units - families, society and the state is true that in Hinduism there are scriptural regulations relating to adoption of caste. Primarily a social Institution, Islam is perhaps more specific and direct. It speaks of how the unit of family should be organized and how it should function. Likewise it speaks of the brotherhood of Islam "UMMAT" and finally about the principles that govern the state as an institution. Thus, in Islam determines the human relations within the family, the society and the state.

The other major religions do not have such an all encompassing view of the social life of its people. This has given Islam and the Muslim society a sense of specificity. Environments may differ even civilizations pattern may differ but not these prescriptive norms. Therefore we are required to look into how a female is viewed within the Islamic society. At this point it is important to realize that some of the environmental and social factors arising out of the area within which Islam was founded and developed first by the Prophet himself.

The Arab society at the time of founding of Islam was composed of tribes which in terms of geography and economy of the area had to be patriarchal. The position of women in all partriarchal societies has been down graded because they could not play an effective role in the functioning of those patriarchal societies. The human anatomy of the female and her role in reproduction of life especially the nursing of the children in such conditions necessarily imposed certain restrictions of behaviour between the male and the female. [The position of women in agricultural societies had been different. In those societies she was the first agriculturalist] Thus in terms of the socio-economic and cultural background within which Islam arose and developed first there had to be status differences between the male and the female. The exclusive dress stipulated for women should be understood in this background. It is equally important to see the female dress in terms of the male Arab dress itself. The male Arab costume covers the head and the body from shoulder to feet. There has been a universalisation of this dress norm where ever Islam spread.

But the regional variations noticeably seen among Muslim societies in the tropical areas show that the concept of "HIJAB" was accommodated within the norms of the tropical society. Thus in an average TAMIL NADU or Sri Lankan Muslim household the females would use the saree itself to be used as the "PURDAH". It is important to recall that the concept of "HIJAB" which Muslim women all the world over practice with fevour today has been an effect of the Iranian Revolution of 1979. One could also observe that with modernization and with the spread of middle level and higher education among Muslims women in our own countries (Sri Lanka, India) the Muslim women are suitably changing their dresses without infringing on the concept of HIJAB.

Muslim women are today employed as Doctors, Lawyers, Teachers and clerks in government services. The dress they wear while being compliant with the religious norms does not hamper them in their public life. At this juncture, reference should be made to the fact that in Pakistan, Bangladesh, Sri Lanka Muslim ladies are occupying important positions in political life. Even in Saudi Arabia the principle of female representation and the right to vote can now accepted. Thus one has to be very careful in rushing to conclusions about the positions of Muslim women.

The religious norms relating to attire and behavior in

the public arena have been feasible enough maintaining none the less a balance between the religious norm and the contemporary social needs. Therefore the examinations of the place and role of the women should be viewed in terms of the social norms it prescribes for the female especially as the life's partners. Before setting about to do this it is important to take into count the question of the socio psychological satisfaction that the members of the group, whether family or other institutions draw from their interactions.

The sense of psychological satisfaction is very essential to the continuity of the institutions and the tradition. It is true that the socio cultural norms do condition the life of the people in terms of both acceptance and expectations external conditions affect these norms. But the continuity socio psychological factor is important. It is this satisfaction that enables a sense of belonging. Keeping these facts in mind let us now go into the position of the female in Sri Lanka Muslim society. The female as the child, as the sister, as the bride, the wife, the mother, the mother-in-law and grand mother has an integrated role in the day to day life and the over all continuity of the family.

While on one hand the norms of patriarchy are widely prevalent it is also true that only a family with a female child is considered worthy of being ("BARAKATH") affluence bestowed. A similar norm is prevalent in Hindu Tamil homes. It is normally held that a female child helps enable the strengthening of the neculear family as a unit. It is worth repeating here female education is a popular and sought for among the Tamils and the Sinhalese. However at the school level the Muslim female child is expected to and is given the rights to preserve its identity in terms of the attire it wears. It should be noted the wide spread use of KAMEEZ and SHALWAR in Sri Lanka today tends to bring about a certain sense of uniformity. The position of the Muslim girl as a bride is quite interesting.

The Islamic practice of "MAHAR" is really in the tradition of the BRIDE PRICE found among the SEMITIC TRIBES. But in Sri

Lanka the Dowry is crucially important in getting educated young men with prospects of highly paid jobs as bride grooms. It is interesting to note that in the patriarchal tradition the residence of the couple is part local. But in the case of Sri Lanka with heavy dowry the bride grooms generally lives in the house of the bride. More interesting is the KUDI system found among the Muslims of Batticaloa. The KUDICCLAN is determined by matrilineal descent and marriages in the KUDI system are exogamous. But this tradition is not found among all the Muslims of Sri Lanka.

In the matter of marriage conventionally it is the father of the bride who takes all decisions. But today with availability of space for interactions, between young Muslim boys and girls the love marriages have become an integral aspect of Muslim life. It is significant to know that the Muslim bride/wife has her right to sue for a divorce this right for seeking divorce is called "KUL-OO". The wife has a right to "KUL-OO" if the husbands develops deformities after marriage or has habits which go against family living. However this right is only very very seldom used.

The need to mention this is because there is a wide spread belief among the non-Muslims that Muslim husbands are permitted to obtain divorce very freely and that they can get married to four women. But within the Muslim society this cannot be done that easily at all. It should be remembered that the request for either the "Kul-oo" or the "Thala" has got to be made first as the "QUAZI COURT". KUAZI are judicial officers inquiring into problems related to marriage. They examine the cases in terms of the Islamic laws and practices and pronounce the verdict. Sri Lanka "A KUAZI" has in his area of jurisdiction the powers of a judge of the district court.

The proceedings of the KHAZI court are open to both parties. It should also be noted that "TALAQ" is not that easily obtainable. There are in fact three stages. There are chances of the husband and wife coming together again in the first two stages. On the question of marrying a second, third and fourth time it should be remembered that the second marriage cannot be had without the consent of the first wife. Besides the husband should be affluent enough to support each of them. Anthropologically speaking polygamy has been a feature of Semitic tradition.

This type of marriage system in which a woman in eligible for re-marriage takes away the concept of widowhood which Hinduism advocates. There again it should be noted that among the many castes and tribes in South India widow re-marriage is an accepted norm. In regard to property rites in Muslim families' sons are entitled to two shares and daughters one share of the father's estate. The wife is entitled for one-eighths of the husband's property. It is true that there are some differences in claim to property. In conclusion it is necessary to note that any analysis of the position of women of the Sri Lankan Muslim society should be done at two levels. a. at the level of a corporative analysis with the other ethnic group of Sri Lanka b. in terms of the Islamic society outside the South Asian Countries.

The study of identities of the marginal groups like the refugees has not received the kind of attention that it deserves. Right from the time of displacement to the phase of rehabilitation/incorporation refugees are forced to reject their old identities and accept the new ones. During the time of exile their identities remain in a flux. A refugee camp could be an ideal site for the study of changing identities, especially when the camp life becomes a long-drawn one. This chapter examines the trajectories of identity formation in refugee camps in the southern Indian state of Tamil Nadu where some 65,000 refugees have been living for more than a decade in about 111 refugee camps.

This chapter examines how the memories of displacement, martyrdom, and the state policies played a major role in shaping new identities of the refugee women. The past, the memories of war, the life of an ideal Tamil woman in Sri Lanka's North and the Northeast all contribute to the formation of new identities. Besides, the segregated camp life, restrictions on movements, lack of job opportunities, the exclusionary policies of the state too need to be explored I the study of women's identity in camps.

At the outset let me point out that instead of using the broader markers of identity like ethnicity, gender, occupation, language, caste and so on I am considering the new markers that gained prominence among the women during camp life. In a camp setting, women who carry on their day to day life with courage and dignity are referred to as 'the ideal women', women who sacrificed their near and dear ones in the war are called 'the mothers and sisters from the family of the martyrs', and women who try their luck elsewhere and migrate to the Middle East for jobs are known as 'the deserters', and those surrendered their chastity as 'fallen women' so on. These are some of the new identities of the Tamil women living in refugee camps.

With the help of case studies, I would like to show how some of these identities are constructed over time and what these constructions would mean to the women in camps. Many sociological studies have shown that the state plays an important role in constructing identities. E. Valentine Daniel, for example, describes the role of the state in the following way: "...faced with the threat of Tamil separatist movement, the state....does like to highlight the differences among Tamils. In this mode, it differentiates Tamils of the Jaffna Peninsula from those who live along the east coast, from those who live along the northwest coast, from those who work on the tea estates in the Island's south-central hills, and so on.

On the other hand, the state, at various time to various degrees, fuels the more. This is how the Sri Lankan state sharpened the existing divide between the Tamils of the Jaffna Peninsula, the estate Tamils, and the Muslim Tamils. As opposed to this when almost all the Tamil militant groups emphasized the participation of women in the national liberation struggle, the new identity of women as warriors gained currency. The Liberation Tigers of the Tamil Eelam's (LTTE) call to women to take part in the war clearly led to the shift in the construction of women from 'brave mother' to that of 'women warrior' or 'woman guerilla'.

The Sri Lankan Tamils in India were seen as inheritors and part and parcel of a great Tamil culture and tradition, who became 'victims' of a bloody ethnic war, and now 'living in exile'. From time to time, Tamils in India were reminded by the politicians and the intellectuals of the great ethnic bond between the Tamils in the Island and the Indian Tamils.

However, the state went out to prove that this earlier construction was more 'fictive' than 'real' since the Sri Lankan displaced Tamils were involved in killings of political leaders including the former Prime Ministers of India, Tamils from the Island were branded as 'subversive elements', 'potential terrorists'.

Nearly 64,000 Sri Lankan refugees are now residing in 111 camps in Tamil Nadu. These camps are located in 23 out of 29 districts in the state. Some are large camps accommodating more than 1000 families. In the following six districts the number of families in camps exceeded 1000: Tiruvalur, Vellore, Tiruvannambalai, Erode, Madurai, and Shivaganga. Each of these districts accommodated 3,500 or more persons. After 1983 exodus of the Sri Lankan refugees, the then chief minister of Tamil Nadu, M.G. Ramachandran drew up a plan to send refugees to as many districts as possible so that they are not confined in a few places.

Accordingly, the district collectors were informed to allot land for their rehabilitation. This kind of dispersal gave them more space and job opportunities especially to those who managed to get shelter near the district headquarters or a small town. However, one of the drawbacks of the plan was meeting relatives and friends living in far off places. Many camps were located far away from the city or in unhygienic and congested cyclone shelters. Large-scale exodus of Tamil refugees took place on three occasions. The first influx began in 1983 and continued till 1987. During this time about 1,40,000 refugees arrived in Tamil Nadu to escape ethnic violence in Sri Lanka.

Out of these refugees, 43,000 were repatriated between 1987 and 1989, after the signing of a peace accord between India and Sri Lanka. The second exodus took place in 1989 when the Indian Peace Keeping Force (IPKF) withdrew from

Sri Lankan war-torn areas, most of these refugees were repatriated in 1991-92, after the assassination of Rajiv Gandhi, The third and the final influx began in April 1995 and it coincided with the declaration of Eelam War III, the battle between the Sri Lankan army and the Liberation Tigers for Tamil Eelam (LTTE). The influx can be divided into three phases. The story of Sri Lankan Tamil refugees rotates around three large-scale displacements, rehabilitation, and repatriations on two occasions.

THREE CATEGORIES

Sri Lankan refugees in Tamil Nadu can be divided into three broad categories. First, 'the camp refugees' or those who took shelter in camps, mostly located in the rural areas. They were sent from the Mandapam transit camp to different locations. The 'non-camp refugees' are those who are living in rented house with relatives and friends without any assistance from the government. Nearly fifty thousand refugees lived outside camps, most of them are staying in big cities. The third group consisted of those who supposedly posed security threats since they were involved in subversive activities in Sri Lanka. They were sent to 'special camps' where they had to live under constant surveillance. These special camps came into existence in 1991.

This chapter deals with the first category of refugees only. Following Kunz (1981) Sri Lankan Tamil refugees can also be classified in terms of degree of alienation. There are refugees who believe that their opposition and antagonism to events at home uprooted them. They are paying the price for the principle they cherished. These refugees retain a strong bond with their homeland and they will be the first to come forward in the case of repatriation once the cause of their exile is removed. They are the heroes among the displaced.

There are refugees who leaving their homeland for a long time feel alienated from the people back home. Long periods of asylum had caused such alienation. They are less likely to have a strong desire to return if they see no change in social and political conditions that alienated them. There are also 'self-alienated' refugees who exiled themselves rather than society alienating them. They are less likely to return. The degree of alienation from the community or from one's self is particularly relevant for the study of camp refugees. We shall return to this point later.

IDENTITIES: OLD AND NEW

Let me begin by stating that identities take forms, erode, reconfigure over time and this is all the more so in the case of refugees. Marker of identities that are not important any more may lose relevance. The village in South Asia remained a reference point of identity for centuries. The village, following Daniel, may be described as a 'place'. One is linked to a place by a sense of identity with and belonging to that has roots. This may be contrasted with 'space', which is an "epistemic unit", it provides with a way of seeing the world. The space has a deeper and larger connotation, more stable than place.

The sense of belonging to a village gradually disappears among the people experiencing liminality, and it becomes a fluid marker of identity. When thousands of villagers are displaced from the place that they shared for many generations, they look out for other appropriate markers of identity. Sometimes, one's district becomes an important marker that remains with them throughout their journey as displaced and during their stay in refugee camps. Another marker of identity, namely 'caste' too loses its meaning with the displacement.

Circumstances make it difficult for displaced persons to hang on to this traditional marker of identity. In congested boats that bring them to India and camps, following of caste rules and practices becomes extremely difficult. Thus in marriages or in other forms of social interactions caste ceases to carry any weight. In some extreme cases, linguistic and community identities undergo changes too. This happens when lives in exile turn out to be a long one. The displaced people get assimilated with the local social milieu, speak in the language of the hosts and adopt culture of the local communities.

Many examples of this kind of assimilation can be cited from recent South Asian history. For example, Afghans migrated to many parts of northern India several years ago, today old markers of their identity can hardly be found among the Afghans. Several Chinese and Burmese had migrated to India since the early fifties. For them too the traditional markers of identity carry little meaning. However, recent studies on diasporas have shown that there remains a space between the rejection of the old markers and the acceptance of the new. This space gives uniqueness to the community. The core elements of identities that stay on and give uniqueness to diasporas is now a popular subject for sociological research.

THE 'IDEAL WOMEN' IN CAMPS

As mentioned earlier, the construction of identities of refugee women has been studied here in the context of harsh camp life, which to a large extent is a result of the exclusionary policies of the state. The new identities of women that are associated with hard life in refugee camps are labeled by the camp refugees as 'the ideal women', 'the deserters', 'the women from the home of the martyrs', and so on. Let me examine the case of the ideal women first. These are the women exemplifying an ideal and often taken as a model for imitation by the rest as they are role models for many in an extraordinary situation. The ideal that they exemplify is simply keeping high morale in the midst of adversaries.

The loss of husbands and elderly male members in the war forced these women to act as the heads of their households. Some of them do all the household chores, look after the children and also go out to earn extra money. Some of these women are married but most of the time lives alone because their husbands go to far off places in search of work and show up only at the time of distribution of doles. Here are some case histories of women, widows who are considered as 'ideal'. Let me now cite some examples. Laxmi lives with five children in a camp located in the southern Tamil Nadu. I entered Laxmi's house to find her in the kitchen what is a luxurious 4 feet by 4 feet space, an extension of the small room in which they live.

Her three daughters, all looking alike, and one in the cradle were all there. Laxmi told me that her only son was out playing. Although Laxmi lives with her husband, she is literally a single mother since her husband goes out to work and comes back only after a week or a fortnight. He needs to be here at the time of disbursements of loans. He earns Rs.60.00 a day and brings it all home, with five mouths to feed. She often borrows money from the moneylender at Rs.10 interest for 15 days for a principal of Rs.100. With debts and hardships life hardly moves for Laxmi. Her neighbour says, "she looks after the children as best as she could.....the children come first when it comes to the question of feeding the hungry."

Although she comes from a well off family in Sri Lanka, Laxmi has dealt with the hard life in camps in an exemplary manner. Like Laxmi, another ideal woman is Jaya. In 1992, Jaya and her family had to leave their home at Mud road, in Mannar District, after her husband was killed in crossfire. A month later, helped by her neighbours she reached Manar. Time was difficult for her as uncertainty clouded her mind for not having a single pie at hand and having to protect three children. She shielded them through the forests: She recollects with gratitude the favour she received from her neighbours who helped her with the bus fare, food and also provided necessary protection: They even paid the boat fee for the family.

She spent nearly ten years in camp and weathered crisis after crisis with determination. Rajalakshimi, the eldest daughter, was married when she was 16. She was once again diagnosed with a cyst and was recommended an operation. A camp refugee points out, "she refused to get operated fearing the expenses since she has two other children to look after." She is unable to lift heavy loads now, walk or even perform the daily chores. The illness has deprived her of daily wage job. However, her son works very hard to educate the two kids and feed her. In the eyes of the camp resident, Jaya showed courage, brought up children with her sweat and blood, an out and out an ideal mother. Nageshwari is another ideal woman in the camp. She and her family lived in Omandhai in Vavunia district. For war and continuous bombing they decided to flee. They walked a distance of 45 kilometers for five days to reach Madu and for twenty-five days to go to Gramam.

On reaching Rameshwaram, the family of six had to look after an ailing child aged 2. The officials saw the child and paid immediate attention and sent the family along with the child to Palayamkottai hospital where he died. She suffers from chronic asthma and is unable to perform her home duties Her eldest daughter has epileptic attacks, the third daughter developed tuberculosis and the husband was wounded by thorn which grew septic, he was unable to move his fingers or grip anything with his hand. He goes to work only when he is well. The family had a debt of Rs.48,000. After meticulous effort she managed to reduce the debt to Rs.18,000.

Despite frequent illness Nageshwari wants to go out and work to save the sinking family. These are the women of courage, struggling hard to make both ends meet against all odds. A camp resident says, "....against all odds she stood like a rock, did all that was necessary to look after other members of the family...." Another person remarks, "she personifies high moral and ethical standard for other women in the camp." Indeed, these are exceptional women carrying out struggle with dignity. For camp residents, they know how to strike a balance between adversaries and moral life. Laxmi lives alone, carrying all the burden on her shoulder, Jaya suffers from ill health, and Nageswari too is unwell and sinking in debts. Valorization of ideal living does not take note of the suffering in silence. The ideal womanhood finds expression in a culture of silence, poverty, and hardships. They make an ideal ground for this culture to thrive on.

WOMEN OF THE MARTYR'S FAMILY

The war in Sri Lanka restructured social relations, redefined the role of women in a war- ravaged society. Many women sacrificed their husbands, sons, daughters, and relatives for the cause of 'Tamil Eelam'. These women occupy special position among the Tamils in refugee camps, they are treated with honour and dignity. These are 'the women from the family of martyrs' In the mid-eighties, almost all the Tamil political outfits carried out campaign to recruit as many women as possible into their organizations. They were not only needed in the battle fields but also to nurse wounded soldiers, to carry out campaign for the cause. The political pamphlets valorized Tamil women and their sacrifice. The appearance of Tamil women in the print media wearing military outfits and with a gun in the hand presented a new image of women.

Women who sacrificed their lives as suicide bombers became martyrs, the role model for other young women. Peteel noted how terms like 'thuuwar' (revolutionaries), 'fedayeen (guerillas), 'munadaleen' (strugglers) became signifiers of a reconfigured self and community in the case of Palestinian women. One can see parallels here. A few cases may be cited. Mary Jesentha lived with her husband in Akaturchi northern Sri Lanka. The IPKF men were around these areas and they harassed the men living close to the IPKF camps. One day, the IPKF caught Mary's husband and charged him for supporting the LTTE. They beat him up and kept him in detention for a few days. Ever since he was beaten up, he developed chest pain and finally expired. At that time Mary was pregnant. Her in-laws took her and cared for her and the baby. Eventually she was asked to leave.

Today she works in an iron factory to bring up her children. But she is from a martyr's family. The camp refugees know that her husband died for a cause. Manjula is from Vavunia district. Due to army occupancy and heavy shelling they were forced to leave the place. Manjula's husband was taken by the army for his links with the LTTE and was beaten up severely.

When he came back he fell sick and was not in a position to work. They traveled from Vavunia on foot for three days and nights without food amidst heavy shelling and aeriel bombing. They rested in temples and churches, on the way.

In April 1990 they reached India. They were transferred from Mandapam transit camp to Thapathi. On reaching India her husband fell ill, he died shortly after arrival. The children were educated in the neighbouring school. Manjula is sick with a series of intestinal problems. She says that the doctor instructed her not to work. Burden of poverty forces her to work hard every day. Back home she cooks and takes care of her children. She looks grimly at the future and say's that "I am worried."

Manjula occupies a special place among the camp women. Camp refugees know that Manjula's husband sacrificed his life, thus she is a member of the martyr's family. All such women of martyr's family enjoy prestige, honour and dignity within the camp. A woman whose husband had been killed in action, who lost sons, daughters or relatives for Eelam is always regarded as a 'woman who has made sacrifice for a noble cause'. This is not unique only in camps, even in Sri Lanka, in the areas under the control of the LTTE, such women are treated with honour and deference. A family that sent a male or female member to the battle field is regarded as 'a freedom fighter's family' and the family that sacrificed a member in the war is 'a martyr's family'.

The 'ideal women' and 'women from the martyr's family' are to set high moral and ethical standards against all odds. As stated, these high expectations are difficult to fulfill in refugee camps. These women are expected to handle crisis at any cost for the sake of ideal ethical and moral life since they are the cut above the rest. As one refugee puts it "...come what may, these are women with brave hearts, they are not going to tilt..." This often puts an added burden on the shoulder of these women as they work hard to meet expectations from their new roles. Most of them pay the price, physically and mentally and they suffer in silence.

THE DESERTERS

Economic hardship has forced many refugee women to take up jobs in the Middle East in a clandestine manner, often by obtaining false passport and by forging one's name. Since the journey is undertaken secretively, it is difficult to get an exact figure of women who had been to the Middle East and now living in the camp and those who have not returned yet. These women who leave camp to take up jobs elsewhere are called *'kaividugiravau'* or the deserters. Several steps need to be taken before a prospective refugee woman leaves India. First, she needs to establish contact with the local agent who acts as a conduit between the main agent in Colombo and his client in Tamil Nadu. These agents are refugees who are in the age group between 25 and 40.

Second, financial matters have to be settled, and once the deal is struck the agent takes step to obtain 'clearance' or exit permit with the help of the local 'Q' branch official, and the Revenue Inspector. Third, once the clearance is obtained, the agent applies for an emergency passport to take his client to Colombo. He purchases the air ticket and establishes contact with the main agent for necessary action there. Once this is over, the woman begins her journey from Chennai to Colombo and from there to Riyadh in Saudi Arabia or to Kuwait or to other countries in the Middle East. At the place of arrival a contact person takes the woman to her employer or the employer himself turns up at the airport to pick up the maid himself. In financial terms, these jobs are lucrative since each maid earns minimum Rs.4000 a month. But for money they have to forego several things like their religious identity, since the employers take only Muslim women as housemaids.

The women take fictitious names, surrender their rights to live in the camps as refugees, forego doles and any other assistance from the state. Anandakrishna, an agent residing in one of the refugee camps, provided the details in the following way: A prospective immigrant to Saudi Arabia will have to obtain an emergency passport from the Sri Lankan High Commission at a price of Rs. 310. For an emergency passport, one has to pay an additional amount of Rs. 1000 to the broker. Most women prefer an early delivery of their passports and thus end up paying Rs.1310 in all. One of the major expenses is the amount payable to the Sri Lankan agency at Colombo that arranges the deal. His commission is Rs.4,500 initially. The air ticket from Chennai to Colombo and from Colombo to Riyadh would cost Rs.13,500, in addition one has to pay a visa fee of Rs.100 in Colombo.

In Riyadh, each maid receives a monthly salary of Rs.6000 per month, from which the agent in Colombo deducts Rs.2000 each month. The job pays off only in the long run." Anandakrishna finds out suitable women from camps. For each deal his commission is only Rs.2000. However, as a middleman Anandakrishna becomes a party to fraud and deception since Hindu women migrating to Saudi Arabia take fictitious names in their passports. A few cases may be cited here. In 1996, Asai and her husband traveled from Mannar by cycle to Madu and then by boat to Rameswaram transit camp. After spending a few months in a camp, she decided to work in Saudi Arabia for two years as a domestic maid.

For this, she had taken a loan from a family friend who collaborated with an agency in Sri Lanka to set up the job and issue a passport. For this placement, the Saudi family that took Asai paid 400 riyals to the Sri Lankan Agency. In addition, it was agreed that 200 riyals from Asai's salary of 600 riyals would be deducted by the agency every month. She then returned to camp in 1998 on a six-month tourist visa after the termination of her two-year contract. In the same year she again went to Jeddah for three years and finally returned to Sri Lanka and then to India in September 2001 on a six-month tourist visa.

Though her visa has expired, she continues to live in the camp illegally without registration. She pointed out, "earlier in 1998, a few women who had returned along with me were in jail for four days for staying in camp exceeding visa time limit. But I have spoken to the 'Q' branch officials about my status and they guaranteed that I won't have any problems in future". She remarked, "though I have spent almost five years abroad, my husband was not wise enough to save any money. One of the camp refugees remarked, "why doesn't she stay back like other women? How can she leave husband and children behind for such a long time?" In 1997, Jayalakshmi went to Riyadh for a maid's job for two years, in order to earn money and educate her children.

Upon her return in 1999, the collector of Vellore sent a letter to Jayalakshmi stating that she was not entitled to stay in India and she has to go back because her visa was not valid anymore. She did not take that letter seriously and one day police came to her house and arrested her and similar other women who went to Saudi for work. They were taken to police station and were asked to stay there for seven days. Jayalakshmi with the help of a lawyer came out of the police station. The lawyer charged her in all Rs.1000 for her release. When she was working in Saudi, she was earning Rs.4000 and what all she earned for her children's education, was spent in renewing her stay in the camp, paying bribe and paying fees to the lawyer.

The journey to the Middle East has led to more hardship and complications. One immediate consequence of taking up jobs abroad is that a refugee loses his right to live in India and right to receive dole. When they return with the tourist visa, they are allowed to live in the country as long as the visa is valid, normally for a period of six months. Once the visa expires, they encounter trouble from the authorities. They end up paying large sums of money as bribe for staying in the camp. The hard earned money goes for the payment of bribe. Jayalakshmi points out, ".......once you are back you feel like a stranger......the camp members do not come forward to help you....and the sharks are all around.."

Finally, in camps some are considered as 'fallen women', those who have surrendered their chastity. The women belonging to this category are those who had to take prostitution for living. Some of these women have their clients within the camp, some go out to cities for better prospect. These are the women who differ from a community's dominant ideologies, and they are condemned for moral weakness. Even in most liminal situation, control over sexuality by women is considered as non-negotiable. Liminal position of refugee women in camps provides an ideal opportunity for the study of identities. New identities take shape and become important markers in everyday life. The identity formation is always in flux, changing constantly depending on the changing social situation. It is also a process of negotiation, always eliminating or accepting, and in some cases compromising.

In the case of Tamil women refugees the old markers that got eliminated were caste, village, kinship, region and so on and the markers that got acceptance were ideal womanhood, martyrdom, desertion, sexual immorality and the like. In a perceptive essay on the Moors in Sri Lanka Q. Ismail noted "identities cannot be taken for granted; that they are fluid, transient, always in flux, never permanent; and that they alter (discursively) precisely because they are constructs. If they were "real", stable and eternal, they couldn't change."

This indeed is the case with the Tamil women, the new markers of identity now play a significant role among the women in the refugee camps. These markers are byproduct of the exclusionary policies of the state, and of the war and martyrdom. However, the stories of configuration and reconfiguration of identities of refugee women would tell us very little unless we take note of the issues of silencing the women and the suffering in silence, the former is linked with the latter in a complex way.

4

Women's Roles in India

A Sociological Review

Developmental policies and programmes that do not address gender disparities miss critical developmental opportunities. Education of girls is vital not only on grounds of social justice but also because it accelerates social transformation. Promotion of gender equality in education is essential for human resource development. By educating a woman you educate the whole family. Given that a woman has the responsibility of the whole family on herself, an educated woman is better capable of taking care of the health, nutrition and education of her children and more so be an active agent in the social and economic development of the country.

It is evident that economic success everywhere is based on educational success. Literacy is the basic building block of education. It is a basic component of social cohesion and national identity. It leads to an improvement in the depth and quality of public opinion, as well as to more active participation of the marginalized in the democratic process. No society has ever liberated itself economically, politically, or socially without a sound base of educated women.

Education has a direct impact on women empowerment as it creates in them awareness about their rights, their capabilities and the choices and opportunities available to them. Studies have indicated that there is a strong correlation between female education and several developmental indicators such as increased economic productivity, improvement in health, delayed age at marriage, lower fertility, increased political participation, and effective investments in the next generation.

POLICIES AND PROGRAMMES

In India, providing education to all the citizens is a constitutional commitment. The principal of gender equality is enshrined in the Indian constitution, in its Preamble, Fundamental Rights, Fundamental Duties and Directive Principals. The Constitution not only guarantees equality to women, but also empowers the State to adopt measures of positive discrimination in favour of women. Just after Independence, in 1951, literacy levels were very low (25% for men and 9% for women), In the next ten years there was not much progress in the literacy levels.

It is only after the recommendations of the Indian education commission (1964) and the National policy of education (1968) that the education of girls was seen as a means of accelerating social transformation. The policy placed special emphasis on initiating programmes to give equal educational opportunities to all the groups and both sexes. The constitution also gave primary responsibility for elementary education to the state governments, while the central government was given responsibility for technical and higher education. This situation changed in 1976 after the 42nd Amendment to the constitution was passed, making all education the joint responsibility of the central and state governments.

One of the consequences of this was that the foreign assistance, so far restricted to technical and higher education, now began to flow into primary education as well. Between the mid-1960 and the early 1980s, the proportion of resources going into elementary education showed a steady increase. National Policy on Education (NPE), 1986 and its Programme of Action (POA) gave high priority to gender equality and committed the entire educational system to work for women's empowerment. The National Perspective Plan 1988-2000 reiterates this point of view and states that women themselves must overcome their handicaps. Thus, there has been a careful articulation of education for equality for women, which is reflected in the educational policy discourse.

Central and State governments attached lot of significance to actually operationalising the NPE's Programme of Action and in a series of regional meetings with the State Governments, a special review of gender issues in education was undertaken. At the same time it was emphasized to the States, that gender concerns must be built into all educational processes. Monitoring committees for women's/girls' education at the Ministry of Human Resource Development level and also state level were formed to monitor the indicators of gender concerns in all policies and projects.

Emphasis was laid on enrolment and retention of the girl child in formal and non formal schooling; recruitment of rural women teachers and removal of gender bias in the curriculum. Mass literacy campaigns in different parts of India were launched which brought out volunteers from all sections of society as instructors, master trainers and organizers. Adult Education Programmes, Total Literacy Campaigns, Post Literacy Programmes, and continuing Education Programmes were also started. Nation wide gender sensitization programmes were undertaken to cover a large number of educational personnel to include educational administrators, teachers and teacher educators.

Complementary to this strategy, media campaigns and parental awareness programmes for generating a positive climate for girls' education were also started. Mobilization of women's groups and projects like Mahila Samakhya (Education for Women's Equality) with focus on the constraints that had so far prevented women and girls from accessing educational inputs were launched.

The purpose of these groups was to address issues of self image and self confidence of women and alter societal perception about them. Its overall goal was to create circumstances to enable women to better understand their predicament, to move from a state of abject disempowerment towards a situation in which they could determine their own lives and influence their environment, and simultaneously create for themselves and their family an educational opportunity which enhanced the process of development.

PROFILING GENDER GAP IN EDUCATION

Gender gap has been well documented and analyzed by governmental agencies, international organisation, university departments, NGO'S and individual researchers. Some recent publications that provide a panoramic view of this subject include, World Bank (1997), which charts the terrain occupied by primary organisations; Ramchandaran (1998), which provides the comparative perspective on girls and Women's education in South Asia; Shukla and Kaul (1998), Bhattacharya (1998), which looks more generally at the status of education in India; and finally Haq and Haq (1998), which analyses education within the context of human development in South Asia.

The past five decades have produced mass of information on innovative practices and experimental programmes. There are also innumerable guidelines and policy statements on why gender gaps persist in education and how these can be reduced. Negative cultural and societal attitudes, different standards-roles for boys and girls, competing demands on the girls time, economic reasons like -lack of resources, distance from school, lack of facilities in schools for girls, lack of female teachers, lack of security both in and outside the school, curriculum not relevant and flexible, gender stereotyping in curriculum, gender unfriendly classroom environment, early marriage and child bearing, absence of women role models, fear of deterioration of social structure, are the most frequently quoted stumbling blocks to female education.

In response to this, developing flexible school calendars, encouraging community participation, promoting parental awareness, creating gender neutral textbooks, training teachers for promoting gender equality, promoting girls access to science and math's education, reliance on multiple delivery systems and increasing resources of primary education are the strategies most often recommended for overcoming these hurdles. In fact, there is a certain degree of agreement about the constraints to education and about strategies that "work". But despite this convergence, these problems persist. The discourse on strategies needs to be located in a dynamic perspective. Revision and reflection are required to analyze this changing scenario, to identify its impact and to develop strategies to adjust to it.

The 93rd Constitution Amendment with the insertion of new article (21A)"The state shall provide free and compulsory education to all children of the age of 6 and 14 years in such manner as the state may, by law, determine." enables any citizen to seek the enforcement of the right by way of resort to writ Jurisdiction under Article 32 and 226 of the Constitution. Thus the 93rd Constitution Amendment fulfills the mandate of the CRC (The convention on the rights of the child which was adopted by UN General Assembly on November 20, 1989).

This initiative of the government has had far reaching consequences and has been a major catalyst in increasing the number of enrolments in primary classes. Data from Demographic and Health Survey (DHS) shows that the primary school attendance rate has increased by more than one percentage point annually since the beginning of the decade. In 2000, 76 per cent of all children of primary school age (6-10 years) were in school. By 2006, this value had increased to 83 per cent.

The attendance rate of girls increased by 9 per cent over the 2000-2006 period and the attendance rate of boys by 6 per cent. School attendance rates also grew in urban and rural areas, and across all household wealth quintiles. However, close to 17 per cent of all children of primary school age still continue to be out of school.

RURAL-URBAN DIFFERENTIAL

Experience of the last sixty years has shown that placing a high priority on education in policy statements has, to a certain degree ensured availability of adequate resources, but it does not ensure that marginalized groups benefit by national programs The expansion of the educational system has been uneven and inadequate There is a gender gap in the educational status of boys and girls and more so amongst the disadvantaged castes and tribes. Wage labourers have lower literacy levels than other occupational groups.

There is also a marked rural- urban differential. The lowest educational achievement can be expected among rural women belonging to scheduled caste or tribe. India represents a picture of contrasts when it comes to education and employment opportunities for girls in the rural and the urban areas. Cultural, social and economic factors still prevent girls from getting education opportunities and so the question of equality is still a mirage. The status of the girl child has been a subject of much discussion, controversy and debate.

While more and more families are beginning to value girls as equals to boys, there are still overwhelming cultural and economic reasons why female children are not receiving the same medical, emotional and educational attention as their male counterparts. From the start, girl child is seen as burden rather than a blessing, bearer of exorbitant dowry, who will eventually move into the home of her husband.

As a child; a girl receives less food, attention and emotional support than her male counterpart; as an adult, less attention is paid on developing her potential and more on matrimony and motherhood as these are regarded the essential and overarching goals of her life and all education is a preparation for that. In the rural areas, the girl child is made to perform household and agricultural chores. This is one of the many factors limiting girls education. Cleaning the house, preparing food, looking after their siblings, the elderly and the sick, grazing the cattle and collecting firewood are some of the key tasks they have to perform.

Households are therefore reluctant to spare them for schooling. Physical safety of the girls, especially when they have to travel a long distance to school and fear of sexual harassment are other reasons that impede girls' education. In the urban areas, however, there is a discernible difference in the opportunities that girls get for education and employment. There is an element of awareness of gender issues in the more educated sections of society in certain regions. Moreover, urban spaces permit greater opportunity for personal autonomy to girls.

Though the figures for girls would still be low as compared to boys, what is heartening to see is that whenever given the opportunity, girls have excelled more than boys. For instance, in the Central Board of Secondary Examinations for grades 10 and 12, which are at an All India level, girls have for over a decade now, bagged all the top positions and secured a higher over all percentage compared to boys. In employment opportunities too, women in India today have stormed all male bastions.

Be it piloting aircraft, heading multi-national corporations, holding top bureaucratic positions, leading industrial houses, making a mark as doctors, filmmakers, chefs, engineers and even as train and lorry drivers, women have made it to all hitherto considered male bastions in India. However, this is not reason enough for us to cheer. For the number of girls and women who have been left out of education and employment opportunities still far outweighs those who have got them. It is important to realize that fewer girls survive in the system long enough to reach the end of secondary education. And what is needed to change this scenario is not just governmental efforts but a change in societal norms, in cultural and traditional biases and in general mindsets of people. And in this the media, the civil society, and the youth, the women and girls have a lot to contribute.

HIGHER EDUCATION FOR GIRLS IN INDIA

Indian higher education system is one of the largest in the world. It consists of colleges, universities, institutions of national importance (such as Indian Institutes of Technology, Indian Institutes of Management and Indian Institutes of Science, etc.), and autonomous institutions with the status of deemed universities. In 2002-03, there were 300 universities; of which 183 were provincial, 18 federal, 71 deemed universities, and 5 were established through central and state legislation and 13 institutes of national importance.

The enrolment was 9,227,833 (about 7.8% of the relevant age group). There were 436,000 teachers in 2002-03 as against 457,000 in 2000-01. Of these nearly 83% are in the affiliated colleges and 17% in the universities. Gender wise data is not provided by the UGC. However, the 2001-02, MHRD (2001-02) provides information on the women teachers in the 12 open universities which is 18.4% and 21.5% in the institutions offering correspondence courses. There has been phenomenal expansion of educational opportunities for women in the field of higher education both general and technical.

Women education at the university-both college levels has been diversified and reoriented in tune with the changing requirements of the society, industry and trade. The number of women enrolled in institutions of higher education increased from 40,000 in 1950-51 to about 14, 37,000 in 1990-91 recording an increase of more than 36 times over the forty-year period. And in the year 2004-05 the number increased to 3,971,407. Proportion of women entering higher education 1950-51 was 10.9 per cent and in 2002-03 it was 40.04 per cent. The number of women per 100 men in 1950-51 was 14 which increased to 67 in 2002-03.

There are also wide disparities in enrolment by region, caste, and tribe and by gender. These differences impact on women from the disadvantaged groups. In 2001-02, the proportions of SC/ST students were as follows: Scheduled Castes 11.5 per cent (1,016,182) SC men 8 per cent (7, 06,769) and SC women 3.5 per cent (309,813). The ST students constituted 4 per cent (351,880) of total enrolment; men 2.7 per cent (240,495); women 1.3 per cent (114,168). In M.Phil/ Ph.D. programmes, there were 53,119 students all over the country. Of these 36.3 per cent (19,299) were women; 5.9 per cent (3,133) SC students; and 1.80 (951) ST students.

There were 824 SC women and 344 ST women, i.e. 4.3 per cent and 1.8 per cent respectively of all women research students. It is quite well known that inspite of a very well formulated policy of positive discrimination, the representation of SC/ST students is not adequate and the proportion of women is negligible. They generally join general education courses and are denied access to elite/courses and institutions.

Further, disciplinary choices are affected by socio-economic factors especially in the case of Scheduled Caste/Scheduled Tribe students whose representation remains marginal in higher education. But they too, are better represented in states in which women have better representation and in which higher education facilities have expanded in recent years.

DISCIPLINARY CHOICES FOR WOMEN

The relationship between availability of disciplinary choices and women's ability to access them are not directly related, nor are they dependent on women's academic achievement. The reasons cited for this are mainly due to social ethics. Large majority of women may be deprived of exercising free options in selecting subjects of their choice in school, as in case of girls, parents generally take the decision regarding the academic stream to be pursued .This decision is guided by the consideration that girls are not expected to work or earn before marriage and education is only an investment to fall back upon in case of the daughter becoming a widow or being deserted.

The poor parents have another problem; even though they perceive the significance of education, many a times they are not able to finance it. Besides, there is lack of role models and socialization support at home. Women from these social categories are the most affected by the stratification of disciplines, programmes and institutions. Further, the social and economic disparities are reflected not only vis-à-vis caste and tribe but also at the regional level, i.e. in different provinces.

Discipline boundaries not only limit choices but choices are further limited by future options of "life chances" of women.

Higher Education is further denied to the disadvantaged groups and especially women from rural poor homes. Because of social and economic reasons, parents may be unwilling to spend on education as well as the dowries of their daughters. A perusal of the disciplinary choices depicts that the proportion of women in some of the masculine disciplines was miniscule soon after independence and remained so till 1980's.

This is evident as the proportion of women in science decreased from 33.3 per cent in 1950-51 to 28.8 per cent 1980-81. This was the period when natural science was at a premium, especially physics and chemistry. Till the eighties they were the first choice for male students and while competing with men, women were pushed out. It is also possible that science was not, in any case, the first preference for young women whose parents perceived marriage as a priority over higher education.

An undergraduate degree of any kind only helped in the marriage market by raising the social status. A science degree required a longer investment of time and other resources, therefore was not desirable. The young women were also socialized to perceive higher education from that view point. The proportion of women in 2002-03 in arts was 44.2 and has been increasingly steadily since 1970-71. The proportion of men, on the other hand, has decreased gradually during the same period from 83.9 per cent to 54.6 per cent. In teacher's education, another feminine discipline the proportion of women has gone up from 32.4 to 50.6 per cent. Science, a masculine discipline, provides an interesting insight on disciplinary choices of young women and men.

For example, in science the proportion of men which was around 80-90 per cent till 1980-81, has come down to 59.8 per cent in 2002-03? Higher education for young women is taken for granted nowadays among the upper and middle strata in the cities but it is still not viewed as an immediate investment in their careers. Social role expectations affect the aspirations of women. For example, in the patriarchal social structure, parents are not expected to use the income of their daughters.

Therefore, even educated daughters are not encouraged to work and if they do so, it is for a short period before marriage. After marriage It is the right of the groom's family to decide whether she will work or not. Therefore, for a majority of young women in the academia, higher education is not linked to careers. This is the reason why women join arts and humanities as they are cheaper, softer, and shorter than the professional courses. But lately the number of those who are entering the professional subjects is growing.

PUBLIC VERSUS PRIVATE EDUCATION

Until the liberalization of the economy in the early nineties, higher education was publicly funded by the federal/central and provincial/state governments. However, since 1991 the policies of the government have dramatically changed with regard to seemingly privileged position of higher education. The government began to remove public support to higher education and make it self financing while privatizing it. Higher education has also become a non merit good.

However, since the early nineties, private autonomous institutions were permitted to be set up on a liberal scale without a clearly defined policy to regulate the private institutions. Most of the private institutes offer professional courses as these are more popular and lucrative. Privatization of education has increased the intake capacity of specific kind of professional education; especially skill oriented undergraduate degrees, which lead to a career and a job. Earlier an undergraduate degree, except in engineering and medicine, was a step to further higher education and was not a finishing degree.

Young men and women were not expected to work and earn soon after finishing undergraduate education. Those who did so, belonged to the lower middle strata and needed to work and to earn to support the family and themselves. The middle and upper strata, on the other hand, could postpone income generation until further education. This was more applicable to most women across strata, that is, they were not studying in order to earn and to take up jobs. It was an investment in their social status as well as additional criteria for marriage. Privatization has deepened the gender gap further.

Professional Education is denied to the disadvantaged groups and especially poor and rural women because of social and economic reasons. Resultantly, more women are taking up courses in general education as these are easily available and are cheaper as compared to professional courses. Professional education requires several years of studentship and higher financial investment than the general education.

Many women join general courses as these provide them an opportunity to enhance their qualifications as well as wait for the right match for matrimony. Secondly, parents may be unwilling to spend on education of their daughters as they are expected to spend money on their marriages. According to Indian tradition, it is obligatory for a girl's parents to offer gifts and money to the grooms family at the time of marriage.

RECENT TRENDS

In recent times there has been a change in the aspirations of young persons. Both men and women are in a hurry to finish studies and start earning. Money making has become the most important value for them. For this reason, they prefer to take up courses which are linked to jobs and pursuing studies for academic purposes is no longer the aim. The revolution in values cuts across strata, i.e. young persons even from the upper and middle strata want to earn as early as possible. The daughters of city based professional parents have really undergone a sea change in their socialization. Parents are giving the best education to their daughters and expect them to be independent and follow careers.

This revolution in values contrasts with those values which dominated prior to the nineties, i.e. education and its linkage to the job market early on in life was only for those men who needed jobs and was certainly not for women. In this changed situation, the priorities of women have also changed. They too want professional education and are, therefore, entering the so called masculine disciplines.

There are two simultaneous trends of clustering and dispersal that can be seen in the participation of men and women in higher education. During the first three decades while women tended to be clustered in the general disciplines of arts and sciences (nearly 90 per cent); men's participation was characterized by both clustering in arts and sciences disciplines but also significantly dispersed in others such as commerce, engg/tech and law. Lately, however, women's participation too is marked by clustering as well as dispersal. Once women enter higher education at the undergraduate level, they move on the next two levels, namely, the graduate and research level.

In other words, their transition from one level to another has increased which highlights their staying power. In 1991-92,14,79,231 women were enrolled for undergraduate programmes which increased to 3,285,544 in 2002-03; 169,267 women were enrolled for graduate programmes in 1991-92 as compared to 355,893 women in 2002-03; from and 19,894 in 1991-92 to 23,609 in 2002-03 for research programmes. During these years their proportion has also increased from 32.8 per cent to 39.9 per cent in undergraduate programmes; from 34.7 per cent to 42.0 per cent in graduate level progammes; and from 37.1 per cent to 38.0 per cent in the M.Phil and Ph.D. programme.

Their proportion is highest at the graduate level while their proportion in research programmes has marginally declined from 39.2 per cent in 1995-96 to 38.0 per cent in 2002-03. Until 1950-51, only 20.2 women had enrolled for research degrees which increased in the next three decades to 8,780 in 1980-81. Their number nearly doubled to 15,018 in 1988-89. Now it stands at 23,609 in 2002-03. The University Grants Commission has been providing financial assistance to universities for undertaking well-defined projects for research in women's studies and also for the development of curriculum at the undergraduate and postgraduate levels and relevant extension activities.

The Commission has also created positions of part-time research associate ships for women candidates in Science and Humanities including social Sciences and Engineering and Technology. Research projects related to the theme of women's studies were approved. Also assistance was provided to 21 universities and 11 colleges/university departments for setting up women's studies centres and cells. The slightly higher percentage at the graduate level indicates that more women are transiting from undergraduate to the next higher level courses. It may also have something to do with the popularity of master's programmes in management, computers and IT, media, advertising, fashion technology etc. which are proffered in the metropolitan cities. But in the absence of statistics, it is difficult to arrive at a conclusion.

In fact, there is a general trend of moving away from the general courses to the professional courses which lead to jobs and careers. There is also a big demand for vocational courses at the undergraduate level. As observed in the departments of Management, women seem to prefer human resource management (HRM) and development (HRD) as fields of specializations. It is likely that jobs involving public relations, personnel management, marketing, and advertising in the corporate sector, such as the banks, IT firms, BPO companies are becoming feminine jobs and specializations.

It seems that women are moving from discipline choices to specializations within disciplines. One could treat post 1991 phase as a period which set forth a change which increased the social demand for specific kind of professional education, especially skill oriented undergraduate degrees which lead to a career and a job. Earlier boys and girls were not expected to work and earn soon after finishing undergraduate education.

Those who did so belonged to the lower middle strata and needed to work and to earn to support the family and themselves. The middle and upper strata, on the other hand, could postpone income generation until further education. This was more applicable to most women across strata, that is, they were not studying in order to earn and to take up jobs. It was an investment in their social status as well as additional criteria for marriage. Although this may still be true of a large majority of women and their parents, that is, they do not expect their daughters to earn after receiving a degree, there are changes in the expectations of parents and of young women in big cities.

Therefore, parental expectations and young women's aspirations have been push factors in the shift of disciplinary choices in the mid 90s. It is related to the change in values as mentioned earlier and as a response to market demands in the post liberalization phase. More women are enrolling in engineering and law but the preference for management degrees and computer related degrees and skills are higher.

These subjects are available in the fast expanding private sector which responds quickly to the unmet demand for specific skills. Informal discussions with key persons reveal that computer applications and software computer engineering as compared to other specializations are popular among women. It will, therefore, have to be seen if women are getting professional training which leads to jobs and careers? There are hardly any micro studies for macro data to fall back upon to answer this question. But as mentioned earlier, there are now differences in the specialisations within disciplines which have career implications.

For example, HRM requires interaction with the public and there are several others of this kind. In the last few years women have become visible in the call centres; telemarketing; front desk jobs in the multinational/private banks, hospitals, hotels, etc. Quite a few of these jobs are short term and contractual and, therefore, suit the social role expectations of women. Current framework of National Development recognises women as a unique power unit and a potential resource and has played crucial role in social reforms, economic development and also in the political process. Women's development is a pre requisite for all the round development of the society. In a package of developmental inputs available to community, education should form an effective means to improve the physical quality of life of the masses.

Many studies have shown that there is a strong correlation between several developmental indicators and level of literacy of the population. Correlation is particularly strong with the level of female education. It is found that the relation between the age of marriage of a girl and her achievement in education is positive. On the other handy infant mortality rate, birth rate and total fertility rate are negatively correlated. Though school enrolment ratios have been rising, high rate of drop outs, particularly of girls, still continues to be a major problem.

The Mass scale Adult education programme for women in the age group 15-35 years, Non- formal education for the age group 6-14 years and the formal school system- these three systems of education have to be integrated and coordinated to eradicate illiteracy among females. Continuing education centres should be strengths to provide training and for retention of literacy skills. Corrective measures must be taken to increase public awareness for the value of the girl child, to ensure their participation in programmes of Child development, health, nutrition and education and to create a positive environment to allow girls to develop into productive young women.

The biggest challenge before the Government and NGO's is to create awareness and sensitization among people of all levels, especially in rural areas, about the special needs of women and girls. They need to be made aware that imparting education to women is a great service to society. This vital section of society has remained bound in the shackles and been deprived for far too long. There is a need for affirmative and real action in their favour which will ensure the women to right to food, shelter, health, education and employment.

However, the recent changes and developments are kindling hopes for better and promising future. In spite of the well known biological advantage enjoyed by women, India remains one amongst a handful of countries where females outnumber males. Much of this disparity can be attributed to higher child mortality faced by Indian girls as compared to boys. While this fact is well documented in the literature, what is even more surprising is that the disparity has widened even as India has experienced record growth rates and a steady decline in poverty. This ratio, which is slightly over 1000 for most countries, has steadily fallen below 1000 in India indicating a widening disparity between girls and boys.

DETERMINANTS OF IN CHILD HEALTH

While considerable attention has been directed to this issue and a number of studies have been directed to this topic, the research in this area has been piecemeal and the results are often contradictory. While most researchers agree that a strong preference for sons over daughters underlies this phenomenon, there is little agreement on the major causes underlying these preferences. Consider the following:

1. Poverty

Since males are more economically valuable in Indian society than females, it seems reasonable to assume that poor parents faced with many demands on their meager resources may prefer to invest these resources in sons by providing them with better food and health care. However, there seems to be little correlation between poverty and gender disparities in health and mortality. While the four large and poor Indian states, Bihar, Madhya Pradesh, Rajasthan and Uttar Pradesh (famously dubbed BIMARU - killers of women — by Ashish Bose, a noted Indian demographer) have always shown poor sex ratios, wealthy states of Punjab, Haryana and Delhi have now joined this group.

Moreover, sex ratio in India has worsened even as India has experienced considerable economic growth and poverty rates have fallen from nearly 50% to under 30%. Providing more support for these observations at the macro level, Kishor (1993) finds that in more developed districts, survival chances of girls are reduced. Similarly, Murthi et. al. (1995) findings suggest that districts with higher levels of poverty decrease female disadvantage in child mortality. Furthermore, at the household level, it appears there is less discrimination of girls in poorer household. Literature from the neighboring Bangladesh suggests that gender discrimination is lower among poorer households than among the richer ones.

2. Education

It has often been argued that women's education is the key to reducing discrimination against daughters. However, female literacy rate has risen from 15% to 54% even as juvenile sex ratio has fallen. Furthermore, some studies have shown that educated mothers are far more "efficient" in discriminating against their daughters than uneducated mothers. Other studies have shown that higher levels of maternal education decreases mortality for both boys and girls, the effect is larger for girls, thus providing evidence that higher levels of maternal education decreases gender differentials in child mortality.

On the other hand, there is also evidence that maternal education at the district and household levels is weakly associated with increases in female survival. At a macro level, in general high female literacy states – Kerala, Andhra Pradesh, Karnataka and Goa– each with relatively high female education levels have shown less discrimination towards girls but in the past 20 years, high female literacy has not stopped Delhi and Tamil Nadu from showing increased discrimination against female children.

3. Women's Employment

Literature on women's status often argues that women's labor force participation increases women's value to the household resulting in higher investments in female children in spite of a cultural preference for sons. However, empirical literature has failed to show a strong direct connection. The indirect relationship, established at a regional rather than individual level, shows that districts characterized by higher female labor force participation are also characterized by more equitable sex-ratio. However, this appears to be more a function of poor health outcomes for all children - including males — than an improvement in girls' health status.

4. Fertility

International literature on micro consequences of high fertility argues that in families with large number of children, implicit choices have to be made regarding which children to invest in, and often daughters lose out in favor of sons. This would suggest that high fertility may be one of the causes of discrimination against daughters and would be consistent with Muhuri and Preston's (1991) findings in Bangladesh that girls who already have one or more sisters are more likely to experience child mortality than first born daughters or sons.

However, in view of worsening sex ratio even as fertility is declining, argue that fertility decline, without a change in son preference, is precisely the trigger that leads to greater discrimination against daughters. As long as families insist on having one or more sons, and fertility declines, one of way of accommodating a preference for boys with lower fertility is to discriminate against girls and either engage in female infanticide or sex selective abortion.

5. Women's Autonomy and Power

Sex differentials in mortality are substantially different across different parts of India with southern and northeastern India exhibiting far less discrimination against daughters than northern and central states. One of the predominant explanations for these differences focuses on regional differences in marriage and kinship patterns and consequent differences in women's status across different parts of India.

Research on women's status suggests that an increase in women's autonomy and decision making control leads to higher investments in children overall and daughters in particular which should result in reduced sex-differentials in health and mortality. Macro level data indicates that where female autonomy is low, the survival of male children is increased and female child survival is reduced. At the same time, direct individual level analysis linking women's status to child mortality has found only a weak link between the two, although this study was based on relatively small sample and given the rarity of child mortality, a larger sample size may be required to adequately study this link.

INDIVIDUAL AND CONTEXTUAL EFFECTS

As we try to interpret this patchwork of results, one problem area becomes clear. Discrimination against girls is carried out at the household level with households engaging in a variety of practices that diminish girls' health and reduce their survival. These include reduced length of breastfeeding, lower nutritional intake and lower access to health care. At the same time, a lot of analysis is carried out at a district level or aggregate level, increasing the dangers of ecological fallacy.

For example, showing that areas in which women work have lower sex differentials in child mortality is quite different from arguing that women's work leads to lower preference for sons. In fact, it is quite likely to be the case that women may be more likely to work in areas that predominantly agricultural and these same areas may be associated with poor quality health services, increase mortality for both male and female children and reducing the gender gap. Thus, children of both working and non-working mothers may suffer from higher mortality on the one hand and benefit from a lower gender gap on the other.

An error in the other direction is also likely. Since the action takes place at the household level, there may be an excessive reliance on the household as a site of discrimination. However, households are embedded in the society in which they live. Whether the mother is herself in control of the household resources or not, in cultures in which women are valued, fathers will also value their daughters and invest in their health and well-being.

Conversely, in areas where mothers' well-being and social status is intricately tied to having sons, mothers may be even more likely to engage in discrimination against girls than fathers. Using data from the National Family Health Survey-II, a demographic and health survey equivalent for India, this chapter addresses the following questions:

1. To what extent are higher female infant and child mortality rates linked to household level poverty, family size and women's empowerment (measured by women's education, labor force participation, control over resources and autonomy of decision making)?
2. Whether these household level effects are independent of the effect of poverty and women's empowerment at the level of the community (district)?

The data for this study come from the National Family Health Survey - II conducted in 1998-99. This is a nationwide survey with a random sample of 89,199 ever-married women aged 15-49. In addition to information in birth history, survival status of children and age at death, this survey also collected information on parental education, employment status, household ownership of land a large number of consumer assets. The unique characteristics of this survey in comparison to its predecessor NFHS-I (1992-93) is its focus on variables measuring women's empowerment, particularly women's role in household decision making, their control over resources and experience of domestic violence.

The current paper focuses on all children born in the past 10 years, giving us a sample of 108,002 children. Of these, 8,144 children died before reaching age 5 and 1,443 children died between age 1 and 5. In general, infant mortality is less preventable than child mortality and hence, we expect gender disparities to be more important for child mortality rather than infant mortality. Indeed this is the case; controlling for household wealth (as indexed by ownership of consumer durables), region, and parental education, female children experience higher mortality at all ages following the neonatal period.

Between months 1 and 12, girls are 20% more likely to die than boys, between ages 1 and 5 years, girls are 40% more likely to die than boys. In our ongoing work, we examine the impact of independent variables of interest, wealth, parental education, family size, mother's work status, and several measures of gender empowerment (control over resources, autonomy of decision making and freedom from sexual abuse) on gender differences in mortality. These effects are examined at both individual and community level using hierarchical linear models (estimated by HLM).

5

The Roles of Women in Indonesia

Immediately after the colonial period, countries in South East Asia expressed a general commitment to constructing a "new society" with primary concern and priority to eliminate poverty and inequality. Development planners, in their efforts to achieve these goals, have embarked on a development approach taking western industrialization processes as their model. As a result, views with regard to gender roles and the status of women, current in western industrialized societies, have been taken as one of the important references in finding a suitable, if indeed desirable goal for their society as a necessary indicator and measure for their social progress.

Under that premise, it was very often the case that the unique potential of women to play their true, genuine and central roles in their society was not fully recognized. The development stereotype has been that women have been regarded as having the same interest and nature of participation as men. Moreover, women were regarded as dependent upon men and their specific needs are still, generally, not attended to in development planning. Therefore, what was generally felt as one of the negative impacts of the development effort on women's potential was the widespread displacement of women from their true sources of power and influence in all sectors of society.

One important impact of the introduction of capitalism in developing countries was its ability to undermine women's traditional spheres of power and influence, while at the same time creating new conditions for the further dependence of women on men. As result of this introduction of inappropriate development ideology, with its corresponding values and practices, the traditional and unique role of women in societies in developing countries has been severely displaced. Compared to men, the role of women has been almost universally altered, displaced and reduced, as development, industrialisation and modernisation proceeds.

The awareness of integrating women in the development process only later became popular, when planners realized the potential of women, regrettably however, as an abundant supply of 'less utilised' labour. Efforts to increase the economic contribution of women was meant not only to make fuller use of all available human resources, but also as a way of improving the society's quality of life and income distribution. Current discussions on issues of integrating women into development indicate that only limited success, if any, has been achieved. For until now, the position of women in South East Asia has not improved very much at all.

WOMEN IN THE DEVELOPMENT PROCESS

Perspectives for women in the development process have, until now, varied on a wide-range of issues. Some writers examined the effect of economic development programmes on the status of women and argued that women's contributions to the production of goods and services had been ignored. Researchers are also concerned with the issues of women in poverty and women's productive roles. They point out that the relative importance of women's productive roles increases with poverty, as the survival of poor households are generally directly related to the economic activities of women in those households.

A lot of attention has recently been focused on the study of women and technology. Technology has been shown to be a potentially powerful force in promoting economic development.

However, the positive impact of the adoption of technology, is not coupled with due attention to its social implications, and can be undermined by negative and unanticipated effects in the social sphere. Much of the existing work on South East Asian women is descriptive and concentrates on the difficulty that women have in obtaining adequate resources and services. Studies of women tend to be focused on gender as an isolated issue.

There is a lack of investigation into the consequences of rapid economic growth and social change on women and on gender relationships. We do not know much about the reaction of women to these changes and how these changes affect them in terms of stress, conflict and contradiction, both at the macro and micro levels. In short, the effect of socio-economic dynamics and dilemmas of rapid change on women and their relationships has been poorly documented. Based on the limited amount of available information, I would like to examine the consequences of the rapid economic growth on the situation of women and to reveal the reaction of women to these changes. The focus of my attention will be on the situation of women in urban areas.

THE SITUATION OF URBAN WOMEN IN INDONESIA

In 1990, nearly one-third of the Indonesian population lived in urban areas, distributed throughout the country. Half of the urban population were women. Evidence suggests that the toughness of urban life may fall particularly heavily on women. In discussing the situation of urban women in Indonesia, factors such as discrimination in employment opportunities and disparities in the level of compensation relative to men, their multiple role as workers and as women of the household are very important issues which must be addressed. The overall environment - social, political, cultural, economic and physical - also has a profound impact on her world and on herself.

Women in most communities in Indonesia have, throughout history, had well-defined roles in the family and sometimes in the community as well. Women are now experiencing an unavoidable, far-reaching and rapid change which is both planned and spontaneous. Given the attractiveness of some new options, changes are sometimes embraced with enthusiasm. In other cases, being able to meet the necessities of daily life involves changes which are only reluctantly accepted. The contest between change and continuity is dynamic, ongoing and never ending, evolving as people and the situation changes.

Change itself is not new. What is new and needs more attention is the number of changes going on at one time and the intensity of pressure felt by society or the individual to accept the imperative to change. In urban areas, change happens very fast and often in a disorientated manner, compared to what might be taking place in rural areas. There are some indications that stress and hardship caused by this change falls particularly heavily on urban women. Social, economic, family, occupational and political changes all interact, triggering and responding to each other.

As women, they have been objects of which assumed that their appropriate role in society was clear and trivial, and therefore their priority needs were also known. In both cases, the focus was generally defined as revolving around the household, supporting husband, raising children and nurturing society. As city residents, women's unique urban needs and challenges have generally gone unrecognized and unaddressed. In the national effort to meet the needs of Indonesia's vast rural majority, urban / rural distinctions were ignored in many aspects of public policy, planning and programming.

Women make up more than 50 per cent of the urban population. They constitute a substantial portion of the urban workforce, particularly in the less skilled and lower paid occupations. They manage the household and at the lower socio-economic level their financial contribution to family income is often a decisive factor in maintaining the well-being of the family. Problems of urbanization and urban poverty affect people in almost every province of the country. Migration, both permanent and circular, has been and continues to be an important factor in the growth of urban areas.

The pace of change in urban areas often outstrips the capacity of formal systems and regulations to manage and provide the necessary services, such as water, electricity, transportation, housing etc. Informal systems evolve and become a key mechanism for the production and distribution of goods and services needed by large sections of the population who fall within the category of the lower income group. The informal sector often plays an essential supporting role to the formal sector, being a source of cheap labour and location for low-cost piece-work processing of commodities.

The informal sector is particularly important as a place of work for poor urban women, who capitalized on its lack of rigidity in working conditions. On the other hand, precisely because of this, women are often exploited: they have to work under conditions of great hardship and have few avenues of appeal in the event of difficulties. The relative restriction on mobility makes them particularly vulnerable to lay-offs and they are only recruited as temporary employees. Family responsibility for women in Indonesia is heavy. As in other parts of the world, Indonesian women are generally considered to be responsible for all aspects of household management and child-rearing.

The multiple roles of women are generally grouped into three categories - the family, work and the community. Despite this "overburden", it was found that many women choose to join the workforce for economic reasons. The percentage is higher amongst the lower income group. In addition to women entering the paid workforce, many find themselves compelled by obligation or social pressure to invest substantial amounts of their time to community activities. There is a compulsory wives organization for the wives of civil servants and there is also a semi-government organization called the "family welfare movement" which is primarily run by women.

These concern, in particular, maternal and child health, as well as broader family welfare. In the urban setting, women are compelled to participate in community activities. It is becoming fashionable now that women become the preferred choice for officers of neighbourhood organizations. From the previous pages, it has been shown that women are playing a central role in the true process of social change. The role of women is affected by the development process. Although central to their societies, women have often benefitted unequally from opportunities and the resources of development in comparison to their male counterparts.

The decision-makers very often assume that women's interests are the same as those of men. As a result, special consideration of women is not considered as particularly necessary, because they can always be included in various groups that the government plans, e.g. workers, farmers etc. Yet on closer examination of the reality of social discourse, one finds that women are different. This lack of concern for women at the planning stage has resulted in exacerbating several problems, such as an increase in women's work burden, more losses of existing employment opportunities and a significantly lower level of participation in the labour force in comparison to men.

One of the reasons why many governments neglect the role of women in the development process is because development planning is basically a political process. Because women are politically weak, in the sense that substantial leverage of women in the decision-making processes has not been achieved, their true voices have not been significantly heard in the process of formulating policies affecting women. It is uncommon that the interests of women are explicitly considered in either the economic or political aspects of development planning. Women's interests have been overshadowed by broader allegiances and other interests.

The process of integrating women's issues into development planning has been slow and the national machinery for the organization of women has been relatively ineffective. While there has been some progress and some change in the status and participation of women, the effort to include women tends to remain compartmentalized and isolated from the mainstream of development itself. The integration of women's issues into development plans, when it is successfully fought for, provides no guarantee that there will be follow-up in terms of the successful implementation of women-oriented development processes.

Plans must be formulated based on the reality of women's lives and society's perception of the importance of the role of women. Attempts must be made to consider information on the sexual division of labour in work roles outside the usual measured labour force participation rates. Besides paying attention to quantitative data, national development plans must be designed to respond to qualitative information, dealing with the needs of women in their multiple roles. Policy makers must no longer assume that women and men are identical. They have to appreciate also the notion that different groups of women will not automatically benefit equally from a well meant political decision.

In the urban economy, where women face problems of poor prospects for regular employment, and many disadvantages, the strategies available to planners to deal with this problem is not so easy. One of the reasons is that the economic problems in urban areas are also entrenched in the broader political and ideological context. The obstacles facing women in the informal sector, for example, are not only their lack of employment alternatives, but also the fact that they are unorganized and unprotected and that attempts at organizing these workers have met with hostility from many sections of government.

Protective legislation for women in this sector needs to be initiated, because women working in this sector are not protected by any form of regulation pertaining to their working conditions, on wage levels and benefits given to them and the nature of employer and employee relationships. Moreover, very often some women are also involved in what has been classified as illegal activities within the informal sector. Planners can reduce the excess by liberalizing and reducing the burden of illegality of some informal activities in which many women are engaged and generating their income for their livelihood. Energy has a vital role in supporting human's life. However, the traditional energy resources, namely fossil fuels are non-renewable energy resources that its availability is restricted and subject to constraints because it needs a very long time to generate by natural processes.

If the usage of this energy is not in a wise and responsible manner and if there is no alternative energy to develop in the islands country like Indonesia, accordingly this will create many problems not only in the long run but also in the short term. Recently, the price of such kind of energy is getting high due to some respects such as economic and political instability in some oil producer countries. In Indonesia, which has potential areas for agricultural farming for cleaner energies is projected to self-sufficient in producing energy alternatives besides the conventional energy.

The Jatropha has some advantages that are it can grow in a wide areas of conditions, it is not need a lot of water, no need fertilizers (only at the first time its planting), this can grow optimally at several altitudes, usually from 0 to 800 above sea levels. Animals are not eager to eat this Jatropha. It is very resistant to pest and disease. This can be harvested after five months, and it is in stable conditions after five years of age until fifty years. In an optimum condition, one hectare of land can produce 10 ton of Jatropha seeds, this can be produced locally to serve the need of local energy. To improve the soil quality, the waste of Jatropha after oil production can be used as an organic fertilizer. The end product of this oil production can be used to produce soaps and medicines. The most important thing is this can create jobs for people living in rural areas.

The number of poor people in Indonesia is 36,146,900 (16.66%). The poor women are 18,076,900 and the men are about 18,070,000 (BPS, 2004). This is one of the countries that suffer very huge number of poverty in the world. By creating new jobs for people that integrate the women participation is useful for income growth. Not only learning a successful story of South Africa and India in empowering and encouraging women involvement in developing policy and technology that have been applied but also the drawbacks of this expansion should be take into account.

Furthermore, community development in the rural areas should be formed to expedite the economic growth. Investors, landowners, and labors are the actors for operating the projects. Investors can invest the money, landowners will get rental cost, and the labors will get the wages. Even though this is not a gender case but the women contribution to the projects will generate the trickle down effects to the household welfare including access to education for themselves, their children and all families.

This means there is a hope for their future because if they have relatively high educated kids so in the prospect for better live will be possible. As we know that in developing country like Indonesia, income support system for the poor and elderly people is not readily available. It is not uncommon that elderly people usually hoping their children to spent their income support to sustain their parent's lives. So, the role of women in rearing their children is very important to maintain their family. The role of women are developing alternative energy they can get benefits such as rising income, gaining skills in production technical processes and its management.

Another advantage that can be got is they can still doing household daily jobs for example cooking and electricity. In this chapter we discuss about the position of women in Indonesia to participate in developing substitute energy in some energy production processes: selecting land suitable for Jatropha farming, encouraging motivation in sharing their knowledge and ability to support energy national program. It is not so clear whether there is a bias gender or not in developing sustainable energy in Indonesia, because when we discuss with an energy development expert in Indonesia, he stated that every person have the same access to technology development and the energy technology development usually developed in principle as easy to operate as possible both by men and women.

Finally, one of the most important things to develop an alternative energy in Indonesia is to think about the culture of the regions or island inhabitants because Indonesia has many different ethnic and different cultures that can create different treatment when we try to unite women to interact with this energy progress. For example, in Bengkulu, it is generally unacceptable if women working to help their husband in raising income but in Bali or Java it is tolerable. So, the cultural knowledge integration to the energy development strategy is also a critical issue in Indonesian archipelagic country.

Women's work in agriculture has become more visible over the last few decades as women farmers become more involved in agricultural activities, increasingly assuming the responsibility for household survival and responding to economic opportunities in agricultural production. This has made rural development in Asia considerably dependent on the capacity enhancement of women farmers as they increasingly provide a vital contribution to the development of rural communities. A look at recent trends and prospects for 2010 for developing Asian countries reveals a striking point: the number of women economically active in agriculture is increasing and growing faster than the number of males economically active in this sector.

This phenomenon is dubbed as the "feminization of agriculture," referring to women's increasing participation in the agricultural labor force, whether as independent producers, as unpaid family workers, or as agricultural wage workers. Yet, despite the growing importance of the women farmers' role in agriculture, as well as in overall rural development, the lack of access to and control over productive resources deprives them of opportunities for their own capacity building and improved quality of life. In addition, the long tradition of gender gap and inequalities seriously restricts women's right to legal, institutional and policy support services.

They are disadvantaged through limited access to land, credit, technology and information, and especially in the remuneration of their activities resulting to a wide underestimation of women's economic contributions. Also, there are very few programs for enhancing women farmers' welfare and their empowerment under a new rural environment. Recognizing the need to overcome gender issues in agriculture and rural livelihoods, the international seminar on enhancement of women farmers' role in the development of rural Asia was organized with the overall goal to understand the situation of women farmers in agriculture in order to improve their status and enhance their contribution to rural development.

The seminar also aimed to promote the integration of women's concerns in rural development policy agenda, particularly of developing Asian countries. During the paper presentations and deliberations, the participants looked more deeply into gender-demarcated responsibilities in agriculture in terms of social and economic activities, access to resources, and decision-making authority. A field observation tour of rural women organizations' agricultural and livelihood activities provided the participants with an insight into Korea's policy to encourage income-generating activities and volunteer works among rural women.

ISSUES AND CONCERNS FACED BY WOMEN FARMERS

The countries that make up the Asian region are characterized by considerable diversity in terms of geography, culture, religion and political systems, as well as economic performance and social development. Hence, programs and policies in gender equality in support of women farmers differ considerably among countries. The more developed Asian countries are much ahead in terms of enhancing women farmers' welfare and their empowerment under a new rural environment. However, in other less developed countries, rural women continue to struggle with dual responsibilities of economic production and domestic labor, and most are confronted by poverty, illiteracy, high health risks, inadequate access to productive resources, and lack of credit/market access.

The common issues among Asian countries which can form the basis for further deliberation and future action may be categorized into four major categories:

- Economic issues such as rural women's lack of title to productive assets and access to "inputs" (land, credit, water, fertilizer, seeds, information, technology, training, etc.) and markets; the increasing drudgery and time spent by women in agricultural activities which is not compensated by increases in value added; and the limited availability and/or relevance of technology and other aids for women.
- Program/planning issues such as inadequate gender-differentiated and disaggregated data, as well as data gaps with regard to rural women, which results in overlooking gender issues for planning; and lack of appropriate methodologies that recognize and value women's contribution, actual and potential, to productive activities resulting in women's marginalization in projects and programs.
- Political issues such as institutional barriers to women's political participation and organization (patriarchy, non-organization of women, rural isolation).
- Sociocultural issues such as low status and disadvantaged position of women resulting in lower education; little access to training; non-participation in decision making; lower income; poor nutrition and health; few property rights;

Rural women in their dual roles as producers in the farm and the home and as caregivers need appropriate technologies to ease their work stress and to improve productivity. In developing countries, technology development and extension programs have not been responsive to household drudgery associated with different production activities undertaken by women. Hence, rural women's demand for technology that improves their productivity while reducing drudgery must be recognized.

Most countries still lack adequate provision for women to hold land rights independently of their husbands or male relatives. Statutory laws often do not ensure independent land rights for women. In traditional or under customary practices, women's direct ownership access to land may be limited, yet they may have greater management and use rights than men. Land ownership in rural areas determines the asset for production as well as access to credit and agricultural support services and the social power to negotiate for resources and membership in decision-making agencies. Hence, rural women must be empowered with legal and institutional measures to secure land and other productive resources.

The development of women's groups should be promoted as a strategy to expand women's access to information, increase their comparative bargaining power, and create opportunities for collective action to access economic inputs. In reality, however, persisting gender biases, deep-seated community dynamics and women's time constraints prevent women from actively participating in these organizations intended to bring about social capital benefits and female empowerment.

Literacy has serious implications for the future of the agriculture sector's productivity and the food security in many countries across the region. Prevailing shortfalls in rural female literacy achievement, coupled with trends towards the feminization of farming, underline the urgency to improve the skills and knowledge of rural women as a means to advance their technological and economic empowerment.

SUCCESSFUL CASES OF WOMEN EMPOWERMENT

A country's economic and social development is a significant factor in creating recognition of the role women farmers play in rural development, and in bringing about gender-sensitive policies in the agriculture sector. The Korean government provides vital support to the Rural Women Leaders Federation (RWLF), an organization of rural women playing lead roles in promoting healthy rural home and prosperous local communities.

Government organizations like RDA have also been introducing various approaches in the promotion of rural values and enhancement of living standards among women's organizations through non-formal adult education, support for nonfarm income activities, and capacity building activities. Korea's agricultural cooperatives also support rural women by organizing them into cooperative work programs, giving them the means and opportunities to buildup their own capacities in order to have access to extension/credit/ marketing services.

Japan's "Farm Management Agreement" which rationalizes women's role in the farm through appropriate division of roles, ownership of property, share in income, and improvement of working condition, has considerably raised the status of women farmers in the country. The agreement is an effective tool in building a comfortable environment for farm families under a new social system in the rural areas, focusing on the promotion of gender-equal society in the aspects of agricultural production and daily living, and a more efficient farm management.

Recognizing the importance of creating jobs or favorable environment for woman entrepreneurs, the Taiwan government has been sponsoring projects to increase the financial viability of rural women for income generation and entrepreneurship. The projects make extensive use of internet marketing or even virtual shops as additional income sources, allowing women to work from their home while taking care of the family. The project named "Tien-Ma-Ma" initiated in 2001 has become a model for creating job opportunities by embracing modern communication and marketing channels.

What are the needs of Asian women farmers given their increasing role in the development and stabilization of rural communities in this new era, and what are the strategies, policy and program interventions needed to refocus attention on the situation of rural women in agricultural development? Technical and extension support is vital, especially in consistently providing women farmers with gender-specific practical technologies and information on agriculture and rural livelihood. Education opportunities for women are also critical not only in the fields of agriculture and in nonagricultural gainful employment, but also in the sectors of health, nutrition, children's education, and family planning.

Women must also be given institutional and legal assistance toward having equal access to and control over productive resources, particularly land; make it possible for them to participate in business activities; and guarantee them a right to membership and voting in labor/credit organizations. Measures facilitating household work and care of the children should be introduced to increase the chance for women to participate in economic and training activities. The importance of women's unpaid work in the home and farm production systems should also be clearly recognized.

In the Asian region, more efforts should focus on the integration of gender considerations and gender-differentiated indicators in the policy formulation process and in designing strategies to improve opportunities for rural women. Toward this end, sex-disaggregated data and gender-differentiated information for all aspects of agriculture and rural development must be collected to be used in policy and program formulation for the advancement of rural women.

6

Yesterday and Today in Laos

Lao women's concerns were first formally addressed by a national government in 1975, with the ascendancy to power of the Lao People's Revolutionary Party. The new communist regime had earlier promised to realise equality between men and women in all fields, political, economic, cultural and social, and to do away with all acts of contempt or oppression toward women. On taking power, the LPRP encouraged women to participate in activities of national reconstruction and the building of socialism.

In spite of the Government's formal commitment to eradicate and its promotion of women's economic participation, Lao women today have far from achieved parity with Lao men in the areas mentioned. Considerable advances have been made in women's access to education and employment since 1975, but women's social status and political representation remains low. Furthermore, the dire economic situation faced by the country has imposed increasing demands on the time and energy of women. This report begins with a brief overview of the political, demographic and economic situation in Laos in the 1975-92 period.

Following this is a short section on Lao women's participation in economic development after 1975. Women have made a vital contribution to both the rural and urban economies, particularly the former. The discussion of the rural sector will concentrate on agriculture and small scale industries, and that of the urban sector will cover the formal and informal sectors. Despite women's essential contribution to the development of Laos, gender disaggregated data on education, health and political representation show that women still lack access to basic services and political power.

Nonetheless, women are organised at the local, provincial and national levels through the Lao Women's Union (LWU), an organisation with a membership of more than one third of the female population. Even so, it has only been in the last few years that this organisation has focused its attention specifically on women's concerns and not simply those of the revolutionary state. This organisation faces several challenges in its attempts to redress women's subordination in Laos. Some of these constraints have been tackled recently with the assistance of the international community.

The nature of this foreign assistance will be outlined, and followed by some policy recommendations. This report is limited in nature due to the lack of research on the socio-economic situation of Lao people, and particularly of Lao women. Most of the literature written on Laos to date has focused on the military and strategic aspects of the country. Furthermore, the little information which does exist on Lao women is almost exclusively concentrated on Lowland women who make up only one half of the female population. However, an attempt will be made to incorporate information on the situation of Highland women where possible.

A brief overview of the recent political, demographic and economic situation in Laos is necessary to provide a context for the following discussion. Laos is presently governed by the Lao People's Revolutionary Party (LPRP) which assumed power in 1975 after more than thirty years of armed struggle against the French colonialists and later against American forces in the Indo-china conflict. Women were active in all spheres of work during the wars, from militia activity, to health care of soldiers and food production (UNESCO, 1989: 5).

The three decades of war, and the half century of French colonialism before it, has left Laos one of the poorest countries in the world. The economy remains predominantly agrarian with a gross national product per capita of a mere US $ 180 in 1989 (UNDP, 1992). Laos has a population of 4.2 million, and a sex ratio of 96.1 males per 100 females. Eighty-five per cent of the people live in rural areas. The country has a total area of 236 800 square kilometres, but only 12 per cent of the land area can be cultivated due to the mountainous terrain, impenetrable forests and to the massive destruction caused by US bombing in the 1960s and 1970s in which exfoliation agents were widely used.

Ninety per cent of the labour force is concentrated in the agriculture and forestry sectors with only two per cent in industry and construction. Urban dwellers are concentrated in four major centres: Vientiane, Savannakhet, Pakse and Luang Prabang. The most densely populated city is the country's capital, Vientiane, which has a population of 442 000. Laos has an extremely varied ethnic composition with over 68 distinct groups. These diverse peoples are often put into three categories. The largest group is the Lowland Lao, or Lao Loum, who make up 55 per cent of the population and inhabit the plains and valleys. The Midland Lao, or Lao Theung, live on the plateaux and mountain slopes and constitute 27 per cent of the population.

The remainder of the population is Upland Lao, the Lao Soung of the mountain tops. Because of poor infrastructure and communication systems, most of the Lao Theung and Lao Soung people still live in virtual isolation from the other more developed parts of the country. This study will perforce focus primarily on the situation of Lao Loum women. As far as economic development is concerned, Laos is currently undergoing a major economic transformation. In order to address the dire economic situation and to gain access to external financial assistance, the Lao Government enacted the New Economic Mechanism (NEM) in 1986.

According to government sources, reforms introduced by the NEM include:

- Decontrol of prices and distribution of goods and services;

- Elimination of subsidies;
- Unification of the exchange rate;
- Reform of the tax system and government expenditure;
- Restructuring of the banking system and enactment of a new Central Bank Law;
- Refinements in money and credit management;
- Passage of a Law on Foreign Investment;
- Reduction of import duties;
- Revamping the tax and customs administration;
- Privatization of the means of production including some state enterprises;
- Formation of the policy apparatus for further privatization.

These reforms contain many elements which are standard in structural adjustment programmes. The impact of such programmes elsewhere has been subject to a gender analysis which reveals a very mixed picture. Adjustment programmes have several potentially negative outcomes for women. For example, price decontrol and subsidy removal creates pressure on household budgets, the burden of which is often borne largely by women; in other parts of Asia (e.g. Sri Lanka) trade liberalisation policies under adjustment programmes have led to the displacement of women working in handloom and other home based production.

No study has yet been made of the gender effects of these macro- economic policy changes in the Lao case. Some consequences of the reform programme in Laos to date are a fall in real urban incomes resulting from price rises, and increased unemployment through public sector retrenchment. Women are thought to have been particularly hit by reductions in public sector employment because they generally occupy lower ranking positions.

In December 1991, the Medium Term Policy Framework and Public Investment Programme (1991-5), was approved. This does not incorporate any specific gender analysis or concerns. However, there is a strong emphasis on human resource development, particularly through investment in health and education. In parallel with the economic reform programme begun in 1986, there have been a number of legal reforms and a new constitution was enacted in August 1991. The constitution provides the legal basis for equality for women in the political, economic, social and cultural fields and in family affairs.

Several of the new laws relate to gender concerns, for example, the Property Law, the Inheritance Law, the Labour Law, the Family Law and the Election Law. Along with men, women have inheritance and voting rights. There is insufficient information available to discuss the precise gender implications of these changes. In any event, due to the recent implementation of these legal reforms and also to the fact that much of the Lao population lives in isolation from major centres, its seems unlikely that these changes have yet had a major impact.

ROLE IN THE NATIONAL AND HOUSEHOLD ECONOMIES

Lao women have played a central role in the country's economic development over the past two decades. Women's participation exceeds men's in the economically active population. Women made up 52.8 per cent of the active labour force (15-44 year olds) in 1985. Women compose 60 per cent of the labour force in the agricultural sector; 60 per cent of the handicraft sector; 50 per cent in commerce, public health and education sectors; 25 per cent in the public sector and 20 per cent in the industrial sector.

Aside from this enumerated work, a gender division of labour exists in Laos which assigns women the major responsibility for childcare and housework. As household size averages seven people, these tasks require numerous hours of work each day in addition to women's work outside the home and yet domestic labour continues to be excluded from labour force statistics. Lao Loum women are generally thought to enjoy a higher status than women of other ethnic groups (e.g. the Yao and the Hmong), among whom son preference is quite strong in accordance with kinship and inheritance structures.

The Lao Loum have bilateral kinship systems and inheritance patterns, as well as a matrilocal tradition, whereby the married couple live with the wife's parents at least for some years after marriage. In many cases, the youngest daughter and her husband remain with the parents to look after them in their old age. Thus, females often inherit property from their parents. By contrast, the Lao Theung and Lao Soung tend to adhere to patrilinear kinship rules and patrilocal traditions, whereby the woman is considered a member of the husband's clan upon marriage. Where women are isolated from the support networks of their natal families, they are more likely to be dominated by the men in the household.

All ethnic groups have traditionally observed bride price, although the Government has discouraged this. In some minority areas, polygamy is practised, but rural poverty is tending to limit this. In spite of their major economic contribution, women are generally not considered as workers. However, women, particularly older ones, do control household budgets and share in financial decision making.

WOMEN'S ROLE IN THE RURAL ECONOMY

Agriculture Agriculture is the largest sector of the Lao economy accounting for 60 per cent of GDP (1989) and employing 90 per cent of the total population. General activities include rice cultivation, slash and burn cultivation, animal husbandry, vegetable growing and forest collection. Women compose 60 per cent of the active labour force in the agricultural sector. The division of labour in the rural areas is such that all women, regardless of their ethnicity, are disproportionately over- burdened with work.

The male household head generally organises and directs family paddy production. In family rice cultivation, women typically perform the following tasks: transplanting, weeding, sowing and almost all post-harvesting tasks including the gleaning and cleaning of the rice. Men prepare the land for cultivation with the help of buffalos, and thresh and harvest the rice along with women. In areas where slash and burn cultivation occurs, women traditionally weed while men cut down trees and burn the stumps in order to clear the land for cultivation.

The division of labour described thus far, however, is not absolutely fixed as women often also perform tasks which are traditionally male, possibly because of the predominance of women in the rural provincial population due to the wars and to male out-migration. Men sometimes also perform traditionally female tasks such as transplanting or tending gardens. In some areas, cooperative groups carry out all the paddy rice work collectively, from seed-bed preparation to harvesting.

Women and children still carry out the post harvest processing and prepartion. Women also cultivate vegetables and some cash crops, and collect roots, shoots, firewood, and small animals from nearby forests mainly for subsistence purposes. Men hunt, collect timber and build and repair houses. Both sexes fish and gather river produce. Women are usually responsible for marketing family produce, except when there are large quantities of surplus rice and when large animals are to be sold.

A further activity of Lowland rural households is animal husbandry. Raising small stock (pigs, goats, chickens and ducks) is women's responsibility while cattle, buffalo and horses are men's domain. Children are also involved in feeding and grazing stock. Animals are one repository for family wealth, with the larger animals raised by males commanding the highest prices in the market.

Land, however, is often inherited by daughters among the Lao Loum, but this is not the case among the other ethnic minorities. Aside from the responsibilities mentioned above, women of all ethnic groups perform the tedious and time-consuming chores associated with household management and child care. Some of these duties include water collection, which may take two to three hours a day; husking rice for family consumption, which may require two hours of work; milling rice; and caring for the sick and the elderly.

Girls assist their mothers with these chores and they are often made responsible for care of younger siblings. It is clear that women farmers have made a vital contribution to both household and national economies. However, women face a number of constraints which deny them access to the means required to increase their labour productivity. Aside from the burden of housework, Lao women lack skills training in agriculture as there are no government extension services in the country. Even when this service did exist prior to 1975, women were denied access to agricultural training. Instead, they were taught sewing and cookery. This reflects traditional stereotypes which view only males as farmers. In Laos, however, female farmers actually outnumber the males.

A further constraint faced by women farmers is a lack of access to the credit needed to expand production. Government agricultural credit schemes carry extremely high interest rates. Moreover, although some machinery has recently been introduced into farming activities, it is predominantly men's tasks which have been mechanised. The most common machines include tractors to facilitate the ploughing and harrowing of land and rice threshers. Women's access to credit facilities, agricultural training and appropriate technology have nonetheless increased since the imposition of the NEM in 1986 as several external agencies have initiated projects targeted specifically at addressing women's productive needs.

Finally, women face increasing time and resource constraints resulting from the escalating deforestation which has occurred in Laos. The primary causes of this environmental degradation are logging and the clearing of land for shifting cultivation. It is estimated that 70 000 hectares of dense forest and 200 000 hectares of less dense forest are depleted each year. This loss of forest has serious consequences for women as it forces them to travel greater distances to collect wood and other essential forest products. Deforestation has particularly adverse effects on women in the Highland areas where household survival depends almost solely upon forest food and medicinal plants.

The Lao Government has begun to address the problem of deforestation by imposing bans on the export of logs and timber, first in January 1989 and again in August 1991. However, much more concerted efforts will be needed to enforce these policies as illegal logging is prevalent in Laos as it is all over South East Asia.

COTTAGE INDUSTRIES

In most cases, agricultural activities barely meet the subsistence demands of rural families. Employment opportunities are scarce in the rural areas and thus, in order to supplement family income, women engage in the production of handicrafts in their spare time and during slack agricultural periods. These small-scale activities include the production of cloth, clothing and blankets for both domestic use and sale.

The domestic demand for woven products was high before 1987 as the Lao Government had imposed strict controls on most imports including clothing. Women were encouraged by the Government to dress in the traditional cotton or silk made sin (sarong) instead of Western attire, for ideological as well as economic reasons. Since trade restrictions have been relaxed with the introduction of the NEM, cheap manufactured clothing imports from Thailand have been increasingly available in Lao markets.

The implications of this for the demand for domestically woven garments, produced mainly by women, are as yet unclear, but it seems likely that a shift in demand away from domestically produced garments could occur, without special measures to protect or promote such cottage industries. Nevertheless, home-based weaving will continue to be an important economic activity for women particularly in isolated rural areas. Women are also largely in charge of selling their products in local markets. Although the supply of a product may exceed the demand in rural areas at any given time, poor transportation systems make it virtually impossible for marketing to occur over great distances.

WOMEN'S PARTICIPATION IN THE URBAN ECONOMY

Formal Sector Laos is a predominantly rural subsistence country and urban areas are still underdeveloped. Where women have found employment in the formal sector, their jobs are often gender typed and concentrated at lower levels. In factory employment, men outnumber women in all areas except for garment production. In the civil service, women are well represented in the education and health departments but seldom occupy directorial or managerial positions even in these ministries. Similarly, in the industrial sector, women are but rarely, if ever, managers. One exception to the normal gender typing pattern is the significant involvement of women in road construction and maintenance.

The recent change of economic policies by the Lao Government will probably result in increased employment opportunities for women in the cities, but it is likely that they will continue to occupy the lowest rungs of the employment ladder. Laos comparative advantage in the world economic market is undoubtedly its cheap labour and in Laos as elsewhere, women's labour is likely to be available at lower cost than men. Furthermore, given Laos budgetary constraints, it is likely that the country will try to develop small scale export industries including textiles and electronics, drawing on foreign investment.

These industries typically favour the employment of young women. Employment opportunities have opened up for women in such industries all over Southeast Asia, due in part to the activities of multinational corporations in the region and their specific demand for female labour. Whilst such new opportunities may increase the quantity of female employment in the industrial sector, doubts have been raised in the context of other Asian countries about the quality of this type of female employment, particularly with regard to job security, working conditions and skills development.

Women's participation in the commerce and the service sectors may grow at a higher rate than men's with the expansion of tourism and trade. This has been the case for Laos neighbour Thailand where women have come to predominate in the commerce and service sectors. There are plans to encourage women's employment in tourism especially as guides.

INFORMAL SECTOR

Women are active participants in the thriving informal sector markets in the urban areas. Trading in these areas is lucrative as state stores are unable to fulfil the demand for goods of the urban dwellers. Informal sector activities in which women predominate include: the sale of food along roadsides; providing domestic services for foreigners; small-scale retailing; and handicraft production.

Many women are said to have left jobs in the public sector in order to engage in informal sector activities. Although employment in the civil service is more prestigious, salaries are much lower than the incomes women can earn from trading. Men, however, prefer to remain in the higher status government service jobs. In doing so, they retain access to other benefits including subsidised goods and rice rations.

Women should be able to take advantage of new trading opportunities resulting from economic liberalisation as they already have established marketing networks and a sense for market trends. Increased income for women from informal sector activities may improve their bargaining position in the household and provide them with increased independence from men. However, other factors could counteract this, for example if the number of informal sector workers increases rapidly as a result of formal sector unemployment, there may be downward pressure on informal sector incomes.

INDICATORS OF WOMEN STATUS

EDUCATION

Overall primary and secondary school enrolment ratios in Laos improved between 1975-6 and 1983-4 (from 67.5 per cent to 85.4 per cent for primary level and from 10.8 per cent to 26.5 per cent at lower secondary level) and the primary enrolment ratio is now average by Asian standards. Data are incomplete but show that the trend to improvement slowed and may even have been reversed between the early and mid- 1980s. Secondary school enrolment was still extremely low at 13.9 per cent in 1983-4, indicating the low education level of children in absolute terms.

A UNESCO study conducted in 1985 showed that out of 1,000 children who had enrolled in first grade, only 139 students completed fifth grade. This was due to the poor quality of education and to domestic responsibilities imposed on children. The educational status of women in Laos has advanced considerably since 1975. The percentage of female students in Lao schools increased from 37.6 per cent in 1975-6 to 45.3 per cent in 1980-1. By 1984-5 the percentage of female students was 46.7. However, the general educational level of Lao women is still very poor, and the gender gap, though narrowed, persists, particularly beyond primary level.

Female school enrolment is consistently lower than male enrolment at all levels of education. The percentage of female enrolment in 1985-6 at the primary, lower secondary and upper secondary levels were 44.9 per cent, 42.8 per cent and 40.1 per cent respectively. Furthermore, regional variations in overall primary school enrolment are great ranging from 10 per cent in some areas to 94 per cent in others.

Whereas the female primary school gross enrolment ration is 48 per cent for Lao Loum groups, it is only 26 per cent for Lao Soung groups. Highland women are the most poorly educated people in the country. Laos has four universities as well as professional schools. In 1985-6, women accounted for 28.05 per cent of total enrolment at the higher education level. Female students were relatively well represented in health sciences (53.1 per cent in 1985-6) and teacher training (37.7 per cent in 1984-5) but constituted less than 20 per cent of the total enrolment in architecture, and at the polytechnical college.

Literacy rates are further indicative of Lao women's educational disadvantage. A UNESCO study, carried out in

15 of the 17 provinces in 1984-85, determined that 56 per cent of the population was illiterate, despite government assertions that illiteracy had been eradicated by 1984.

The study showed that illiteracy was acute among Laos ethnic minorities; that it was higher in rural areas than in urban areas; and also higher for women than for men. These claims were further confirmed by a Food and Agricultural Organisation study on literacy in Laos which recorded a specific sex inequality in literacy rates for three provinces: Vientiane, Luang Prabang and Champasak.

The overall literacy rate for Lao women is estimated at 35 per cent, compared to 65 per cent for men. The low education level among females results from two basic factors: inadequate overall educational provision in the country, and continued gender discrimination faced by girls and women. The education system is Laos is highly inadequate for two major reasons. Firstly, it lacks the proper funding required for minimal infrastructural requirements, such as school buildings and teaching equipment, as well as for recurrent costs, particularly salaries.

The Government has realised the need for increased financial support for the education system and this is reflected in the share of its budgetary expenditure on education which has increased from 3.7 per cent for 1981-1985 to 8 per cent for 1986-1990. However, development analysts have reported that this allotment is still too low. Secondly, the lack of qualified teachers in Laos contributes to the poor quality of education. Laos was reported to have lost 90 per cent of its educated population in 1975 due to the massive outflow of refugees after the Communist takeover.

Systemic barriers to women's equal participation in education are numerous. Traditionally, women did not attend school as education was provided by monks in the pagodas and girls were prohibited from attending these lessons. This bias in attitudes still persists today. Boys consistently receive priority over girls with respect to education. Although girls and boys enrolment rate in primary and secondary education is moving close to equality, sources suggest that the drop-out rate for girls is higher than it is for boys. This may be due to greater domestic and other labour responsibilities of girls.

A 1982 ILO study of Hat Xai Fong district in Vientiane Province showed that 8.6 per cent of girls in the 6-15 age group, compared to 3.3 per cent of boys, were engaged in crop production, livestock rearing and related activities. Women's household responsibilities greatly limit their ability to attend adult non-formal education classes. Even if government campaigns to eradicate literacy had been sustainable and systematic, which they were not, women would have still not benefited fully from them. This is due to the male biased assumption often inherent in literacy campaigns that all members of society have equal amounts of time to devote to education.

Health General health conditions in Laos, and women's health standards in particular, reflect trends similar to those in education levels. Life expectancy at birth was slightly higher for women, at 50 years compared to 47 years for men. In 1970, women's life expectancy had been only 41.8 years, demonstrating a gradual, real improvement in health conditions for women (WHO, 1989).

However, the maternal mortality rate in 1988 was still one of the highest in the world at 750 deaths per 100 000 live births. This ratio is as low as 150: 100 000 in Vientiane and as high as 900: 100 000 in the rural provinces. Laos infant mortality rate is also very high at 104 deaths per 1 000 live births in 1990. Again, in Vientiane the ratio approximates 50:1 000 while in some mountain districts it is as high as 299:1 000. Very many children do not survive until their fifth year. The under-five mortality rate in 1990 was 152 deaths per 1000 live births. Regional variations in infant and child mortality rates are marked. In some upland provinces as many as one third of babies die before their first birthday.

A further indication of the difference in the quality of health care between the urban and the rural areas is number of population served by a doctor in different areas. In Vientiane this ratio is 1: 1400 whereas in other parts of Laos the ratio is as high as 1:12600. Most maternal deaths could be easily prevented as they result from treatable causes, for example, lack of immunization against diseases such as tetanus and tuberculosis; diarrhoea; lack of spacing between pregnancies; and malnutrition. Malaria is less easily preventable, and is the prime killer of Lao children. Other main causes of death among children include gastrointestinal and respiratory diseases, and malnutrition.

Poor health conditions of women are further exacerbated by public health constraints such as shortfalls in access to health services, safe water and sanitation. The proportion of people with access to these services is 67, 29 and 12 per cent respectively. Approximately ninety per cent of all births take place at home with untrained attendants. Past government efforts in collaboration with the World Health Organisation (WHO) and UNICEF to expand immunization programmes have failed to make a significant impact on the eradication of childhood diseases. Some obstacles encountered by this programme included poor management and implementation by ministry officials; infrastructural constraints such as poor transport and communication systems; and financial limitations.

Until recently, the Government has invested little in improving health care in Laos. Public expenditure in this sector increased only slightly from 0.5 per cent of GDP in 1960 to 0.6 per cent in 1987, rising to 2.0 per cent in 1992. In spite of this significant increase in health expenditure in the last five years, which is now above the (1.4 per cent) average for developing countries, the level of expenditure is still too low for the provision of adequate health care systems. The Lao Government has had a strongly pro-natalist population policy due to what it sees as the need to increase the small population size in order to encourage increased economic growth. The sale of contraceptives was banned in Laos until 1988.

Pro-natalist policies have had a negative impact on women's health as contraceptives are required to prolong birth intervals. In 1990, the total fertility rate was 5.7 births per woman, a figure which although decreased from 6.2 births in 1970, is still too high. Inadequate birth spacing continues to claim hundreds of mother's lives. In recent years the government's position on birth control has improved slightly with the recognition that the high birth rate was having detrimental effects on population growth as mortality rates remained high. Seven programmes to promote child spacing were introduced in 1991.

The low awareness and use of contraception in Laos has a second serious corollary: the likely rapid spread of HIV/AIDS. Although there have only been a few HIV/AIDS cases reported to date in Laos, the incidence of HIV/AIDS is likely to increase in light of increased trade and other contacts with Thailand, which has one of the most serious HIV/AIDS problems in Asia. A study on family planning conducted by UNESCAP showed that 65 per cent of the women interviewed had no knowledge of any form of contraception.

Of the less than 20 per cent of women who used contraceptives, the pill was the most common form at 45 per cent while condoms were the least used at less than one per cent. It can be safely concluded that at present a minute number of people use condoms in Laos in which case the risk of the rapid spread of HIV is acute. Other factors may also contribute to the increased risk of a rapid spread of HIV, such as the promotion of sex tourism which is now said to be being diverted from Thailand to Cambodia and Laos. In 1991, a Mid Term Plan of Action for Control of AIDS was set up, apparently with a strong emphasis on women's role in AIDS control.

POLITICS

A third indicator of women's status in Laos is their representation at different levels of political organisations and institutions. Laos has a dual political structure which consists of the Communist Party and the Government. The Communist Party is a hierarchical organisation controlled by a seven member all-male Politburo, the key policy making body of the country. The next most powerful decision making group in the party is the Central Committee of which five out of 59 members are female. The final tier in the party is the ordinary membership of 60000 and women make up 40 per cent of this group.

Women's representation in the Government follows much the same pattern. The only female minister is the president of the LWU. Overall, women are fairly well represented in the civil service; but they are under-represented at director level in ministerial departments, although quite a few do become vice-directors.

Those who do occupy such posts are found in traditionally female sectors such as health and education. Below the ministries are the provincial, district, sub-district and village offices. Sources suggest that even at these levels, women are barely represented, except as Women's Union representatives on district, sub-district and village administrative committees. Village heads appear to be almost exclusively male and external agencies have experienced difficulties in drawing women into discussions due to the dominance of men in public roles at village level.

By law women are eligible to stand for public and administrative posts at all levels of Government but this right are not exercised for several reasons. Although the Government is nominally committed to gender equality, many political leaders continue to believe that women are only suitable for employment in certain nurturing sectors such as health care and education.

This bias was clearly demonstrated by the General Secretary of the Party's Central Committee when he stated in 1982 that: In the new revolutionary stage, work among women is aimed at achieving equality between men and women ... We should assist our women ... [to] participate in the management of the affairs of the country, especially in jobs suitable to women such as those in health services, education and so on. A further reason for women's lack of presence in the broader political hierarchy is that those women who are active in formal politics tend to operate within the Lao Women's Union.

One of the largest barriers to women's participation in

political activity, however, is time. The major prerequisites for nomination to party membership and to leadership positions are active participation in state organised activities; and punctuality, good attendance and willingness to perform overtime duties in the workplace. Women, who are over-burdened with domestic concerns, are often prevented from meeting these qualifications. Those women who have attained high positions in politics are in most cases related to powerful men in the country and have the resources to hire other women to perform their domestic duties. Finally, there is a strong socio-cultural bias against women's active or vocal participation in public life, which seems to persist, particularly at the village level

INSTITUTIONAL MECHANISMS FOR CHANGE

Lao Women's Union: The Lao Women's Union (LWU) is a mass-based organisation with a membership of 500132 women, almost half of the female population of Laos aged 15-60 years. The organisation extends from the national level where it has the status of Ministry, through to the village level. The LWU has links with every ministry, state organisation and government sector.

Given the size and level of organisation of the LWU, it appears to be the only viable institutional channel through which to mobilise women, or implement projects or programmes specifically aimed at women. The LWU was established by the LPRP in 1955 under the name of the Lao Patriotic Women's Association. For many years the primary task of the organisation was to mobilize women in support of the revolutionary struggle.

From 1975 onwards, the Patriotic Women's Association mobilised women in the tasks of national reconstruction and building socialism. Defending women's specific interests was only a secondary concern. In fact, the organisation's slogan of the three goods and two responsibilities'contradicted their goals for women's emancipation. Women were encouraged to be good citizens, good mothers and good wives. Furthermore, they were expected to seek employment outside the home and to actively participate in national construction and defence.

Nowhere in the LWU programme was there any mention that men should equally share in household tasks. In 1984, the LWU held its first national congress and changed its name. A second congress was held in 1989 where the tasks and roles of the LWU were more clearly defined. A small group of more educated women assumed leadership positions at this time, and the organisation has more recently been shifting its emphasis to directly addressing the needs of women, particularly poor rural women.

The Union is presently involved in several activities to promote women's interests. These include collaboration with the Ministry of Education in campaigns to combat female illiteracy especially among adult women and women of ethnic minorities; training for women in general health care, hygiene, child/natal care and nutrition; and introduction of time saving technologies for women and providing skills training for income generation. The LWU, however, faces several constraints which include lack of adequate funding and lack of trained personnel to implement projects. These needs are now increasingly being addressed by international donor agencies and some of these efforts will be discussed in the following section.

INTERNATIONAL ASSISTANCE

Following the adoption of the NEM, several non-governmental agencies, UN organisations and some bilateral donors initiated women's projects in Laos. Funds and technical assistance are being directed towards programmes related to agriculture, health care and sanitation, income generation, child care and institution building. UNICEF and the Lao Government have set up a Women's Development Programme (1992-6) working through the LWU, with an emphasis on women and child survival, health and development. Interventions are planned in the health, education and water and sanitation sectors.

The institutional and information base for women and

development activities will also be addressed by: enhancing the capacity of the LWU; improved gender disaggregated data collection; gender sensitization of policy makers; and women focused community development projects. In spite of the long-standing political priority given to gender equality by the LPRP and the central role of women in the national and household economy, women in Laos continue to be marginalised by male dominated social and political institutions and restricted in their educational and employment opportunities.

They also continue to have the major responsibility for domestic labour, at the same time as engaging in numerous activities to maintain household living standards often under conditions of extreme hardship. Women of the highland ethnic minorities are particularly disadvantaged due to the isolation and underdevelopment of these areas and to more male dominated socio-cultural institutions and attitudes.

Furthermore, whilst some women may be in a position to benefit from the current thrust towards economic liberalisation, it is important to be aware that many maybe negatively affected by the wide ranging economic reforms. Interventions are required at various levels to ensure that women's interests are kept at the forefront of the current processes of economic and political change in Laos.

MACRO POLICY AND INSTITUTIONAL INTERVENTIONS

1. To promote more systematic consideration of gender concerns at the macro policy level, for example, in decisions on the allocation of government expenditure (inter- and intra-sectorally); in changes in trade policy, given the possible impact of this on women's productive activities; in the promotion and regulation of export oriented industries where women are likely to constitute the major part of the labour force.
2. To provide financial aid and institution building assistance to the LWU, in particular to enhance its adminstrative and

managerial capacity and its ability to lobby and liaise with technical ministries;

3. To assist in developing a reliable data base for women in Laos especially for assessing the situation and needs of Midland and Highland women.
4. To encourage more participatory assessment of women's needs at local levels and provide women with the training and resources to organise their own development activities and to intervene in local decision making and resource allocating institutions more effectively.
5. To prioritise investment in health and education in order to extend and improve the quality of provision, particularly in underserved minority areas.

HEALTH

To fund and support the development of appropriate health care programmes which integrate nutrition, sanitation, education and preventative measures such as immunization. This should be prioritised over institution based health care which would be inaccessible to the majority of the population. The improvement of women's and children's health status, particularly ethnic minorities, should be a major priority within this.

To promote an integrated approach to reproductive health, incorporating family planning, maternal and child health and HIV/AIDS prevention activities. Experience elsewhere has shown that men also need to be drawn into family planning and AIDS awareness activities for them to be effective.

EDUCATION

To provide incentives to encourage female attendance and reduce drop out rates of girls. Scholarships, school feeding programmes, more local provision of schools and flexible timing are possible ways to encourage increased female enrollment and reduce drop out rates. This should be in the context of an overall drive to improve the coverage and quality of educational provision. Renewed efforts are needed to combat female illiteracy, possibly in the context of other local development efforts (e.g. in health or agriculture). These need to be sensitive to the multiple demands on women's time.

AGRICULTURE

Women should be recognised as farmers and provided with credit and training in new production techniques so that they can reduce their work burden and increase their labour productivity. Programmes should be sensitive to women's time constraints which are in part determined by seasonality in agricultural requirements and by regional differences.

SMALL SCALE INDUSTRY

Women's home based handicrafts production needs to be supported and promoted (possibly for export), particularly in view of increased competition from imported manufactured goods.

MARKETING

Women are already heavily engaged in small scale marketing operations in both rural and urban areas. This activity should be supported by the provision of credit facilities, combined with training in business and information skills, and the formation of women's marketing organisations.

7

Women in Malay Society

Studies on influential women in antiquity have revealed that they "neither had nor sought political power, but worked through their husbands or father or sons". Even if a few of these women seem to defy the norms of what is expected of feminine behaviour, it has been documented that "women take political action only under certain closely defined conditions, and that unless they do so at least ostensibly on behalf of a male relative, they and others around them come to a bad end". Lefkowitz's findings, drawn from Greek myths and history, confirm restrictions to female power. Since the concern of this chapter deals with a group of women of influence in Malay historical works, Lefkowitz's findings can perhaps yield some light on the matter.

Malay historical works (sastera sejarah) prospered as a courtly narrative tradition between the late thirteenth century and the early nineteenth century. The two works chosen in this chapter represent two ends of a continuum; The Malay Annals (hereafter referred to as MA) were commissioned by Sultan Alau'd-din II, not long after the fall of Melaka to the Portuguese in 1511. The Precious Gift (hereafter referred to as PG), started around the 1860s and finished in the early nineteenth century, and was not commisssioned by a ruler, but emerged out of the writer's own initiative to "trace genealogies, expeditions, dates and most important of all, the narrative of the Malay and Bugis Kings and of all their children".

Unlike other works in the same genre whose scribes are unidentifiable, the compilers of these two works have been identified, and they are male court dwellers, relatives of the rulers, and are well-versed with the goings-on in the two courts. Malay historical works trace the origin and genealogy of Malay rulers, describe the founding of kingdoms, glorify expansions of geographical boundaries, and give an account of the elaborate etiquette of royal households. The titles of these works commonly begin with either sejarah (history), silsilah/salasilah (genealogy), and hikayat (lengthy traditional tale).

Due to the nature of the works, and the reasons for writing them, women do not figure prominently in these narratives. Most women are nameless and voiceless, incognito. They normally appear as somebody's wife or daughter, for example, "Sultan Mahmud Syah begat three children: the son was called Sultan Ahmad and it was he who was to succeed his father on the throne: the other two are daughters". The scribe does not identify the consort, or the two daughters as they are considered unimportant to the reading public (which is limited to the court/elite sector of a feudal society). Women are utilised as peace-weavers, or valued as pawns in political alliances, either by marrying them off to foreign rulers/ diplomats or sealing alliances within one's own kinship.

The women discussed in this chapter, however, do not appear as the passive political tools as do most of the women in the court. There is a group of them who attempt overt participation in court politics, especially in a delicate matter such as the succession of rulers to the throne. This is an extremely important position, because a ruler carries with him sacral sovereign power. The Malays, whose ancestors can be traced to worshipping the Hindu Gods, adopt a belief in divine kingship. The coming of Islam gives birth to another form of sacral sovereignty which regards a ruler as "a shadow of God upon earth".

Therefore, the power which comes with the position gives rise to a power contest between eligible male siblings. The general trend which can be discerned from most historical chronicles is that the ruler decides who is going to succeed him, and the power normally passes to the eldest son of a royal consort. However, Malay rulers in these works do not practise monogamous marriages, and although they have all adopted the Muslim faith which allows up to four wives at any one time, some of them even have up to six, not to mention numerous concubines. Therefore, the question of who is going to replace the ruler becomes contentious, because several princes might claim their eligibility.

This provides the opportunity for female court-dwellers to intervene, especially those who are in the position to determine the outcome of the succession battle. The first instance of a woman's overt participation in Malay court politics occurs during the reign of Sultan Muhammad, the third Sultan of the Melakan dynasty. He has two consorts - the Princess of Rekan, who is the Queen, and the daughter of the Bendahara (Prime Minister). Both give birth to a son, however the eldest son is the offspring of his secondary wife. Although the Sultan wishes his oldest to succeed him, the Queen wants her own son, who is only seventeen months' old, to ascend the throne:

"The latter [Raja Kasim] was older than Raja Ibrahim, but it was the desire of the Queen that even so Raja Ibrahim should succeed his father, and Sultan Muhammad Syah acquiesced despite his fondness for Raja Kasim. Such was the deference that he paid to the Queen's wishes that he was helpless, allowing Raja Ibrahim to do just as he pleased but chiding Raja Kasim if he took so much as a bit of sireh leaf from anyone".

Although the Sultan heeds his Queen's wish, how and what methods she has used to manipulate him are not specified. Obviously, she is influencing the outcome of the battle for power by working through her husband. Ironically, her overt intervention is merely described; her voice is decidedly absent. The scribe, who can pick and choose to tell a story as he sees fit, cannot appear to offend the royal patron who has commissioned him to write the history of kings. Yet he implies that the Sultan has violated an established custom, and erred in his decision: "The people, however, hated Raja Ibrahim and liked Raja Kasim".

By conceding to his Queen's wishes, the ruler is indulging her, and giving licence to women to participate actively in a male domain. The consequence of her intervention causes an uproar - that her son is still a minor gives an excuse for the Queen's own cousin, the Raja of Rekan, to act as a regent, while Raja Kasim is made to earn his living as a fishmonger. An Arab trader, Maulana Jalaluddin, foretells Raja Kasim that he is the true ruler of Melaka, and pushes him to claim his throne, although the trader puts a condition that the Queen must be given to him as a reward, which Raja Kasim agrees to fulfil.

The prince manages to gather the support of the masses, overthrows the regent, who, in the event, stabs the child-ruler. The Queen's life is spared: she is neither killed nor given away to the Arab which Raja Kasim could have easily done to humiliate her for her meddling. Instead, Raja Kasim orders a palace maid to be adorned like a princess whom the Arab trader has mistaken to be the Queen herself. By saving her that ultimate humiliation, Raja Kasim is shown to be a nobler man, while the Queen is presented as a vindictive woman. Although she tries to take part in politics because of her son, her involvement does not follow closely defined conventions: firstly, by allowing the older step-son to ascend the throne, and secondly, by allowing the court elders to act as the regent, not her own cousin. Her meddling causes internal strife, and brings destruction to her close family members.

Female participation is described as more intruding as the chronicle progresses to narrate the reign of Sultan Mahmud. His father, Sultan Alauddin, chooses young Mahmud to be the successor although he has two other sons from a marriage with a princess. In one instance, the child-ruler gets chronic diarrhoea, and is almost at the point of death, and the message is relayed to his grandmother, the queen dowager. She wishes her older fully royal grandson, Raja Menawar, to take over the throne, and contrives to murder the present ruler by suffocating him: "Let me get to the palace and I will lay myself down on Sultan Mahmud Syah and weep over him, so that he may die while I lie upon him".

However, when she tries to approach the bed, the two caretakers rush forward to attack the old woman. She reminds them of her own sovereign power, endowed through her position as the previous Queen. But both men reply: "Yes, this once Malays will be disloyal! If your highness persists in going near your grandson, nothing shall stop us attacking you! Raja Tua accordingly abandons the idea of approaching Sultan Mahmud". The scribe further says ".... and he was preserved by God Almighty: his alloted span in the Book of Life was not yet rubbed out". One can make two interesting observations in this episode.

The queen dowager is presented like a raving mad woman with dishevelled hair which indicates that she is not in the right frame of mind, and therefore her sovereignty can be discarded. The scribe also seems to scorn the idea of a woman trying to assert her sovereignty and influence. In this case, she is given a voice, but the fact that the scribe allows us access to her thoughts is a device used to show the transparency of her treachery. Moreover, the favoured grandson does not even contend the kingship of Melaka. The queen dowager is an independent agent who is bent on working on behalf of a relative who is not even remotely concerned with the position.

The reign of Sultan Mahmud also records an explicit kind of female power as shown by Tun Fatimah, daughter of the Bendahara. The king is well-known for his liaisons with women, married or maiden. He has many consorts, and even attempts to marry a fairy (non-human) Princess, Princess Mount (Gunong) Ledang, though she thwarts his proposal by asking, besides a bridge of gold and a bridge of silver from Melaka to the mountain, seven trays of mosquitoes' hearts, seven trays of mites' hearts, a vat of young areca-nut water, a vat of tears, a cup of the Raja's blood and a cup of his son's blood.

Strangely enough, the Sultan says he is able to fulfill all wishes except a cup of his son's blood. This is obviously a myth to show the ruler's preoccupation with women, but only a woman in non-human form is able to reject his proposal. His first consort, whose name is not mentioned, bears him a son, Raja Ahmad, whom he makes his heir apparent. One event, however, changes the whole scenario. He sets eyes upon Tun Fatimah on her wedding day, and conceives a passion for her. His desire is so insurmountable that he orders the execution of all the males in the Bendahara's family after a malicious rumour that the latter plans to dethrone him. The Sultan marries her, even makes her his Queen, but Tun Fatimah, throughout her married life with the Sultan, "never once did she laugh or even smile. As was her sadness, so was the king's; and he bitterly repented what he had done. And he abdicated from the throne in favour of his son Sultan Ahmad, to who he made over his officers and the regalia". Tun Fatimah's anger at the Sultan is implied through her repeated abortions that puzzle the Sultan: "Why is it that when you are with child you cause abortion? Is it that you dislike bearing a child to me?" And Tun Fatimah answered, "Why should you want children of me any longer when you already have a son on the throne?" And Sultan Mahmud Syah said, Even so, if you conceive by me, let the child be born: if it be a son, it is he that we will make Raja".

It so happens that his son, Sultan Ahmad, mistreats court elders which gives the excuse for Sultan Mahmud to commission someone to kill his son. He later appoints another son, Raja Muzaffar Syah from his marriage with the princess from Kelantan, as his successor: "When Raja Muzaffar Syah sits in the hall with people before him, there was laid for him first a spread-out mat and then a rug. On the rug there was a sitting-mat and on top of all the royal cushion. Thereon he sat". However, Tun Fatimah, after giving birth to two daughters, now gives birth to a son, Raja Alau'd-din Shah.

Soon after the son is born, the royal cushion of Raja Muzaffar Syah is removed, then the rug, until he is left with nothing to sit on except a mat such as ordinary people use. When Tun Fatimah's confinement period is over, which is forty days, her son is proclaimed as the successor. The Sultan easily abdicates his throne, and as easily does away with his two sons to follow the whims and fancies of a woman. The fact that she cannot possibly forgive a murderous ruler, who gives way to his lust, and kills all her male family members, is not elaborated. The act of killing her unborn babies becomes an act of selfishness; but the fact that she cannot carry to term a progeny of violence is passed over in silence.

Tun Fatimah has no control over her marriage, however, she seems to hold the trump card for her own offspring to take over the dynastic lineage. She works through her husband, and adapts to patriarchy by using her femaleness and sexuality until she gets what she wants, but at a great cost. The ruler loses two sons, and more importantly, the Melakan empire loses all its glory to the Portuguese. The fall of Melaka is indirectly attributed to Tun Fatimah's active participation in court politics. Does time change the perception of women's participation in Malay politics? The Precious Gift, which comes nearly three centuries after The Malay Annals, describes the pattern of events that leads to the Bugis intervention in Malay politics, and how the covenant between the Malay-Bugis is broken time and again by a selfish Malay faction.

A Malay princess plays a large part in making way for the Bugis to launch themselves in Malay politics, which later becomes a sore point with Malay aristocrats who see themselves losing power to the military might of the Bugis clan. The Sultan of Johor, a former Bendahara, finds his position threatened by the son of the assassinated ruler. The Sultan is of non-royal descent who has gained his royalty through regicide. The previous ruler, Sultan Mahmud, has murdered his chieftain's pregnant wife. This is how the story goes:

"This is the account of the reasons why the sovereignty of the Kings of Malacca passed to their Bendaharas. According to the story, the last descendant of Seri Teri Buana and the Kings of the Singapore, Malacca and Johor periods was Sultan Mahmud, a Johor king. It is said that he took a peri, a type of genie, as his wife, and so had no desire for marriage with a human spouse. Once, when the ruler was sleeping, someone brought him a ripe jackfruit as a gift, which the palace steward kept until the king should wake. By chance, Megat Seri Rama's pregnant wife came by. She had a craving for jackfruit, and begged the steward for a slice. He gave her one, and she went away.

When the king awoke, he wished to eat the jackfruit, so the steward brought it to him, and said, Something unfortunate has happened; I have just given some to Megat Seri Rama's wife, rather than turn her away. On hearing this, His Majesty was furious and ordered Megat Seri Rama's wife to be summoned. He then ripped open her belly and pulled the child from her womb. Thus Megat Seri Rama's wife died". The chieftain, with the Bendahara's help, assassinates the Sultan as he is borne aloft on his retainers' shoulders. The Bendahara proclaims himself as the Sultan of Johor. After nineteen years of peaceful reign, the Sultan is faced with an intruder, Raja Kecik, who claims that he is the son of the murdered Sultan Mahmud, and there are three versions given of how he is conceived:

1. Sultan Mahmud desires his fairy wife, ejaculates, and orders Encik Pung, a concubine wife, who happens to be in the room, to eat his semen. She becomes pregnant.
2. The Majesty dies with an erect penis because he desires Encik Pung before he dies, so she is requested by the court officials to have sex with the dead man whose penis only relaxes after the act. She then becomes pregnant.
3. Encik Pung is already pregnant when the Sultan dies.

Obviously the scribe, by telling the three versions of the existence of Raja Kecik, is trying to raise doubts about the legitimacy of the claim. The men of the ruling Sultan, however, appear too weak to oppose the charges; Raja Kecik has managed to convince the sea-people that his conception is attributed to divine power which is endowed upon the rightful monarch. At such a critical period which seems to paralyze the male court officials, Tengku Tengah, a daughter of the Sultan, decides to take charge. She implores a family of five Bugis princes, immigrants from another part of Malay Archipelago, who have great military might, to restore her father's honour:

"... Tengku Tengah stood at the entrance to the guests gallery, opened the screen and threw down her ear stud, saying: O Bugis Princes, if you are truly brave, avenge the shame of our family. When that is done, I shall willingly be your slave, and even if you ordered me to cook your rice, I would do it".

One of the princes, Opu Daeng Parani, takes up her offer and makes her his second wife, and promises to avenge her family's shame. The same prince goes on to marry two other women; each time the group of brothers restores peace to a city-state, he marries one of the daughters of the rulers. The Sultan's honour is restored; Tengku Tengah is seen as courageous, a woman warrior who even dares to face her father's assailants with a sword. She adopts the masculine stance of the aggressive avenger, symbolized in the throwing of her ear stud.

However, after revenge is done, she voluntarily abandons her masculinity, and goes back as a domesticated female - the woman who cooks rice for her husband. This transformation from femininity to masculinity to femininity again correlates with Lefkowitz's framework that an act of courage, a streak of masculinity, is but ephemeral - the influential woman "takes action to preserve and then returns to her families". We can draw some conclusions here about women and power, based on the two texts. There seems to be two types of participation - the honourable way of female intervention, and the dishonourable way. Tengku Tengah is an example of an honourable assertion of power; she acts to preserve her family's royalty, not her own son, from a dubious claimant.

She does not seem to get any immediate reward; in fact, her husband dies quite soon after her marriage. Tengku Tengah stops interfering when order is restored. However, the chronicler gives a warning to his readers of the possible repercussions from the behaviour of assertive women: "The reader knows what women will do; when they are angry or full of hatred they act rashly, heedless of consequences". Thus, for all her courage, there is still a lack of confidence in prolonged female political participation. The women in The Malay Annals, on the other hand, indicate the dishonourable way of assertion of power. Their methods of participation are dangerous.

The scribe provides his readers with the other side of the picture - what women are capable of if they get the upper hand. His examples confirm that women should stay away from politics. It is clear that the authors of the court narratives believe that women do not and should not have executive power. Gender distinction exists as part of the formal structure of a feudal society, and I believe that the scribes give warning signals to the audience of the repercussions of female intervention. The fact that the women seem to wield power in their domestic capacity shows their innovation and adaptibility to the restrictive condition, yet, their participation is at best perceived as an intrusion, and is not at all favourable to men. The typical male reaction is a confirmation of the subordinate status of the women in feudal Malay society.

Women constitute half of humanity, and it follows that any decision-making, whether at the personal, family, societal or public levels, should be mindful of and involve the participation of women in the making of those decisions. Women's political, social and economic rights are an integral and inseparable part of their human rights. Democracy is an inclusive process, and therefore in a functioning democracy, the points of view of different interest groups must be taken into account in formulating any decision. The interest and opinions of men, women and minorities must be part of that decision-making process. Yet far from being included in the decision-making process, women find themselves under-represented in political institutions. Numerous challenges confront women entering politics.

Among them are lack of party support, family support and the "masculine model" of political life. Many feel that Malaysian society is still male dominated, and men are threatened by the idea of women holding senior posts. In the political sphere this is compounded by the high premium placed on political power. This makes some men even less willing to share power with women. Based on the Malaysian experience, this case study will explore some of the obstacles that hinder the participation of women in parliament, and propose strategies that may be used to overcome them.

THE MALAYSIAN CONTEXT

Malaysia is a federation of thirteen states and three federal territories. Nine of the states are headed by sultans, the other four by governors appointed by the king, known as *Yang Dipertuan Agong* (YDPA). The YDPA is elected from among the sultans by the Council of Rulers made up of the sultans themselves. The position is rotated among them for a five-year term. The YDPA rules with the advice of the prime minister and the sultans rule in their various states with the advice of their chief ministers. Malaysia is a constitutional monarchy that follows a system of parliamentary democracy. The prime minister and chief ministers are elected by the people through general elections held regularly every five years.

The current YDPA is the twelfth since the nation's independence on 31 August 1957. At independence the nation was made up of eleven states and was called the Federation of Malaya. In 1963, Sabah and Sarawak joined the Federation to form the Federation of Malaysia. Women constitute over 50 per cent of Malaysia's 23 million people. Famed as a multi-ethnic country, rich in its variety of cultures, Malaysia's population is made up of more than 30 ethnic groups. Less than eight per cent of the population was classified as living below poverty line before the 1997 economic crisis; the literacy rate is above 85 per cent and life expectancy is comparable to developed countries. It has a bicameral parliamentary system composed of a lower house (*Dewan Rakyat*) and upper house (*Dewan Negara*).

While members of the Dewan Rakyat are elected, members of the Dewan Negara are appointed either by the states or directly by the YDPA acting on the advice of the prime minister. The National Front (Barisan Nasional or BN), a coalition of about fifteen political parties established in 1974 in the aftermath of 13 May 1969 racial riots, forms the government. BN's core members, the United Malays National Organisation (UMNO), the Malaysian Chinese Association (MCA) and the Malaysian Indian Congress (MIC), that earlier formed the Alliance Party (1955-1974), have been at the helm of the government since the country's independence. While BN dominates Malaysian mainstream politics and the parliament with an almost unbroken record of two-thirds majority or more, the nation has credible opposition parties, including the *Parti Islam SeMalaysia* (PAS), Democratic Action Party (DAP), *Parti Rakyat Malaysia* (PRM) and since 1999, *Parti keADILan Nasional*.

WOMEN IN MALAYSIAN POLITICS

In 2002, Malaysia had three women in full ministerial positions: the Minister of Women and Family Development, the Minister of International Trade and Industry and the Minister of Welfare and National Unity. In addition, women occupy other significant governmental posts that include deputy ministers, political secretaries, diplomats, senior civil servants, elected members of various state assemblies, and senators in the Dewan Negara. In the Dewan Rakyat, there are now 20 women members of parliament, out of 193 total members. If the number of elected women MPs is an indicator, there has been a slow improvement in the status and position of women in Malaysian politics. Nevertheless, the presence of women in Malaysia's decision making process is still far from satisfactory. Some women leaders have talked of gender parity in this context. And for the time being, women still find themselves under- represented in Malaysian political institutions.

There are at least five factors that form obstacles to Malaysian women's active participation in politics: subliminal discrimination against women; time constraints; the notion that "a woman's place is at home"; natural apathy and aversion to political involvement and lack of adequate resources.

According to Rashila and Saliha there are at least five common factors which form obstacles to Malaysian women's active participation in politics. They classify the factors as, social discrimination against women's roles in the public domain, time constraints due to career and domestic demands, cultural and religious arguments that a woman's place is in the home, structural constraints within each political party that do not allow women to advance beyond a certain level, and lack of adequate resources in terms of organizational support, personal influence and finance. Contrary to popular misperceptions, an understanding of Islamic concepts leads one to appreciate the liberating possibilities afforded by the teachings of the religion. In many cases, religion has empowered and enabled women to reach their full potential and capabilities just as much as men. The experience of Malay women at the turn of the last century is a case in point.

MUSLIM WOMEN AND 'REFORMASI'

In the past, Malay women have been active in the public sphere. Che Siti Wan Kembang was a female ruler of the state of Kelantan on the east coast of peninsular Malaysia in the seventeenth century. History tells us that Malay women were also rulers of the kingdom of Aceh. For example, Ratu Shafiuddin, the daughter of Sultan Iskandar Thani, ascended to the throne after the death of her husband, Sultan Iskandar Muda. In fact, Aceh was ruled by a succession of queens for the next fifty years. On the islands of Maluku and Sulawesi, there were other Malay women rulers. A century ago, Muslim reformers like Syed Sheikh Al Hadi, Sheikh Tahir Jalaluddin and their contemporaries in the progressive Islamic movement - popularly known as the Kaum Muda - spread the idea that Malay Muslim girls should receive the best of modern education along with the boys.

Although initially these ideas encountered some opposition from the more conservative minded, Malay society in general embraced this suggestion with open arms. Thus, even before independence, Malay Muslim society adopted this liberal attitude towards its women and an open atmosphere which encouraged education and the role of women in the public sphere. Since then, we have had women in the civil service and in the corporate sector who have attained senior positions. Therefore, unlike other societies, there does not appear to be confusion or significant conflict in terms of the roles played by women in Malaysia. Our society has been fortunate in that we had these visionary scholars and intellectuals who opened up avenues for women more than a century ago.

In many cases, Islam has empowered and enabled women to reach their full potential and capabilities just as much as men. In fact, in Malaysia the most politicized and politically active group of women has always been the Malay Muslims. After independence, the first Malaysian woman to become a minister was Fatimah Haji Hashim, who was appointed to be Minister for Welfare by the country's first Prime Minister, Tunku Abdul Rahman. Since then, women have tended to be assigned either to ministries seen as "suitable" to their roles, such as the Ministry of Welfare or the Ministry of Women and Family Development, or to junior ministries such as Culture, Youth and Sports, now realigned to become the Ministry of Culture, Tourism and Arts.

The only woman who has been given a senior ministerial post is Rafidah Aziz who was appointed Minister of International Trade and Industry in 1987. Even now, the proportion of women ministers or deputies, compared to men, is very small, and still far behind the developed world. There is no quota system in Malaysia to increase women's political representation. At the party level, women are only beginning to take up important positions. In the ruling party UMNO, there is only one elected woman member out of the about forty members on its supreme council, while Parti keADILan has eight women elected its leadership council.

Besides the eight women leaders elected to the policymaking body of keADILan (including the president and the treasurer), two keADILan state committees (in Sabah and Sarawak) are also headed by women. However, what is more important is that the dual political and economic crises of September 1998, acted as a catalyst in galvanizing the latent public mood for reform (*reformasi*). These events also helped sensitize women to take a more active interest in the country's social, economic and political domains. This is proven by the active role of women in the reformasi movement since that year. Women have clearly played at least an equal role with men in activating programs carried out in the quest for change.

Women played an important and active role in the reform movement, sensitizing them to become more active in participating in the country's social, economic and political issues.

Over the past three years, we can see the continuing role played by women in sustaining the endeavors for a more open, just, and equitable society. The vigor with which they are carrying out these efforts disproves the often quoted cliché that women are fickle and easily swayed. The sheer perseverance and tenacity of women in this struggle has in fact resulted in a very natural bonding or synergy in generating strength and enthusiasm to work towards a fairer and more just society and government in Malaysia.

As part of this effort, it is necessary to establish an alternative agenda that includes enabling women to maximize their potential in contributing to their personal well-being and to the development of their society. It is necessary to create an alternative forum that goes beyond tokenism that does not just use women as an accessory of the political machinery to bring in the votes during elections. If women are enabled to maximize their potential, they will be able to contribute to the empowerment of all citizens in society.

This can happen without denigrating the social, cultural or religious obligations that are part of every woman's life. While women's positions in politics are one aspect contributing to development, it is important to remember the role women play in other sectors of society. Malaysia's experience has shown that any discussion on the role of women in politics cannot be confined to only representation in formal institutions.

A great number of women, after having pursued their education to tertiary levels, choose to become homemakers. Although they may not be occupying formal positions commensurate with their training, they are also contributing to the development of society by bringing up their children and family in a more enlightened environment. The common definitions of democracy and politics generally do not lend themselves to a woman-friendly approach. The linking of ideas of democracy and gender is still an arena that needs to be further explored.

OBSTACLES FACED BY WOMEN IN PARLIAMENT

The numerous problems facing women who enter politics in Malaysia deters many from political involvement.

Dual Burden

Women themselves are less assertive and often have to shoulder additional burdens, juggling domestic responsibilities and career concerns thereby making it hard for any but the most determined to succeed. However, a more relaxed attitude is discernable among the younger generation and men now appear to be more willing to see women as partners in both the domestic and professional spheres. Since political leaders tend to be middle-aged, it will perhaps be some years before this change is reflected at the highest levels of politics.

Political Parties

The nature of political parties also hinders the political involvement of women. In general, it can perhaps be observed that the comfortably entrenched parties tend to adhere to more conservative attitudes, failing to see and adapt to the fairly radical changes taking place in society. It is the more dynamic alternative or opposition parties that have on the whole given greater opportunity to women. Also, many political parties have few resources to devote to training and education, including for women, because of the multiple pressures applied by those in authority.

Deterring Environment for Women

It is sad to note that female MPs and women representatives in the various state assemblies still face sexual harassment in the form of disparaging remarks and offensive jokes made during parliamentary or state assembly sessions. There has been no effective action taken to ameliorate such abusive practices and both female and male members of parliament have not been successful in making any concerted effort to change the situation. Another reason keeping women away from politics is that they often consider it as a male realm, and are often daunted by the hypocrisy and "dirty game" of politics.

STRATEGIES TO OPEN ACCESS FOR WOMEN IN POLITICS

Considering the conditions above, it is necessary to explore the strategies that women employ to access the public sphere in the context of a patriarchal socio-political system. There are women who have been successful in subverting the boundaries of gender, and in operating in a very aggressive male-dominated sphere. Could other women learn from this example? It is important to note that many of the women who have been successful come from a background in the political elite. Their background and class is perhaps the most important factor in their successful inclusion into the political system.

We can, however, examine whether socio-political movements provide opportunities for women to use certain strategies that might be able to subvert the gender hierarchy in politics. Certain forms of support within the society are important for the development of women's role in politics, and there are already many success stories of this type. The most important is political awareness. Muslim women who had until recently been relatively invisible in the public sphere are suddenly filling up meeting halls and organising campaigns for women's rights, civil rights, human rights, and for democracy.

Prominent among them were women from the *Angkatan Belia Islam Malaysia* (ABIM), *Jemaah Islah Malaysia* (JIM) and various civil society NGOs like *Tenaganita* and *Suaram*. The second is education, which provides the core of informed and competent female opinion. Thirdly, there are now many women holding senior positions in the country's civil service. This has ensured women's input in the planning and implementation of government policy.

Many of the NGOs aligned themselves with keADILan, and by extension, the Alternative Front, which is a coalition of opposition parties -keADILan, PAS, DAP and PRM - in the fiercely contested 1999 general elections. *Hajjah Zainon Jaafar* (ABIM), Fuziah Salleh (JIM), Irene Fernandez (Tenaganita) and Zaiton Kasim (Women's Candidacy Initiative) were picked to contest on the BA platform. Such alignment between civil society activists and political parties has come to be regarded as a feature of "new politics" in Malaysia post-1998.

It is also important to remember that we should look beyond the often asked question of how to increase the numbers of women in parliament, and move towards presenting examples and experiences of how women can impact on the political process while working through a parliamentary structure. Malaysia, like any other country, needs to have balanced male/female representation in the public sphere, including politics, so that women can participate in high-level decision-making.

Having women at the highest levels of decision- making not only means the articulation of issues generally perceived to be women's issues, but ensures that the interests and needs of women, who are half of the population, are given due weight and consideration. Beyond that, the presence of women at these levels will mean that women's perspectives will be easier to hear and more highly valued in national discussions, in the direction of creating a more just, open, fair and equitable society. Without a sufficiently visible, if not proportionate, presence in the political system - i.e. "threshold representation" - a group's ability to influence either policy-making, or indeed the framing of political culture, is limited.

A POLITICAL CREDO

On a personal note, I would like to end by mentioning that I never aspired nor dreamed that I would be occupying my current position, in helping to bring about change in society. Some commentators have mentioned that it is a unique position, borne out of exceptional circumstances that befell the country when the cataclysmic events of 1998 gave rise to a public outcry for reform. The experience in Malaysia has shown that women tend to take a greater interest in politics in times of crisis. Certainly, Malaysian women have responded strongly to the events surrounding the political persecution of leaders of the opposition. One of the most gratifying aspects of keADILan's popularity is that a substantial proportion of its supporters are women.

As daughters, sisters, wives and mothers, they could readily empathize with the victims of abuses. As an "accidental" politician, I share the view that the struggle for justice must be continued even outside the sanctioned perimeters of elections held once every five years. The cause of justice must be fought for vigorously at all times so as to create ultimately a government and society that is not only just but that provides dignity to the people.

Although my journey into politics was not a deliberate and concerted plan, everyone has the right to use the arena of electoral politics to promote their cause. My cause is justice, especially for women, and for the disenfranchised and other marginalized groups in society. I sincerely believe in what the great sages have said throughout history, that the journey of a thousand miles starts with the first step. A Chinese proverb has it that a mountain is made up of many pebbles and that the ocean consists of millions of drops of water. In short, whatever the adversities and obstacles placed in our paths, Malaysia's women will answer with the universal chorus of common humanity: we shall overcome.

8

Changing Patterns of a Pakistan Family

Pakistani social life revolves around family and kin. Even among members of the most Westernized elite, family retains its overarching significance. The family is the basis of social organization, providing its members with both identity and protection. Rarely does an individual live apart from relatives; even male urban migrants usually live with relatives or friends of kin. Children live with their parents until marriage, and sons often stay with their parents after marriage, forming a joint family. The household is the primary kinship unit. In its ideal, or extended, form, it includes a married couple, their sons, their sons' wives and children, and unmarried offspring. Sons establish separate households upon their father's death.

Whether or not an extended household endures depends on the preferences of the individuals involved. Quarrels and divisiveness, particularly among the women (mother-in-law and daughters-in-law), can lead to the premature dissolution of a joint household. Descent is reckoned patrilineally, so only those related through male ancestors are considered relatives. The *biradari*, or group of male kin (the patrilineage), plays a significant role in social relations. Its members neither hold movable property in common nor share earnings, but the honor or shame of individual members affects the general standing of the *biradari* within the community. A common proverb expresses this view: "One does not share the bread, but one shares the shame."

In theory, members of a *biradari* are coresidents of a single village. In some areas, however, land fragmentation and generations of out-migration have led to the dispersal of many members of the *biradari* among various villages, regions, and cities. Patrilineal kin continue to maintain ties with their natal village and enjoy the legal right of first refusal in any *biradari* land sale. Members of a *biradari* celebrate the major life events together. Patrilineal kin are expected to contribute food and to help with guests in the ceremonies accompanying birth, marriage, death, and major religious holidays.

The *biradari* has traditionally served as a combined mutual aid society and welfare agency, arranging loans to members, assisting in finding employment, and contributing to the dowries of poorer families. There is considerable pressure for patrilineal kin to maintain good relations with one another. *Biradari* members who quarrel will try to resolve their differences before major social occasions so that the patrilineage can present a united front to the village. People with sons and daughters of marriageable age keenly feel the necessity to maintain good relations because a person whose family is at odds with his or her *biradari* is considered a poor marriage prospect.

Although descent is reckoned patrilineally, women maintain relations with their natal families throughout life. The degree of involvement with maternal kin varies among ethnic groups and among regions of the country. The tie between brother and sister is typically strong and affectionate; a woman looks to her brothers for support in case of divorce or widowhood early in her marriage. In those regions where families maintain considerable contact with maternal kin, children, even though they are members of their father's patrilineage, are indulged by their mother s kin. Just as a family's relations with its *biradari* are considered in evaluating a potential spouse, so in these regions may the mother's kin be assessed.

Marriage is a means of allying two extended families; romantic attachments have little role to play. The husband and wife are primarily representatives of their respective families in a contractual arrangement, which is typically negotiated between two male heads of household. It is fundamentally the parents' responsibility to arrange marriages for their children, but older siblings may be actively involved if the parents die early or if they have been particularly successful in business or politics. The terms are worked out in detail and are noted, by law, at the local marriage registry. Marriage is a process of acquiring new relatives or reinforcing the ties one has with others.

To participate fully in society, a person must be married and have children, preferably sons, because social ties are defined by giving away daughters in marriage and receiving daughters-in-law. Marriage with one's father's brother's child is preferred, in part because property exchanged at marriage then stays within the patrilineage. The relationship between in-laws extends beyond the couple and well past the marriage event. Families related by marriage exchange gifts on important occasions in each others lives. If a marriage is successful, it will be followed by others between the two families. The links thus formed persist and are reinforced through the generations.

The pattern of continued intermarriage coupled with the occasional marriage of nonrelatives creates a convoluted web of interlocking ties of descent and marriage. A woman's life is difficult during the early years of marriage. A young bride has very little status in her husband's household; she is subservient to her mother-in-law and must negotiate relations with her sisters-in-law. Her situation is made easier if she has married a cousin and her mother-in-law is also her aunt. The proper performance of all the elaborate marriage ceremonies and the accompanying exchange of gifts also serve to enhance the new bride's status.

Likewise, a rich dowry serves as a trousseau; the household goods, clothing, jewelry, and furniture included remain the property of the bride after she has married. Marriage also involves a dower, called *haq mehr*, established under Islamic law, the sharia. Although some families set a symbolic *haq mehr* of Rs32 in accordance with the traditions of the Prophet Muhammad, others may demand hundreds of thousands of rupees.

A wife gains status and power as she bears sons. Sons will bring wives for her to supervise and provide for her in her old age. Daughters are a liability, to be given away in an expensive marriage with their virginity intact. Therefore, mothers favor their sons. In later life, the relationship between a mother and her son remains intimate, in all likelihood with the mother retaining far more influence over her son than his wife has.

The decade of the 1980s has truly been a decade of the women of Pakistan. A powerful women's movement made a dramatic impact on Pakistan's political scene. The concrete achievements of the women's movement in its struggle against policies of General Zia's military regime which were directed against women in the name of Islamisation, have not been inconsiderable. A number of women's organisations in the country came together in this struggle, which included the Women's Action Forum (WAF) which has been the leading and the most effective of these, the Democratic Women's Association, the Sindhiani Tehrik and the Women's Front as well as the All Pakistan Women's Association (APWA) the oldest of these which has been run by wives of senior bureaucrats and politicians and has had a reformist but rather a patronising orientation.

The decade of the 1980s was also a decade of degradation of Pakistani women. The Zia regime, in its search for legitimacy, in the name of Islam, embarked upon a series of measures that were designed to undermine what little existed by way of women's legal rights, educational facilities and career opportunities - as well as the simple right for freedom of movement and protection from molestation by males. That galvanised women of the country into militant action in defence of their rights.

The military regime's actions, rhetoric and propaganda created an atmosphere which encouraged bigoted and mischievous individuals to take the 'law' into their own hands and harass women under the pretext of enforcing 'Islamic' norms of dress or, indeed, for simply appearing in public. Such lawlessness was allowed to go on with impunity. Women had to defend themselves not only vis-a-vis the state but also against hostile mischief makers in the society at large. Such attacks still continue. The women have fought back. These developments must be viewed against the background of quite far-reaching changes in Pakistan society in the four decades since independence, that have affected women's place in it, both in the rural society and the urban.

It is the latter, the urban society, with which we shall be most concerned here, for this is where the changes challenge most forcefully established social practices and attitudes. It must be kept in mind, however, that everywhere, in both the rural as well as the urban society, Pakistan remains a rigidly patriarchal society in which women are treated as chattel, 'given' or 'acquired' through arranged marriages, to spend their lives in the service of a male dominated social system. By and large women are married within *biraderis (lineages)* and the *biraderi* organisation provides a framework within which women's lives are ordered.

In the case of corporate *biraderis* the power of the *biraderi panchayat* (council) derives largely from control over decisions about whom a woman is to marry. It is not only a single patriarch, the head of a nuclear family, but the whole male dominated kinship organisation which has a stake in the subordination of women. (for an account of *biraderi* organisation cf.Alavi, 1972). No woman, even one with an independent career in a city can set up a home on her own, without the *'saya'* (lit: shade or protection) of a male. A divorced woman or a widow must turn to her father or brother, if they will have her. unless she has a grown up son under whose protection she can live. This is a powerful factor of control over women.

Furthermore, not altogether infrequently, especially amongst the poorer sections of the society, especially in cities and amongst *kammis* or 'village servants'. a daughter is 'sold' for money to a prospective husband and likewise, husbands divorce and 'sell' their wives. A woman who is not prepared to accept such a fate has little choice. She is a valued object, a prized chattel. Demographic statistics provide a measure of the effects of discrimination against women. Pakistan is probably unique in the world in having a lower number of women in its population than men i.e. 906 women for every 1,000 men as against a world average of 111 women to every 100 men.

In the population segment of 15 to 40 years olds there are 75 per cent more female deaths than male. This is attributed to nutritional anemia that affects most women in the country resulting from discrimination against women in the sharing of food. They are given less and have often to make do with left-overs. Because of the lower resistance of their underfed bodies women are more susceptible to killer diseases; malaria, gastro-enteritis and respiratory diseases, especially tuberculosis. Repeated pregnancies also take a heavy toll by lowering their resistance to disease. In the case of urban lower middle class women their condition is aggravated both physically and psychologically by their incarceration within the four walls of their appallingly confined and insanitary homes.

They get little of the sun and fresh air and no recreation at all while their men go about everywhere freely and are not affected therefore quite so much by their poor housing conditions. When attention is drawn to the subordination and oppression of women in Pakistan and demands made for improvement in their lot, Pakistani ideologues are quick to rebut such charges by painting an idealised picture of the high status of women in Islam. But this is a non *sequitur,* a specious line of argument that is intended to obscure the real issues, those of the actual conditions to which women in Pakistan are subject.

It is against such a background that questions about women in Pakistan society need to be looked at. Changes of a variety of kinds are under way, some improving their condition, others worsening them. In rural areas, the place of women in society and their role in the division of labour in production differs very widely from region to region and also between different classes. And there have been far reaching changes everywhere. To give only two instances, in the Potohar area of North West Punjab, for example. which is a region of fragmented bankrupt farms, massive numbers of men of working age have left the villages for jobs in the army, in factories all over Pakistan and, not least, as migrants, for work in Britain and Western Europe and especially in the Middle East where they are not permitted to bring their families to live with them.

This has brought about an extra-ordinary situation in villages of the region, many of which are, as a result, inhabited mainly by old men who are past working age, young children and women. It seems that in these cases women have to carry the main burden of working the land over and above their customary share in the farm economy and their domestic responsibilities. By contrast, in the rich canal Colony districts of the Punjab. in the wake of the Green Revolution, many women have been withdrawn from the farm economy and confined within *purdah.* Until these developments in recent decades (with the exception of landlord families) women have always had an active role in agricultural production in weeding, harvesting and threshing of crops, and other operations.

It is their duty to cut fodder and to look after farm animals. Accordingly these women enjoy freedom of movement and are not confined behind *purdah.* A custom that gives them a degree of economic freedom is their exclusive right to pick cotton . This is being undermined by recent changes). For this women are paid in kind. The cotton that they receive in payment is ritually sacrosanct, their privileged property which men cannot lay their hands on. After the cotton harvest it is a common sight to see women walking to town with a bundle of cotton perched on their heads, going shopping, to barter the cotton for something for themselves or, more likely, their children, without having to ask the husband for permission.

But after the Green Revolution of the 1970s many well to do peasants, who had prospered, withdrew their womenfolk from the labour force and confined them, to the *purdah*, secluded and isolated within the four walls of their homes, as a mark of their new higher social status. In the course of research in Punjab villages my wife and I found that far from rejoicing in this partial relief from the burden of work, the women resented this change. Many of them described their new situation to my wife as the equivalent of being locked up in a prison. They had lost the small degree of economic freedom and with it their freedom of movement.

When one considers the implications of such a change, one is led to a conceptual distinction between *exploitation* of a woman's labour and a woman's *oppression*. While the burden of labour on women has eased, though only slightly, their oppression has increased enormously, a change which the women themselves see as one which has left them feeling greatly deprived. It is in the urban context that women's contribution to the family economy has changed beyond recognition, as compared to conditions forty years ago. These changes seem to be having a greater impact on lower middle class families than either working class families or upper class ones. A large component of the working class, in Pakistani cities consists of migrant workers from the north of the country whose families have been left behind in their villages.

We know too little about the consequences of that fact on the life of single male workers in the city nor about the families left behind in the villages. In the case of workers whose families live with them in the cities, many of the women either do unskilled work in factories or operate in the so-called 'informal economy' or are engaged in domestic employment. They often prefer such employment over home-based work, for waged employment pays better. Despite the great increase in their burden of work and their independent contribution to the family budget, judging from evidence brought up in court cases during the last decade, it seems that the women continue, nevertheless, to be subject to patriarchal domination.

By contrast problems of the majority of upper class women are different. They have servants to do their chores and they do not need to (or are not allowed to) take jobs and have careers. Their worries stem from their total dependence on the husband and consequently insecurity for fear of being abandoned by the husband in favour of a second wife. In the absence of the possibility of an independent job or career, compounded by extreme difficulty for women in setting up an independent household without the *'saya'*, or protection, of a male head of family, their dependence on the husband is total.

They are therefore reduced virtually to the status of well fed, well dressed and well ornamented slaves who depend absolutely upon the whim of their husbands. Where the husband ill-treats or abuses them they must put up with it. Because of the difficulty in setting up an independent household even women with careers share this problem. Amongst the *nouveau riche,* in particular, a familiar pattern is one of a first 'traditional ' marriage to a woman from the *biraderi* (lineage), possibly not very well educated or fashionable.

This is often followed later in life by a marriage to an attractive socialite, a fitting spouse for the *arriviste,* a woman well endowed to perform the duties of a sophisticated hostess who can receive and entertain his friends and associates, businessmen and bureaucrats, in style. The first wife is discarded like an old shoe. She dare not insist on a divorce for, generally, she has nowhere to go and virtually no prospects of building a new life in a society that despises a divorced woman who is invariably blamed for the failure of her marriage. She is lucky if she has grown up sons who might make it possible for her to set up an independent home.

But in general, given such prospects, upper class women are likely to live out their lives in insecurity and anxiety. How common such situations are, would be difficult to quantify. Nor is the problem of dependence upon husbands absent in the case of women of the lower middle classes or the working class. However, in their case, as well as in the case of members of upper classes to a lesser d egree, pressures from *biraderi* (lineage) members and elders tend, to some degree, to restrain husbands from abandoning wives, daughters of their kinsmen.

In Pakistan, unlike the West, the social life of most people functions within frameworks of extended kinship, and the values and norms of kinship obligations cannot be flouted without penalty, except by the rich and the powerful or those who live in cosmopolitan circles. On the whole one gains the impression that the risk of a woman being abandoned by her husband in favour of a more attractive woman is less common, though by no means absent, in the case of lower middle class husbands, who can less afford two wives and are in any case ground down by the humdrum daily routine of their rather ordinary lives for such fanciful indulgence.

In the case of lower middle class families we can identify a two-fold division. On the one hand there are families whose women are educated, sufficiently at least to hold down a 'respectable' job. On the other hand there are more traditional families whose women have not received a good education who therefore do not qualify for 'respectable' salaried jobs. In these latter cases women contribute to the family economy by taking in home-based work under a putting out system operated by entrepreneurs who are only too happy to exploit this extremely cheap source of labour. General Zia's *Islamisation* policies threatened most directly the first category of lower middle class women, triggering off the militant women's movement of the 1980s.

Underlying these developments is the growing crisis of the lower middle class household economy over the last forty years. At the time of independence it was the normal expectation that man was the provider for the family. Joint families were favoured because of economies of scale in the domestic economy. A patriarch and his brothers, with his sons and nephews would all go to work and bring in the income needed to keep the family. Burdened with domestic labour, women of this class were not classified as 'economically active'.

It might be said that urban lower middle class women were amongst the most oppressed of women in Pakistan. being confined to the *'purdah and char diwari'* or the four walls of their home. In villages even those women who are confined behind the *purdah* nevertheless have relatively easy access to the company of other women of the village which is very supportive for them. Likewise, in old cities the layout of the *mohalla* (wards) has provided a similar possibility of social interaction amongst women. But with the explosive expansion of Pakistan's cities such patterns of spatial organisation of society seem to have broken down.

In such circumstances urban lower middle class women became virtually prisoners in their diminutive homes for going visiting would entail an elaborate logistic operation reserved for very special occasions. The continuous inflation in the cost of living in Pakistan over the decades has brought about a situation where a man's wage is no longer sufficient to keep the family. There was therefore a continuous pressure to broaden the base of the family economy. Gradually and steadily, more and more women were forced to find jobs to supplement family incomes. The change is visible and quite striking. Initially only a few occupations were thought to be respectable enough for such women.

As the pressure for jobs increased the concept of a 'respectable job' was progressively broadened to take in a wider range of jobs. Initially, apart from high status professional occupations, notably that of a doctor , what better, jobs in the teaching profession, especially in girls' schools and colleges, were considered to be respectable enough. About a third of the doctors and an equal proportion of school teachers were women. Gradually this changed. The mantle of respectability was now to cover also clerical jobs in open plan offices where women could work with men, but in public view.

The role of the personal secretary was initially suspect although it was much better paid, because it entailed a close relationship with the boss. But that too has changed. Today one finds women in a wide range of occupations, including laboratory assistants or ticket clerks at railway stations or clerks at post office counters and so on, as well as lawyers, architects, engineers, journalists and broadcasters. Needless to add, the numbers in the latter categories of occupations are extremely small. With more and more women taking up salaried jobs and in keeping with an increasing number of women taking to higher education, new values have emerged. Women now desire jobs and careers for their own sake so that an increasing number of wives of well heeled professionals and women from the upper classes take jobs not out of economic necessity but for self-fulfilment.

Education is the key to acceptable and respectable jobs and careers. Lower middle class families would find it degrading to let their women take up jobs as domestic servants or to work on the factory floor (though some are driven to this out of desperation) i.e. jobs for which education is not a pre-requisite. But families who expect their women to take up jobs as teachers or office clerks (or better) tend therefore to put a higher value on women's education than was the case before - though financing the education of sons still takes precedence. There was a time when women's education was thought to be mere indulgence, wasteful of the money spent on it.

There is demand for women's education also from professional men who want to marry reasonably educated wives, although not too highly qualified. There is a concept of an 'over-qualified' woman i.e. a woman who has better qualifications than her potential spouse. Such a woman is positively at a disadvantage. Far too many engagements have been broken when the fiancee has done too well at college or university. Where both spouses are professionals or academics, if the wife's career advances more rapidly it becomes a threat to the false pride of the husband. Because of the heavy price a woman has to pay if her marriage breaks down sometimes she holds back to keep her marriage safe. But some marriages do break down on this account.

Given these social changes and the high degree of functionality of women's education for middle class and lower middle class families the threat to women's education that was posed by Islamic fundamentalism and General Zia's so-called 'Islamisation' policies was a threat to the family economy and to the new values and attitudes. These families have therefore tended to subscribe rather to liberal social philosophies or 'modernist' interpretations of Islam. They tend to be sceptical of dogmatic versions of Islam propounded by ignorant and bigoted Mullahs.

There is therefore a considerable and growing social base of secularism in Pakistan's political as well as social life, a fact that is reflected in the repeated routs of the Islamic fundamentalist Jamaat-i-Islami in three successive elections in the country namely those of 1985, 1987 (local bodies election) and, again, in 1988. There are, however, many lower middle class households in Pakistan where women have been given no education that could befit them for 'respectable' salaried jobs. Traditionally they were relegated to the role of 'housewives'. But, gradually and with increasing rapidity new avenues for exploiting the labour of these women have opened up.

There are factories with women only work force, notably in the ready made clothing trade, where they can go and work as seamstresses or similar tailoring and finishing jobs, which are woefully underpaid. There is, however, another alternative too whereby the labour of women of this category is exploited without their having to leave their '*char diwari*' i.e. the four walls of their home. This is by way of development of a classical form of 'putting out system' whereby orders for the work to be done and the materials that are required are brought to them in their homes and the finished goods are later collected.

For their long hours of labour, carried out in the midst of the demands of a variety of domestic chores and clamour of a multitude of children, they are paid a mere pittance - much less even than the outrageously low level of wages for women who go to work in factories. But for women who have families to look after there is often no choice. We can identify two patterns in such cases, although there are no data available that can allow us to quantify their relative importance. One is that when the family patriarch controls the operation. He mediates with entrepreneurs brings home the materials and work orders. delivers the finished goods and, most important of all, pockets the money paid by the entrepreneurs.

In effect the women of his household are virtually his slaves. He guards their subordination quite as jealously as any slave owner, deploying ideological weapons against the women by a constant invocation of Islamic values, as interpreted by himself and the Mullahs. On the other hand he builds up images of the 'modern' ordinary working women who take up outside employment as corrupt and un-Islamic, which he contrasts with that of his own enslaved kinswomen who are good and pure, unsullied by the eyes of strange men. Ideologically fundamentalist interpretations of Islam reinforce the authority of the patriarch over his enslaved womenfolk. There is also another pattern of the putting out system.

In this case the entrepreneurs employ women agents who go around houses (especially in *katchi bastis* or shanty town homes) distributing orders and materials for work and collecting the finished goods. In this case they are said to make payments directly to the female head in the household. In the absence of research one can only speculate whether in this case the balance of power in the household is shifted thereby (even if only partially) in favour of women. In an interesting study of Muslim women 'beedi' (cheap 'cigarettes' made of rolled tobacco leaves) makers in Allahabad, Zarina Bhatty found that as a result of contributing substantially (over 45 per cent) to the household incomes, the women acquired a "greater importance in household decision making process. ... (i.e.) an increased say in spending money".

It would be hazardous to extend such a conclusion drawn from a study of a community of Muslim rural labourers in India to urban lower middle class families in Pakistan. Clearly there are a number of issues located here which invite systematic investigation. Home-based women workers, denied the freedom of movement and relative independence of their sisters employed in salaried jobs, rationalise their own predicament in ideological terms, through a self-image of their moral superiority. Frustrated by their increasingly straitened circumstances and lack of freedom, they are easily mobilised by their men against women who go out to word.

They are even made to join public demonstrations, suitably enclosed in the *chaddar* or *burqa (the* all-enveloping women's overalls that covers them from head to foot). They parrot the complaints of their men that women's employment takes jobs away from men and undercuts their salaries and that, in any case, it is quite shameless and un-Islamic for women to go about the city and work in offices with men. In their own minds as well as in the minds of the men who control their lives, their confinement to their homes offers a gain in respectability. The life of lower middle class women in salaried employment is subject to rather different kinds of pressures. Her working day starts early, for she must feed her husband and children and send them off to school before she herself rushes off to work.

Traveling to work is itself quite a battle, given the state of public transport in Pakistan cities, especially Karachi. In order to attract women workers whom they need, many large companies maintain fleets of minibuses to pick up their women employees in the morning and take them home after work. In the case of a woman who is the first to be picked up or the last to be dropped home this can add an hour, or even two, to the long day spent at work. She comes home tired. Whilst her husband relaxes with a cold drink under a fan, she has to rush straight into the kitchen to prepare the family evening meal.

And there are umpteen little chores to be attended to, young children to be looked after and the family fed and put to bed. Some chores, such as washing clothes and cleaning the house, are inevitably put off for the weekend which therefore is not time for rest nor for demonstrations in aid of women's rights. Given the race against time only a very few working women can afford the time to go to meetings and demonstrations even though they sympathise solidly with their aims; women who happen to have particularly enlightened and helpful relatives (e.g. a mother-in-law) or a co-operative and politically committed husband (a rare commodity) who is willing to take over some of their chores during their short absence.

Only those who are sufficiently well off to have servants to take care of the domestic front can play an active and continuing part in such activities. Mobility is another major obstacle in their way so that only those women can take part in such activities without too much difficulty who have their own cars or who have women friends or close male relatives who can give them a lift (going with unrelated males is unthinkable). It is because of these difficulties that the vast majority of lower middle class employed women cannot take a regular, not to say an active and leading part in the women's movement. But this does not mean that the vast majority of working women who are not blessed with the advantages which make such activities possible- 'lack consciousness' or that they are unaware of the issues that confront women in Pakistan.

One has only got to go and talk to some of them to get a measure of the depth of their feelings and the clarity with which they themselves see the issues. Under these circumstances the activists and the leadership inevitably comes from women of better off families especially those whom can afford servants and cars, mainly professional women in their thirties. But it needs to be emphasised that they, nevertheless, articulate by and large attitudes and demands that affect all working women. These relatively small number of activists are like the tip of a huge iceberg, their inarticulate sisters being submerged, for the time being, in an ocean of work.

The women's movement in Pakistan thus revolves around educated women, both professionals and those who take up salaried jobs. Official propaganda under the long years of the Zia regime tried to discredit the women's movement by caricaturing it as a movement of English-educated, Westernised, upper class women whose heads are filled with foreign imported ideas and who, the propaganda claimed, had no roots amongst true Pakistani women.

The fact of the matter is that the vast majority of activists in the women's movement are closer to working women of all classes than either the bureaucrats in government or much of the political leadership or journalists, who all sit in judgement over them. Most of these activists are new to the tasks that they have taken upon themselves in organising and leading the movement. In taking up these unfamiliar tasks they have demonstrated quite remarkable qualities of leadership – not only ingenuity and flexibility but also a noteworthy personal humility. This last quality is reflected in the commitment of WAF members to non-hierarchical organisation.

The Zia regime itself had much to do in creating conditions that precipitated the movement and caused it to break out with much force. Problems that confront women in Pakistan today have been accumulating over several decades. The reason why the women's movement suddenly erupted into action in the 1980s has much to do with the outrageous attacks that were actually undertaken or were contemplated by the Zia regime, in the name of 'Islamisation', a policy that was designed (unsuccessfully) by the regime to gain political legitimacy. These policies were calculated to degrade the place of women in Pakistan society and to erode such legal rights that they did possess, and to put up barriers in the way of women's education and their freedom of movement and to obstruct their access to jobs and professional careers.

Among the new 'Islamic' laws that were enacted by the Zia regime was a change in the law of evidence, enacted in October 1984, purportedly to bring the existing law of evidence in line with prescriptions of Islam. Except in the case of the Hudood Ordinances of 1979 (prescribing 'Islamic' punishments) which laid down their own special rules of evidence for *hadd* offences, the new law of evidence provided that two male witnesses or in the absence of two male witnesses one male and one female witness would be required to prove a crime. This law as well as other proposed legislation, equated one man to two women.

This was so, for example, in the proposed new laws of *Qisas* and Diyat which provided for financial compensation to be given to the injured party by an accused in lieu of punishment in cases of murder or bodily injury, it being held that in such cases the 'Islamic' remedy lay not in punishment of the offender but in compensation to be paid to the victim or his family. This law was proposed by the Council of Islamic Ideology and passed by the Majlis-e-Shoora (Zia's legislative institutions). The compensation in the case of women was to be fixed at half that for men. Such laws that put the worth of a women at half that of a man, were a powerfully symbolic factor that set the women's movement into action.

Besides these blatantly discriminatory laws that reduced a woman's humanity by half, there were policies undertaken or contemplated by the Zia regime that threatened the life and prospects of working women more directly. Although the militant activities and demonstrations of the women's movement were, in the first instance, directed against the new laws, there were some no less weighty and more directly felt underlying concerns, especially about the future of women's education. In general laws and policies pursued by the Zia regime were directed towards discouraging women from taking an active part in activities outside the home and to limit the scope for their self-expression.

There were proposals, for example, that threatened women's access to higher education. Perhaps the most important of these was the idea of segregating women within 'Women's Universities'. As proposed by Zia's University Grants Commission, the existing three colleges of Home Economics located at Karachi, Lahore and Peshawar were to be upgraded to University status. Women were to be given the education that was thought to be appropriate for them, namely to be trained as housewives. They were to be denied a wider education that might prepare them for professional or academic careers or jobs in government, commerce or industry.

Obstacles, such as higher required grades, were placed in the way of women seeking admission to science courses in

Universities or places in medical colleges. There was an attack too on women's participation in sports. Pakistani women athletes and the women's hockey team were prevented from participating in international events. Zia's Federal Minister for Sports and Culture explained that women could participate in sporting competitions only before an exclusively female audience or one in which only *mehram* males and no others males were present ! Reporting this, the press translated the term *mehram* inaccurately as 'blood relatives'. That is not the case.

The category of *mehram* defines relatives whom a Muslim may not marry. A woman's *mehram* comprise her siblings, ascendants and siblings of ascendants, descendants and descendants of siblings and, amongst some sects, sisters' husbands. A first cousin, such as father's brother's son is not *mehram* though a 'blood relative'. As *mehram* defines an ego centred kindred, which would be differently constituted for each woman, male spectators are effectively ruled out.

Women could engage in sports only in purdah ! This ridiculous and meaningless rule illustrates only too well the arbitrary and cavalier manner in which religious symbols were invoked to restrict women's activities. The issues of higher education and sports, in a society such as that of Pakistan, affect mostly upper class, middle class and lower middle class families. There are other policies of the Zia government that bore down relatively more heavily on the most vulnerable component of Pakistan society namely women of the poor. It must be said that degradation of women in Pakistan is nothing new and is not the result solely of the so-called 'Islamisation ' policies of the Zia dictatorship. But it reached abysmally low levels in the wake of its legislation and policies.

In the name of fighting against 'obscenity' and 'pornography' the Zia government set in motion a mass campaign against women seen in public. An atmosphere was generated in the country in which attacks against women became commonplace, legitimated in the name of religion. Such campaigns against women are led by mullahs, the custodians of ignorance, and by criminals and mischief-makers in general, who all seem to derive a kind of perverted psychic pleasure from molesting women under the pretext of enforcing morality. A spate of directives were issued by the Zia regime ordering female government employees, women teachers and girls at schools and colleges to wear 'Islamic' dress and the *chaddar* or *burqa.*

As a direct result of such campaigns against women who are depicted as a threat to male virtue, the morality of Pakistani males sunk to new depths. They do not seem to be able to resist the temptation to interfere with and manhandle women, posing as guardians of public virtue. Violence against women has been on the increase behind the cloak of 'Islamisation'. The most obscene examples of such hypocrisy are numerous, widely publicised, incidents where women's noses have been cut off or they have been disrobed and paraded in the nude in public to 'teach them a lesson'.

As a result of public outrage aroused by such incidents, the Zia regime announced punishments for such actions. But his so-called 'Islamic' regime did little to track down the culprits and punish them. Nor did it engage in any public campaign to denounce such actions and arouse public opinion against those who perpetrate them. Such incidents and attacks on women still continue. The Zia regime introduced *Hudood* Ordinances purportedly to lay down 'Islamic' punishments for certain crimes. These were barbaric punishments such as cutting off of hands and stoning to death. There has been some controversy in the country whether these are truly Islamic prescriptions. That, as such, is not a matter that we need to pursue here except to say that even where these were not actually carried out in all cases, they carried a symbolic charge and provided a rallying point to mullahs who demanded their full implementation.

Public lashings however, were carried out before vast crowds and TV cameras, quite savagely - members of the crowd urging the 'executioners' to hit 'the bastards' even harder. These were incredibly degrading sights to watch. The law that concerns us here most directly, however, is the Zina *(Enforcement of Hudood) Ordinance* of February 1979. This Ordinance provided a new basis, as we shall see, for intimidation and terrorisation of women by husbands or male relatives, especially amongst the urban poor, but not amongst them alone.

Ironically, the Ordinance has also created a situation in which women victims of rape dare not even complain about the sexual violence done to them for fear of penalties that they themselves invite under this iniquitous law, while the culprits go Scot free because of its extra-ordinary provisions. The Ordinance provides new weapons to men against women by virtue of making Zina i.e. adultery and fornication, crimes against the state, cognisable offences for which the police can take action. Previously that was not the case, for then adultery was a matter of personal offence against the husband by the male party to adultery and extra-marital sex was not a penal offence at all. Now where a wife leaves her husband, it has become all too easy for the husband to go to the police and file a complaint against her for committing zina whereupon the wife is arrested and jailed.

Given police corruption and the interminable length of time that it takes for such cases to be adjudicated by courts of law (often years) the woman is effectively punished without even going through the due process of law. The husband can bail the wife out of jail. But when that happens. she is totally at his mercy. for he would threaten to withdraw bail which would return her to prison. Thus the woman's position is made worse than that of a slave. According to Asma Jahangir, a distinguished Pakistani woman lawyer and Secretary of the Human Rights Commission of Pakistan: 'it has now become common for husbands to file complaints of *Zina* against wives wanting separation.

There are hundreds of cases every year where women are arrested for *Zina* on complaints filed by husbands' (SHE. March 1989: 81). It is likewise in cases of elopement, where a father refuses permission to his daughter to marry the man of her choice. The father brings charges of 'abduction' in such cases and the law presumes *zina* unless the couple can prove lawful *nikah* or marriage according to Islam. The *Zina* Ordinance has created a 'Catch 22' situation for women victims of rape.

This arises from the fact that the ordinance brings both adultery and fornication *(zina)* on the one hand and rape *(zina-bil-jabr)* on the other, under a single law in a manner that is unsafe. Secondly, the problem arises from the type of admissible evidence that is prescribed under the Ordinance. The offence of rape is defined as sexual intercourse against the will and/or without the consent of the victim or with consent if the consent has been obtained under fear of death or hurt. It also includes under the category of rape sexual intercourse with consent of the victim where the offender knows that the consent is given by the victim because she (or he) believes that she (or he) is validly married to the offender although the offender knows that they are not.

The catch in this law, that affects women victims of rape cruelly, is the specification of the type of evidence that is admissible for *hadood* or 'Islamic' punishment for *zina* and *zina-bil-jabr* which is stoning to death (under certain conditions lesser punishments called *tazir* would apply). The evidence required is either a confession on the part of the accused (for an unmarried woman pregnancy is self-evident proof) or the testimony of 'at least four Muslim adult male witnesses about whom the Court is satisfied ... that they are truthful persons and abstain from major sins ... (who) give evidence as eye-witnesses of the act of penetration necessary for the offence.'

This is a type of evidence that is most unlikely to be found except perhaps in the vast open spaces of the Arabian desert. In effect, therefore, the offence of rape is unprovable and rapists now go about without fear. Reports of such offences have become widespread. The law excludes the testimony of women, so that evidence of the victim of rape counts for nothing. But if she complains of rape (which she cannot possibly prove, according to this law) she is taken to have admitted to having had sexual intercourse with a man who is not her lawful husband, hence guilty of *zina.* For this she invites the heavy penalty of this law.

A woman has not only no remedy under this iniquitous law for the sexual violence done to her; she herself becomes a victim of the law. In one way or another, women have been victimised under the Zina Ordinance. Documenting the phenomenal increase, during the 1980s, in the number of women who are languishing in Pakistani prisons as a consequence of this law, Asma Jahangir points out that about 40 per cent of the convicted women whom she interviewed in Multan Jail had been sentenced for the offence of zina.

Most of the women whom she interviewed belonged to low income families; out of 37 women 16 had a family income of only Rs. 500 per month (the wage of a single labourer) and no one had a family income of more than Rs. 3000 (the salary of an office clerk). Newspaper reports of victimisation of women under this law are legion. For want of space, we will give only a couple of examples to illustrate the different ways in which women are victimised under it.

The most notorious case is that of Safia Bibi, an 18 year old virtually blind girl, the daughter of a poor peasant, who was employed in the house of the local landlord as domestic help. She was raped by her employer's son and then by the landlord himself. As a result the girl became pregnant. Her illegitimate child is said to have died soon after birth. The girl's father filed a case with the police alleging rape. The Court acquitted the landlord and his son for lack of evidence as required under the zina Ordinance, the evidence of the girl not being admissible and four *pious* Muslim witnesses to the repeated acts of rape not being available. But by virtue of her accusation the girl herself, being unmarried, was found guilty of zina, her pregnancy being proof of it, and she was sentenced to three years in prison, public lashing (15 lashes) and Rs. 1000 fine.

In passing this sentence, the Court said that it was being lenient in view of her age and disability ! This case created an uproar and turned out to be an issue on which the Women's

Action Forum began campaigning. In the light of public outrage, General Zia himself intervened and got the Federal Shariat Court to take over the case, *suo moto.* An exceptionally liberal judge quashed the outrageous conviction of the girl on the ground that if in the case of rape the man (or men) were acquitted due to lack of the required evidence, the woman too was to be given the benefit of doubt. But there was no question here of prosecuting the rapists and bringing them to justice.

A rather different type of case illustrates the way in which the law is used by male relatives or husbands to terrorise and control women. A young woman of 25, Shahida, got a divorce from her husband, Khushi Mohammad. The divorce deed was signed by the husband and was attested by a Magistrate. Under the law as it stands, however, the divorcing husband is then required to register the divorce papers with the local council. That he did not do. This was possibly a deliberate omission which was to give him a hold over his ex-wife. Shahida, after spending the prescribed period of ninety six days of waiting (*iddat*), as prescribed for a divorcee, with her parents, married Mohammed Sarwar. Khushi Mohammed, meanwhile decided that he wanted her back or, in any case, he would not allow her to marry again.

So he took the matter to the law, charging her with *zina.* Although Shahida produced before the Court the attested copy of the divorce document which was signed by Khushi Mohammad and attested by a magistrate, the Court did not consider it to be admissible as it had not been registered with the local Council. The Court decided that the divorce was invalid and therefore that the second marriage illegal. As the two accused, Shahida Parveen and Mohammed Sarwar had 'confessed' to living together as husband and wife, the Court found them guilty, under the convoluted provisions of that extra-ordinary Ordinance, of raping each other!

Accordingly they were both sentenced to stoning to death. Happily, due to campaigning by the women's movement that extreme sentence was eventually commuted- but not all victims of this extraordinary law have been so lucky. In cases of eloping couples, parents deprived of the money that they would get for marrying off their daughter (bride price is not a normal custom) file a complaint with the police for abduction. Even if the girl has found refuge with the family of the boy or some supportive family, sexual intercourse is presumed in such cases and both the girl and the boy are penalised for zina.

It is by no means unusual in such cases, especially if the young couple cannot be found, for the police to arrest the families who are believed to have given them support, as accomplices to zina. The fact is that all such cases have affected not only the parties directly involved but have intimidated Pakistani women in general, for they dare not leave an oppressive and cruel husband or greedy and grasping parents wishing to sell them, for fear of the consequences for them under this terrible law. Sadly, the eleven years of the so-called policy of 'Islamisation' under General Zia, have produced in Pakistan a culture of intolerance.

This culture, above all, has persecuted women and subjected them to all kinds of humiliation and ill-treatment, not to speak of inhuman punishment under the *Hudood* Ordinances, as described above. The Government embarked upon a mass publicity campaign, through all the media, exhorting people to order their lives in accordance with Islam, but as interpreted by Zia and his bigoted mullahs. Far more mischievous was Zia's call to the 'people' to ensure that their 'neighbours' did likewise.

This was a charter for the mischief-makers and the bigots who took upon themselves the task of chastising women, total strangers, and molesting them under that excuse. For example, Mumtaz and Shaheed quote an instance, which is by no means unique or isolated, when a woman who entered a bakery in an upper class Lahore neighbourhood, was slapped by a total stranger for not having her head covered. A much publicised and quite horrendous case is that of a congregation leaving a mosque after Friday prayers who found a new born baby on a nearby rubbish dump. The mullah promptly concluded that it was an illegitimate child and, in accordance with the laws of Islam, as he understood them, led the congregation of the pious Muslims in stoning the child to death. Such outrageous conduct was the direct result of incitement by the propaganda of the Zia regime, which has created an atmosphere of bigotry and intolerance.

It was hoped that the democratic Government of Benazir Bhutto would reverse this and, in particular, repeal the *Hudood* Ordinances (including the Zina Ordinance. But a year after it was put in office the Government has shown no inclination to change the laws. This is in part due to the paralysis of the Government, due to a complex set of political factors which we cannot go into here. Meanwhile the terrible legacy of the Zia regime lives on. Prospects before Pakistani women remain uncertain and threatening.

9

Women in the Philippines

The role of women in the Philippines is explained based on the context of Filipino culture, standards, and mindsets. The Philippines is described to be a nation of strong women, who directly and indirectly run the family unit, businesses, government agencies and haciendas. Although they generally define themselves in the milieu of a masculine dominated post-colonial Asian Catholic society, Filipino women live in a culture that is focused on the community, with the family as the main unit of society.

It is in this framework of Philippine hierarchical structure, class differences, religious justifications, and living in a globally developing nation wherein Filipino women struggle for respect. Compared to other parts of Southeast Asia, women in Philippine society have always enjoyed a greater share of legal equality.

PRE-COLONIAL STATUS

The pre-colonial social structure of the Philippines gave equal importance to maternal and paternal lineage. This bilateral kinship system accorded Philippine women enormous power within a clan. They were entitled to property, engage in a trade and could exercise their right to divorce her husband. They could also become village chiefs in the absence of a male heir. Before the arrival of the Spaniards, Filipino women could also achieve status as medicine women or high-priestesses and astrologers.

HISPANIC PHILIPPINES

During the colonization of the Philippines, the Spaniards relegated the Filipinas to a secondary position in society, while glorifying and assigning the Virgin Mary as a model for Filipino women. The arrival of the Spaniards and Catholicism also fixed the native Filipino women's role to the church, the convent and the home.

AMERICAN INFLUENCE

When Spain lost the Spanish-American War in 1898, the Philippines was ceded to the United States of America. America introduced the public education system, a catalyst for the change in women's roles in Philippine society. The democratic concepts of elections and political parties were also influential factors to the psyche of Filipino women. Through the American-patterned school system, Filipino women became professionals.

CONTEMPORARY ROLES

Modern-day Philippine women play a decisive role in Filipino families. They handle the money, act as religious mentors, and could also arrange the marriages of sons and daughters, striving to improve the family's dynastic connections. The emergence of Corazon Aquino, Imelda Marcos and Gloria Macapagal-Arroyo as political figures shows that Filipino society respects women, in spite of its male chauvinism, and in spite of women being often portrayed as surrogates of their husbands.

URBAN SETTING

In the metropolitan work realm, firms and businesses generally hire Filipino women for less pay and lower positions. Typically, a man is hired for the professional position and the women for the secretarial position, despite their having an equal level of education. The Filipina will not only receive smaller wages, but also additional secretarial functions. This "servile mindset" begins in childhood. In school, boys are often elected to organizational positions such as president and vice-president, while the girls are either members or holding treasurer positions.

Young girls try to justify their worth through hard work and by being responsible pupils. Compared to Filipino men, Philippine women carry the obligation of continuing to support their family financially after their school years and marriage. The man, on the other hand, keeps his salary and holds no obligation to the family.

However, current trends in Human Resources Management paved the way in equalizing this perceived notion of inequality. As can be seen by a lot of women holding high ranking positions in both big and small organizations. There are a lot of women holding managerial positions in banks, government and even in multinational companies.

RURAL AND TRIBAL CLAN SETTING

In rural areas, the Filipino woman belongs in the home. The children approach her for money and help. She is the family's treasurer. She supports the children's educational needs. For non-family members who require support, the wife is the person to be approached. However, the wife is neither the person who makes the final decision or the person who hands out the money. In contrast, however, Juan Flavier, a physician, an authority on community development, and a former Philippine senator, described in his book *Doctor to the Barrios*, that "whether some (Filipino) men are willing to admit it or not"... "rural women in the Philippines wield consideratble authority," the housewife in particular.

This is especially if the housewife, who is often referred to as the *Reyna ng Tahanan* (Queen of the Home), is convinced of the benefits that will be gained from a certain practice such as the concept of family planning in the barrios. Flavier also mentioned that "In the Philippine barrio, the one responsible for the home" and its management "is the wife... she holds the key to... household... development."

MARRIAGE AND RELATIONSHIPS

In rural areas, it is rare for a Filipino female to stay single. Permanent or prolonged single status is not always possible. It is only recently in ethnic communities that men and women have arranged their own marriages. Traditionally, the tribal council of elders and the family of the boy arranged the matches. The woman's family had little say, and the woman herself had no say at all. For example, based on Subanen tribal tradition, men can take on more than one wife, and the women are treated as the property of men. This interpersonal process, however, is already undergoing change.

In marriage, rural women, particularly those belonging to tribal communities, do not present their feelings to their husbands, particularly regarding love and sex. This is because traditionally the husband owns his wife and makes the decisions regarding her body. She can neither ask for nor deny her husband's wishes. Because of this cultural mindset, women in Philippine rural areas experience higher rates of domestic abuse than those from urban areas. Women have no control over the number of children they have. As a result, rural communities are confronted with the growing global reality of overpopulation. Socio-economically, there is not enough land or alternative means of living.

Culturally, divorce is viewed as negative and destructive in the Philippines, because of a tradition that stipulates and emphasizes that the family is the core social unit, especially for the Filipino wife. Divorce is not perceived as a solution to any matrimonial-related problem because it hinders the development or progress of the basic community unit. Therefore, husband and wife are obligated to fix problems within the boundaries of marriage. It should always be noted, though, that pre-colonial women in the Philippines enjoyed equal status with men.

Prior to colonization, both men and women could get a divorce for the following reasons: failure to meet family obligations, childlessness, and infidelity. Children regardless of sex and properties were equally divided. Since a man needed to pay a dowry to the woman's family, she was required to give it back should she be found at fault. If the man was at fault, he then lost the right to get back his dowry. The pre-colonial society valued offspring regardless of sex. Female children were as valuable as male ones probably because of their economic implications, which was the family getting a dowry from suitors or prospective husbands and their capacity to help in the family's economic, social and political activities.

CHANGE, INFLUENCES AND INTERVENTIONS

Although the Roman Catholic Church has changed its position on the role of women in marriage, the Filipina as a wife is still secondary to her husband. She is the "servant" and the "helper". In urban areas, single Filipinas have become liberal due to western influences. Although it is still culturally unacceptable for a single Filipino woman to ask a man on a date or to show interest in a man, Filipinas have learned to use body language to show their interest and openness to a relationship. In rural communities, Filipinas are still not allowed to be too liberal. They are required to stifle their personality and sexuality, and should show a total lack of interest in intimacy with men to maintain reputation and self-respect.

FILIPINO WOMEN AND WORK

Traditionally, rural and tribal women do all the work. The scope of their functions include cooking, cleaning, teaching the children, washing clothes, repairs, budgeting, and managing the farm. After the husband has finished tilling the farmland, the wife does the planting, the daily maintenance, the carrying of water, and the harvesting. Normally, the husband helps in the harvesting, but the tribal woman has the responsibility to find food for the family.

She also acts as the mediator between her children and her husband. She manages practically everything but she does not have control over finances or in decision-making. In general, Filipino women find pride in their work. They do not find themselves alienated from their chores because they work with, around, and for their families. This family-oriented mindset gives them a sense of dignity and responsibility. The family and the children are the primary priority in a Filipina's life.

FILIPINO WOMEN AND PHILIPPINE POLITICS

Despite the introduction of an American-based school system and the transformation of Filipino women into educated and professional members of Philippine society, their participation in was slow. This was primarily because engagement in politics is considered "dirty," and due to the traditional concept that holds that women cannot take positions higher than their husbands. But this idea introduced by colonization that Filipino women historically and traditionally belonged in the home, the church, or the convent, is also changing.

A recent study revealed that there is a re-emergence of the empowerment of Filipino women through the political process, just as they were prior to the arrival of the ancient conquerors from Spain. Philippine women are rediscovering their strengths "even if they are not [directly engaged] in the electoral process." Filipino women had been successful in implementing policies by becoming executive staff members, advisers to politicians, and as advocates within non-governmental organizations.

Modern-day Filipinas are making strides in electoral politics by initiating more female-oriented programs. They are performing well as leaders, although generally, Filipino women still often earn political seats by having fathers and husbands who are politically connected, a "dynasty system" that hinders other Filipino women from joining the electoral process. Other factors that prevent full-engagement of other well-qualified Filipinas from the Philippine political scene are the expense in politics and the importance of the family name.

Participation of Filipino women in was encouraged during the Beijing Declaration in 1995 at the United Nations' Fourth World Conference on Women. In February 2005, however, a United Nations review on the progress of Philippine women and their role in politics revealed that despite "an increase in the quality of female politicians, there was not enough increase in" the number of women participants in government activities. From 1992 to 2001, Filipino women had been elected as local chief executives, functioning as mayors, governors, and captains of villages. One influential factor contributing to the increasing number of female politicians, is the elevation of Corazon Aquino and Gloria Macapagal-Arroyo as Philippine women Presidents.

FILIPINO WOMEN IN ART

In his paintings of Filipino women, the Philippine National Artist Fernando Amorsolo rejected Western ideals of beauty in favor of Filipino ideals He said that the women he painted have "*a rounded face,* not *of the oval type often presented to us in newspapers and magazine illustrations. The eyes should be exceptionally lively,* not *the dreamy, sleepy type that characterizes the Mongolian. The nose should be of the blunt form but firm and strongly marked. ... So the ideal Filipina beauty should* not *necessarily be white complexioned, nor of the dark brown color of the typical Malayan, but of the clear skin or fresh colored type which we often witness when we met a blushing girl.*"

Two women have risen to the presidency in the Philippines in the last fifteen years. Corazon Aquino, the first female to ascend to the presidency in the country's history, was elected after the ouster of Ferdinand Marcos amidst charges of criminal wrongdoing. Fifteen years later, Vice President Gloria Macapagal-Arroyo succeeded Joseph Estrada, who had been accused of corruption and plundering the Philippine economy. Not only is it rare for a woman to be elected president, but it is also least expected in countries like the Philippines that have a long history of patriarchy, oligarchy, and subordination of women.

Even though the Philippines has an elected bicameral legislature and elected officials in lower levels of government, there are few female elected officials. In 1939, women were given suffrage and the right to stand for elections. Since then, only 9.8% of the 224 lower- house seats have been held by women (*Who's Who of Women in World Politics* 1991). In spite of the Philippines' patriarchal institutions, narrow elite class, and repression of women, other social variables such as family ties, the Catholic Church, a context of corruption and gender symbolism allow women to enter into the male-dominated political arena.

THE RISE OF WOMEN LEADERS

To understand how women are elected in the Philippines, this chapter is structured as a comparative study that explores Corazon Aquino's and Gloria Macapagal-Arroyo's successions and their interaction with these four variables: family ties, the Catholic Church, the context of corruption and gender symbolism. Previous studies of Southeast Asian women leaders have found that family ties are necessary for women candidates to win elections. Family ties, specifically those to politically active men, explain why Aquino and Arroyo received immediate recognition.

The dramatic death of a prominent political husband was most significant in Aquino's rise to power, while Arroyo's father-daughter relationship with the former president of the Philippines, Diosdado Macapagal, increased her campaign recognition. Family ties might explain how both women attracted voters' attention in their campaigns but does not explain how they successfully managed to work against the assumption that men should be at the forefront of leadership and decision-making. In addition to family ties, scholars believe that without the Catholic Church's support, a woman would not have succeeded.

Even though the Philippines' political structure is modeled after the American system, the Philippines' political culture has its roots in the oligarchic system established during Spanish colonialism. Since the Catholic Church is a male-dominated institution, it is reasonable to question why the church mobilized voters to support a female candidate. Jaime

Cardinal Sin, the Archbishop of Manila, requested corrupt leaders to step down from power. He led the mass non-violent movement against corrupt leadership at Epiphania de los Santos Avenue (EDSA), the focal point for Aquino's and Arroyo's rise to power. While the Catholic Church's involvement explains the development of candidate support, it fails to explain why that candidate was a woman.

The Catholic Church's concept of a woman being morally superior to a man perhaps explains the Church's support of women candidates in movements against corruption. Both Aquino and Arroyo ascended to the presidency after the removal of a corrupt leader. There are two approaches to looking at corruption and how it affects the fate of political leaders. Jon Moran (1999) asserts that corruption is pervasive and affects politics, economics and social relations in general. Social movements arise because corruption affects an individual's economic well-being, and these social movements push for fundamental change. Another view of corruption is that it involves only top political leaders who come to symbolize corruption. In this interpretation, social movements seek to defeat top political leaders.

Like Moran, Wurfel argues that social movements arise because corruption affects an individual citizen's economic well-being and that individual's join together to push for fundamental change, but in this case change means calling for a shift among those who rule. The context of corruption explains the demand for new leadership but does not explain the candidate choice made by elites and voters. Culture also plays a role in determining how elites and voters choose their candidate.

One element of Filipino culture that may explain why people elect a female candidate is the symbolic role of women in Philippine society. Since the colonial era, women have been taught to conform to the behaviors of their ideal mother, the Virgin Mary, upon whom is built a "cult of feminine spiritual superiority, which teaches that women are semi-divine, morally superior to and spiritually stronger than men". Women leaders who embrace the Catholic faith represent a positive image in society and are distinguished by purity. Both Aquino and Arroyo invoked this cultural belief in women's morally superior role in order to legitimize their entrance into public office at a time of political upheaval.

While family ties and the Catholic Church play a role in determining the outcomes of these presidential elections, the cultural construction of women as "Madonnas" allowed first the election of Aquino and then the succession of Arroyo to the presidency at times when political leaders had been charged with corruption. Philippine culture encourages voters to view women as less prone to corruption than men. This means that in times of political corruption, women who seek higher office have an advantage over male politicians.

From Dictator to Housewife Aquino would not have gained immediate recognition nor have been selected to run for office without her relationship to a prominent male politician. Corazon Aquino was the wife of Benigno "Ninoy" Aquino, the candidate who opposed Ferdinand Marcos and exposed his corruption. Marcos had demonstrated his abuse of power by manipulating his men to assassinate Ninoy Aquino. As the widow, Corazon Aquino was urged to run in the election against Marcos.

The political party of her husband was sure that Aquino was the best candidate to defeat Marcos in the 1986 election. Not only was she seen as the victim of Marcos' corruption but "almost as a Madonna, a saint in contrast to the wily, corrupt Marcos". The turning point of Corazon Aquino's rise to power was the involvement of the Roman Catholic Church in the fight against corruption. Marcos' dealings with the church remained cordial until the late 1960s, but following the imposition of martial rule in September 1972, church-state relations began to deteriorate with the loss of civil liberties, increased abuses of human rights by the military, and the rise of graft, corruption, and economic mismanagement.

The Church's inability to lift the poor from their economic struggle gave Cardinal Sin, the Archbishop of Manila, the necessity and urgency to mobilize a nation-wide movement for the poor and fight for socio-economic change. During the election, Cardinal Sin served as Aquino's personal campaign manager and asked the people to "vote for persons who embody the Gospel values of justice, humility, truth..." and thus elect a candidate "immune" from corruption.

Aside from the Church's support in invoking the Madonna image, a woman candidate benefits from her close association with the head of the Catholic Church. Since the Philippines' religious population is made up of Roman Catholics (83%), a devout Catholic woman closely affiliated with the Archbishop of Manila is likely to succeed in elections. According to the Social Weather Stations (SWS) 1991 national election report, 67% of voters would favor a candidate that his or her church supports.

This study reported that 49% of female voters found a church endorsement important, against only 29% of male voters. A relationship with the Church is thus an important asset for women voters. Ferdinand Marcos' corrupt leadership heightened the support for Aquino's candidacy. Aquino was an unusual candidate: a politically inexperienced woman who took the risk to compete against a corrupt leader who had murdered her husband. Ferdinand Marcos' twenty-year rule of corruption pushed people to demand a new form of leadership. The first family's accumulation of wealth, Marcos' manipulation of the army, and the increased economic disparity between rich and poor exposed Marcos' manipulative power and "immoral governance."

At the same time, women were growing more involved in the political process after a large number of women had been recruited to work outside of their home by manufacturing and textile concerns. Women were paid below minimum wage and worked under hazardous conditions. In response to the increasing abuse of women, radical groups of women organized against Marcos' dictatorship. As guardians of morality, these women fought for peace, justice and democracy. Perhaps this explains Aquino's sense of duty to run against Marcos as well as the rise of a feminist movement that supported her candidacy.

According to the 1991 national election report, the reputation of a politician matters in his or her success. Relatives and close associates of former president Marcos were found to be least likely to succeed: only a fourth of potential voters would have favored the relatives of Marcos as opposed to 68% of those who would not have. This study shows that perceptions of corruption affect Filipino voters' candidate preferences. Even though Aquino was accused of being inexperienced and a housewife by her opponent, it was this image that gave her mass support and worked against her opponent. Aquino's campaign rhetoric stressed her difference from her male opponent: "I admit that I have no experience in cheating, stealing, lying or assassinating political opponents".

The media portrayed her as a housewife, a widow of a political leader and a religious woman, suggesting that Aquino was not just "pure" but "immune" to corruption. Another Victory against Corruption Aquino's succession opened a new door for women to run for national positions. Gloria Macapagal-Arroyo was the second woman to rise to power after the ouster of a corrupt leader. She was in the right position to become the Philippines' second female president when she succeeded Joseph Estrada. Legislative elections in the Philippines are based on proportional representation, and the President and the Vice President are elected separately.

This can result in a President and Vice President from opposing political parties, such as Arroyo and Estrada. Estrada was unlike the autocratic Marcos. He was a former movie actor who enjoyed widespread popularity and won the presidential election with the support of the poor. Arroyo ran in 1998 as the Vice Presidential candidate of the coalition that opposed Estrada. This election was described in the media as a race between a *babae* [woman] and a *babaero* [womanizer].

The media therefore identified Arroyo with her gender in such a way as to connote inferiority and undermine her candidacy. Arroyo's political experience prevailed over attempts to weaken her candidacy. Unlike Aquino, Arroyo was a woman accustomed to power. The public recognized Arroyo as a former senator and the daughter of a former president. In 1998 she was elected Vice President of the Philippines with almost 13 million votes, the largest mandate in the history of presidential or vice presidential elections.

Estrada's impeachment and resignation meant that Arroyo succeeded to the presidency without having to run for that office. The question is, what made it possible for Arroyo to succeed Estrada legitimately? What gave her the confidence to take the risk of confronting a sitting president who was popular with the poor? In the 1991 national election study, a slim majority of voters agreed with the statement that a woman is capable of governing the country.

The most interesting result is the large net difference in Metro Manila (GMA) in favor of a woman, which suggests that female candidates in general find most of their support in Metro Manila. The grounds for Arroyo's confidence in confronting Estrada and for her succession to the presidency include the direct support of the Church and its effort to mobilize a second mass movement, EDSA II. Jaime Cardinal Sin, who led the revolution against Marcos, condemned Estrada at mass in Manila and supported Arroyo as "one who epitomizes the Christian, feminine ideal".

Women leaders could not have gained the tremendous support they enjoyed without the support of Cardinal Sin and religious women who joined the movement to oust the sitting president. Having a close affiliation with the head of the Catholic Church turned Arroyo's gender identity into an advantage over male leaders accused of corruption, as had been true for Aquino. Arroyo symbolized opposition to a corrupt leader. Her rise to the presidency began on October 12, 2000, with the disgrace of Joseph Estrada.

Corruption charges against Estrada emerged after a close friend, Governor Luis "Chavit" Singson, exposed him for pocketing millions of dollars in illegal gambling payoffs and tobacco tax kickbacks. Impeachment by the House of Representatives followed. In response to the corruption charges, Arroyo and other members of the Senate resigned from office. Arroyo built the People Power Coalition to call for a peaceful mass demonstration to request Estrada's resignation from office. Aside from the charges of economic plunder, Estrada's past as a womanizer, gambler and an alcohol abuser were made public.

It is possible that women supported their own kind in response to a male opponent who represented the "machismo" character who degrades women; Marcos had stated in public that "women belong in the bedroom," and Estrada had been accused of abusing women. Arroyo represented the democratic choice and a positive image for women in society. Her devout Catholicism helped distinguish her as female politicians who was "serious," "clean" and "pure".

Corruption thus increased support for Arroyo's succeeding Estrada. A Philippine polling organization, Social Weather Stations, has collected data analyzing the links voters make between corruption and female candidacy. In a 1991 survey, voters who were dissatisfied with the government's effort to fight graft and corruption were likely to be in favor of a woman candidate. Sixty per cent of voters who favored women candidates for president were dissatisfied with the government's performance in combating corruption, while 55% of voters who did not favor women candidates were dissatisfied with the government's performance in fighting corruption.

A one- tailed t-test ($p < .05$) shows that although the difference is substantively rather small, it is statistically significant. The smallness of the difference is probably due to voter's disappointment with Aquino's performance in office. The effects of corruption on voters' attitudes are also evident in the 2001 senatorial race. Voters were asked if they believed that Estrada committed economic plunder—46% believed that he had and 53% believed he had not. Among those who believed that Estrada had committed plunder 45% responded that they had much trust in President Arroyo while 22% showed little trust in Arroyo.

Aversion to corruption thus did influence voter preference. On January 20, 2001, the Supreme Court unanimously declared the position of President vacant, and Arroyo was sworn in as the 14th President of the Philippines. Estrada argued that Arroyo's succession was "unconstitutional," an illegal seizure of power. However, like Aquino, Arroyo used statements promoting herself as the "best" candidate to take the place of Estrada.

Arroyo supporters such as the KGMAers (*Kaibigan ni* [Friends of] *Gloria Macpagal-Arroyo*) called for "a leader with compassion, humility, resourcefulness, perseverance, and identity with all sectors of the Filipino community," traits that Arroyo presented herself as possessing. She increased her mass support during her inaugural speech by stating that Filipinos "must improve moral standards in government and society in order to provide a strong foundation for good ".

Arroyo's moral tone differentiated her from male politicians and defused allegations that she was illegally seizing power. While family ties and the Catholic Church gave Aquino and Arroyo the recognition and support to run for office, cultural symbols and the context of corruption legitimized and made it possible for these women to rise to power. Aquino and Arroyo would not have succeeded to the presidency without gender-typing and corruption. Both strategically embraced gendered moral and religious identities in order to differentiate themselves from their male opponents.

In addition, these women rose to power with the aid of prominent political leaders and their alliance with the Catholic Church, which offered them immediate public recognition. Although this study discusses the factors that contributed to Aquino's and Arroyo's presidential successions, the research is still incomplete. Scholars need to further explore how powerful actors like the Catholic Church and political parties manipulate or appeal to gendered identities to bolster support for women candidacies. Further investigation will also need to focus on how gender is constructed in political competitions and how voters differentiate candidates by their gender identities. It is important to keep in mind that women may have been elected to top political positions, but this has not necessarily changed society's patriarchal system.

10

Chinese Women of Singapore
Their Present Status in the Family and in Marriage

Almost all Singaporeans lived in small nuclear families. Although both Chinese and Indian traditions favored large extended families, such families were always rare in immigrant Singapore where neither the occupational structure, based on wage labor, or the housing pattern, characterized by small, rented quarters, favored such family forms. In the 1980s, families were important in that most individuals as a matter of course lived with their parents until marriage and after marriage maintained a high level of interaction with parents, brothers, and sisters.

Probably the most common leisure activity in Singapore was the Sunday visit to the grandparents for a meal and relaxed conversation with brothers, sisters, in-laws, uncles and aunts, cousins, and other assorted kin. Although the age of marriage increased in the 1970s and 1980s, reaching a mean 28.5 years for grooms and 25.8 years for brides in 1987, Singapore remained a society in which it was assumed that everyone would marry, and marriage was a normal aspect of fully adult status.

Both ethnicity and class affected the form and functioning of families. Chinese and Indian families rested on cultural assumptions of the permanence of marriage and of the household as an ongoing, corporate group whose members, bound by duty, obligation, and subordination, pooled and shared income. The continued efforts of Indian parents to arrange the marriages or at least to influence the marital choices of their offspring and the Tamil obligation to provide daughters with large dowries reflected such cultural definitions of family and household. In a similar manner, some Chinese combined the household with the family enterprise, practicing a traditional entrepreneurial strategy that included mobilizing the savings of all household members and allocating them in accord with a long-term plan for family success.

Such a strategy might take the form of a thriving business with branches in the major cities of Malaysia and Indonesia, or of sons and daughters employed in the Singapore civil service, a large foreign bank, or a university in Australia. Malay families, on the other hand, gave priority to the individual and to individual interests. They viewed relations between siblings as tenuous and saw the household as a possibly short-lived coalition of autonomous individuals linked by sentiments of mutual concern and affection.

Malays had traditionally had much higher rates of divorce and adoption than other ethnic groups, and the distinction continued in the 1980s although the divorce rate was lower than in the 1940s or through the 1960s. More significantly, for the Malays divorce was regarded as a realistic and normal, although unfortunate, possibility in all marriages. Because Malays did not define the household as a continuing body, they did not make long-range strategic plans to maximize family income and success. In Malay families, husbands, wives, and children with jobs held separate purses and sometimes separate savings accounts. It was thus difficult for Malays to establish family businesses as the Chinese and the Indians did.

Class affected families in a manner generally similar to many other industrialized societies. In all ethnic groups, lower-class or working-class people tended to be dependent on kin outside the immediate household for a wide range of services, and to operate wide networks of mutual assistance and gift exchange. Throughout the 1980s, kin provided the bulk of child care for married women working in factories. Such relatives were paid for their services, but less than a stranger would have been paid. The possibility of such support often determined whether a woman took a job outside the home, and thus demonstrated the relation between large numbers of kin and material comfort and security.

Substantial sums of money were passed back and forth on such occasions as the birthdays of aged parents, the birth of children, or the move into a new apartment. Family members were a major source of information on and referrals to jobs for many unskilled or semiskilled workers. Relations with the extended circle of relatives were not always harmonious or happy, but they were important and necessary to the welfare and comfort of most working-class families. Middle- and upper-class households were less dependent on kin networks for support. They maintained close ties with parents and siblings, but did not need to rely on them. Indeed their relations with their extended kin often were more amiable than those of the lower-class households, where mutual need often was accompanied by disputes over allocation of such resources as grandparents' childcare services, or of the costs of supporting elderly parents and other dependent kin.

Middle- and upper-class households spent more leisure time with people who were not their relatives and gained much of their social support from networks based on common schooling, occupation, and associational memberships. In such families, the bond between husband and wife was close as they shared more interests and activities than most workingclass couples and made more decisions jointly. Marriages across ethnic lines occurred, but not often. Between 1954 and 1984, intermarriage rates remained at 6 per cent of all marriages. None of the traditional cultures encouraged marriage outside the group. The Hindu traditions of caste endogamy and the Malay insistence on conversion to Islam as a condition of marriage were major barriers to intermarriage.

Shared religion encouraged intermarriage, with marriages between Malays and Indian Muslims the most common form of ethnic intermarriage. Interethnic marriages included a disproportionate number of divorced or widowed individuals. Divorce rates in Singapore were low. Interethnic marriages were somewhat more likely to end in divorce than were marriages within an ethnic group. During the 1980s the divorce rate for Malays fell, while it rose for the other ethnic groups. In 1987 there were 23,404 marriages in Singapore, and 2,708 divorces, or 115 divorces for every 1,000 marriages.

The figures included 4,465 marriages under the Muslim Law Act, which regulated the marriage, divorce, and inheritance of Muslims, and 796 divorces under the same act, for a Muslim divorce rate of 178 divorces for every 1,000 marriages. Marriages under the Women's Charter (which regulated the marriage and divorce of non-Muslims) totaled 18,939, and divorces under that law were 1,912, for a non-Muslim divorce rate of 100 per 1,000 marriages. The differential rates of divorce for ethnic groups may have suggested greater differences than were in fact the case. Situations that for Malay families resulted in prompt, legal divorce were sometimes tolerated or handled informally by Chinese or Indian families for whom the social stigma of divorce was greater and the barriers to legal separation higher.

For all ethnic groups, the most common source of marital breakdown was the inability or unwillingness of the husband to contribute to maintaining the household. This sometimes led to desertion, which was the most common ground for divorce. Almost all Singaporeans lived in small nuclear families. Although both Chinese and Indian traditions favored large extended families, such families were always rare in immigrant Singapore where neither the occupational structure, based on wage labor, or the housing pattern, characterized by small, rented quarters, favored such family forms. In the

1980s, families were important in that most individuals as a matter of course lived with their parents until marriage and after marriage maintained a high level of interaction with parents, brothers, and sisters.

Probably the most common leisure activity in Singapore was the Sunday visit to the grandparents for a meal and relaxed conversation with brothers, sisters, in-laws, uncles and aunts, cousins, and other assorted kin. Although the age of marriage increased in the 1970s and 1980s, reaching a mean 28.5 years for grooms and 25.8 years for brides in 1987, Singapore remained a society in which it was assumed that everyone would marry, and marriage was a normal aspect of fully adult status. Both ethnicity and class affected the form and functioning of families. Chinese and Indian families rested on cultural assumptions of the permanence of marriage and of the household as an ongoing, corporate group whose members, bound by duty, obligation, and subordination, pooled and shared income.

The continued efforts of Indian parents to arrange the marriages or at least to influence the marital choices of their offspring and the Tamil obligation to provide daughters with large dowries reflected such cultural definitions of family and household. In a similar manner, some Chinese combined the household with the family enterprise, practicing a traditional entrepreneurial strategy that included mobilizing the savings of all household members and allocating them in accord with a long-term plan for family success. Such a strategy might take the form of a thriving business with branches in the major cities of Malaysia and Indonesia, or of sons and daughters employed in the Singapore civil service, a large foreign bank, or a university in Australia.

Malay families, on the other hand, gave priority to the individual and to individual interests. They viewed relations between siblings as tenuous and saw the household as a possibly short-lived coalition of autonomous individuals linked by sentiments of mutual concern and affection. Malays had traditionally had much higher rates of divorce and adoption than other ethnic groups, and the distinction continued in the

1980s although the divorce rate was lower than in the 1940s or through the 1960s.

More significantly, for the Malays divorce was regarded as a realistic and normal, although unfortunate, possibility in all marriages. Because Malays did not define the household as a continuing body, they did not make long-range strategic plans to maximize family income and success. In Malay families, husbands, wives, and children with jobs held separate purses and sometimes separate savings accounts. It was thus difficult for Malays to establish family businesses as the Chinese and the Indians did. Class affected families in a manner generally similar to many other industrialized societies. In all ethnic groups, lower-class or working-class people tended to be dependent on kin outside the immediate household for a wide range of services, and to operate wide networks of mutual assistance and gift exchange.

Throughout the 1980s, kin provided the bulk of child care for married women working in factories. Such relatives were paid for their services, but less than a stranger would have been paid. The possibility of such support often determined whether a woman took a job outside the home, and thus demonstrated the relation between large numbers of kin and material comfort and security. Substantial sums of money were passed back and forth on such occasions as the birthdays of aged parents, the birth of children, or the move into a new apartment. Family members were a major source of information on and referrals to jobs for many unskilled or semiskilled workers. Relations with the extended circle of relatives were not always harmonious or happy, but they were important and necessary to the welfare and comfort of most working-class families.

Middle- and upper-class households were less dependent on kin networks for support. They maintained close ties with parents and siblings, but did not need to rely on them. Indeed their relations with their extended kin often were more amiable than those of the lower-class households, where mutual need often was accompanied by disputes over allocation of such resources as grandparents' childcare services, or of the costs of supporting elderly parents and other dependent kin. Middle- and upper-class households spent more leisure time with people who were not their relatives and gained much of their social support from networks based on common schooling, occupation, and associational memberships. In such families, the bond between husband and wife was close as they shared more interests and activities than most workingclass couples and made more decisions jointly.

Marriages across ethnic lines occurred, but not often. None of the traditional cultures encouraged marriage outside the group. The Hindu traditions of caste endogamy and the Malay insistence on conversion to Islam as a condition of marriage were major barriers to intermarriage. Shared religion encouraged intermarriage, with marriages between Malays and Indian Muslims the most common form of ethnic intermarriage. Interethnic marriages included a disproportionate number of divorced or widowed individuals.

Divorce rates in Singapore were low. Interethnic marriages were somewhat more likely to end in divorce than were marriages within an ethnic group. During the 1980s the divorce rate for Malays fell, while it rose for the other ethnic groups. In 1987 there were 23,404 marriages in Singapore, and 2,708 divorces, or 115 divorces for every 1,000 marriages. The figures included 4,465 marriages under the Muslim Law Act, which regulated the marriage, divorce, and inheritance of Muslims, and 796 divorces under the same act, for a Muslim divorce rate of 178 divorces for every 1,000 marriages. Marriages under the Women's Charter (which regulated the marriage and divorce of non-Muslims) totaled 18,939, and divorces under that law were 1,912, for a non-Muslim divorce rate of 100 per 1,000 marriages.

The differential rates of divorce for ethnic groups may have suggested greater differences than were in fact the case. Situations that for Malay families resulted in prompt, legal divorce were sometimes tolerated or handled informally by Chinese or Indian families for whom the social stigma of divorce was greater and the barriers to legal separation higher. For all ethnic groups, the most common source of marital breakdown was the inability or unwillingness of the husband to contribute to maintaining the household. This sometimes led to desertion, which was the most common ground for divorce.

Throughout Asia, marriage behavior and family life are changing. Young people are waiting later to marry, couples are having fewer children, and more married women are working outside the home. Within the region, such trends were observed first in Japan and more recently in South Korea, Taiwan, and Singapore. Similar patterns are starting to emerge in other Asian countries. Trends such as later marriage, lower marital fertility, and greater participation of married women in the labor force are similar to changes that took place earlier in the industrialized societies of Europe and North America.

Yet other aspects of family life in Asia are still quite different from the way family institutions have developed in the West. Fewer Asian couples live together outside marriage, and childbearing outside marriage is extremely rare. Marriage is generally viewed as a permanent arrangement, and divorce rates, although rising, are still quite low in most Asian societies.

MARRIAGE TRADITIONS

Asia's three subregions all have distinct traditional family structures. In East Asia, including China, North and South Korea, Japan, Hong Kong, and Taiwan, traditional families are strongly male-dominated. A woman leaves her parents at marriage and often lives with her husband's parents if he is a first son. Women traditionally have little independence within the family, at least until they are past their childbearing years. With economic development and modernization, however, women in most East Asian countries now enjoy a great deal more autonomy than they did in the past. China stands out as having experienced a series of radically differing social and political systems during the 20th century that have greatly changed family life and the position of women in society.

The traditional family structures of Southeast Asia are more varied. Among the large lowland populations of Indonesia, Malaysia, the Philippines, Thailand, and Vietnam, young couples typically establish their own independent households, or a man may move in with his wife's parents, at least for a while. At marriage, the husband's family often makes a gift to the family of the wife. Although most young couples establish a home of their own, a youngest daughter and her husband may stay with her parents to look after them in their old age and eventually inherit their property.

Family patterns of ethnic Chinese populations in Singapore and other Southeast Asian countries offer a contrast, resembling the traditional family structures of East Asia. In South Asian countries, such as Bangladesh, India, Nepal, and Pakistan, a strong male-dominated family system prevails. Families in Sri Lanka tend to be somewhat less patriarchal. As in East Asia, young women in most South Asian countries have little independence. Traditionally, when a woman marries, she leaves her parents and goes to live with her husband's family. In many parts of South Asia, the bride's parents pay a dowry to her husband's family, which may be substantial. The burden of dowry payments often puts considerable economic pressure on the parents of daughters and contributes in many families to a preference for sons.

CHANGES IN MARRIAGE PATTERNS

In every country of Asia, both men and women are marrying later than they did in the past. Where records are available, as in India and Japan, a consistent trend can be traced back nearly 100 years. Between 1975 and 1995, the average age at first marriage in Japan increased from 24 to 28 years for women and from 28 to 31 years for men, making Japan one of the latest-marrying populations in the world. The average age at first marriage is higher for men in South Korea than in the United States (at 30 compared with 28 years) and the same for women (at 26 years in both countries).

This trend toward late marriage tends to occur in two phases tied in with levels of economic development. At early stages of development, rural populations tend to expand until all suitable land is brought under cultivation. Once this happens, families that have many surviving children are faced with a dilemma: Either they must subdivide their landholdings into smaller and smaller parcels or they must leave their land to one sibling (often the eldest son) and leave the other children landless.

Either option potentially lowers the standard of living of future generations. In the Philippines, one response to this dilemma has been to leave land to sons but to provide education—and thus enhanced employment opportunities—to daughters. The result has been high levels of educational attainment for young women. Other responses to reduced landholdings include delayed marriage, non- marriage (i.e., a higher proportion never marrying), reduced fertility within marriage, and migration to urban areas or overseas. In Asia's rural areas, age at marriage has been gradually increasing, and there has been some outmigration—to the Middle East, for example.

Marriage patterns may not be affected to the same extent if landless siblings can readily find jobs in urban areas so that they, too, can afford to marry. In Japan, the average age at marriage for women actually went down slightly between 1960 and 1975 when the country was urbanizing at a very rapid rate and the economy was booming. At later stages of economic development, longer schooling tends to delay marriage for both men and women. For young women, paid employment also provides a measure of financial independence that reduces the pressure to marry early.

Education and employment tend to expand women's horizons and provide them with previously unavailable opportunities and lifestyles that compete with marriage. With further modernization, a major expansion of the service sector brings structural changes in the labor market, creating large numbers of jobs that are compatible with traditional female roles. The result is a massive shift of women into paid employment outside the home. Young unmarried women usually predominate during the initial stages of this shift, followed later by married women. These changes have already taken place in Western Europe and North America. They are occurring now in many Asian countries, especially in East and Southeast Asia, generally at a faster pace than occurred in the West.

The narrowing education gap between women and men also brings a gradual narrowing of the wage gap between the sexes. This may lead women who work before marriage to attach more value to their careers and less value to their roles as housewives and mothers. Even delayed marriage itself may cause further marriage delay because, as the average age at marriage rises, single men and women have less reason to be concerned that their marriage chances will be reduced if they wait even longer to marry.

A comparison of data from the 1960s and the 1990s reveals a broad pattern of increasing age at first marriage for both men and women. The average age at marriage is increasing in countries where it was already high in the 1960s (right side of figure) as well as in countries where it was low (on the left). The rise in age at marriage tends to be larger for women than for men. It is particularly striking for women in Bangladesh, Malaysia, and Hong Kong and for men in India. By the 1990s, most women in Hong Kong, Japan, South Korea, Taiwan and Singapore were marrying at age 26 or older. Most women in China, Pakistan, Sri Lanka, Indonesia, Malaysia, Myanmar, the Philippines, and Thailand were marrying at age 20 to 25.

In Bangladesh, India and Nepal, most were still marrying before age 20, but even in these countries the average age at marriage had risen substantially over what it was a few decades earlier. The decision to marry and the choice of whom to marry are likely to be quite different for young adults with education and work experience than for teenagers who are still dependent on their families. Thus, an important aspect of the shift toward later marriage in many countries has been a sharp decline in arranged marriages. In Japan, the proportion of marriages that are arranged fell from 63 per cent in 1955 to 7 per cent in 1998.

The collapse of arranged marriages has not been fully balanced, however, by an emergence of social networks where single men and women can meet prospective marriage partners. In Singapore, where the government has been concerned about low marriage and fertility rates since the early 1980s, a Social Development Unit organizes dances, workshops, and holiday trips for single university graduates and runs a computerized matchmaking service. These programs in Singapore reflect a concern that men and women in Asia may increasingly choose not to marry at all. In Japan, for example, it is already possible to predict that by 2010 at least 10 per cent of women and about 20 per cent of men age 50 will never have married.

The proportions never marrying, although low, are rising in other Asian countries as well, particularly in the region's major cities. In 1990, for example, the proportion of women age 45 to 49 who had never married was 5 per cent in Thailand as a whole, but 11 per cent in Bangkok. In Asia's most modern societies, young people may find marriage less important because premarital sex is becoming increasingly acceptable. In Japan, about half of single women age 18 to 34 report that they are currently using contraception. Japan is quite different from late-marrying societies in Europe and North America, however, in that there is much less "living together" than in the West and almost no childbearing outside of marriage.

In 1997, only 5 per cent of single women age 25 to 29 and 8 per cent of single women age 30 to 34 had ever cohabited with a sexual partner. As of 1999, only 2 per cent of births occurred outside of marriage, compared with about one-third of births in the United States. Indeed, Japan has the lowest proportion of births outside of marriage of any industrial nation. Rising divorce rates may also reduce the attractiveness of marriage. In the traditional societies of South Asia, divorce is still rare, but in East Asia, divorce rates— while lower than in the United States or most countries of Western Europe— are rising. Although comprehensive information on divorce is difficult to obtain, it is estimated that one in five marriages in Japan, South Korea, and China will end in divorce. In these societies, awareness of the risk of divorce may strengthen the motivation of unmarried women to obtain good educations and good jobs.

EAST ASIA: WOMEN BALANCE MARRIAGE AND WORK

Despite economic and social modernization, women's roles in East Asian societies continue to be defined primarily within the household. When women marry, their lives are expected to change drastically in terms of employment opportunities, housework, the obligation to bear and raise children, and eventually a duty to care for their parents and parents-in-law. Most young women in East Asia work before marriage. Until very recently, however, most of these women dropped out of the labor market when they had their first child and remained out of the labor force during their prime child- bearing and childrearing years.

Recently, more Asian women have continued to hold down full- or part-time jobs while looking after household and raising children. In 1994, 57 per cent of married women in Japan and 27 per cent of married women in South Korea worked full-or part-time outside the home, com- pared with 66 per cent of married women in the United States. Although expanded opportunities to pursue a career may be viewed as a favorable development, balancing work and family obligations may be an even greater strain for women in East Asia than in Europe or the United States. This is because housework patterns are quite different in East Asia than in the West.

Married men in the United States spend more time on such household chores as cleaning, cooking, doing laundry, and grocery shopping than married men in Japan or South Korea. Asian wives who work full-time outside the home reduce their housework hours somewhat, but elderly parents tend to fill in the missing hours of housework, rather than husbands. In 1994, married women in Japan who worked 35 or more hours per week outside the home spent another 30 hours on housework, compared with three hours contributed by their husbands.

In 1987–88, the equivalent figures in the United States were

26 hours of housework for wives working full-time and nine hours for their husbands. Household obligations may come as a particular shock to young married women in East Asia because very few live on their own before marriage. Most live with their parents well into adulthood (87 per cent of single Japanese women age 20 to 27 in 1994) and contribute little to housework or to household expenses. One important aspect of the marriage burden for women in Japan and South Korea is the system of highly competitive school entrance examinations.

Gaining entrance to a good university or secondary school depends on performance in an entry examination of a do-or-die nature, and the competitive admission process is reaching down to primary school and even kindergarten. In families where fathers rarely come home in time to see their children before bedtime, mothers must spend hours every week helping their children with schoolwork. This situation has led to an explosion of expensive private cram schools (called *juku* in Japan and *kwa-woe* in South Korea) and private tutoring, which take place after normal school hours, on weekends, and during vacations.

In 1991, 48 per cent of Japanese sixth-graders and 58 per cent of ninth-graders attended *juku*. Among pupils in government high schools in Japan, spending on private education now exceeds normal school expenses. Many married women go back to work primarily to pay for cram schools and other private education expenses. Not surprisingly, a study comparing views on marriage among young adults in Japan and the United States (Mason and Tsuya forthcoming) found that single Japanese women hold more negative views on marriage than do single Japanese men or single American women.

Married women in Japan and South Korea are also much less likely than married women in the United States to have a positive attitude about their marriages. These negative attitudes are probably an important reason why women in Japan are postponing marriage or even choosing not to marry at all.

Policy issues

In any society, traditional roles within marriage are likely to change more slowly than other aspects of women's lives such as schooling or employment opportunities. As long as women who are educated and have worked outside the home are expected to shoulder all the traditional house- wifely duties when they become wives, it should come as no surprise that many are reluctant to marry. Women's changing views and behavior have profound implications for in areas such as health, family planning, labor, and support systems for the elderly. For one thing, postponement of marriage has been an important factor bringing birth rates to unprecedented low levels in countries such as Japan, South Korea, Taiwan, and Singapore.

These low birth rates raise serious concerns about population aging and the size of the future workforce. Policymakers in Asian countries faced with low marriage and birth rates need to make it less burdensome for women to marry, raise a family, and continue their careers. For instance, employers can be encouraged to provide part- time positions with employee benefits, and governments and employers can initiate or expand high-quality childcare programs for working mothers. Policy- makers also need to help families provide financial support and care for the elderly. The Japanese government has initiated a number of policies in these areas, but their effects may not be consistent.

SOUTHEAST ASIA: TRADITIONAL MEETS MODERN

Traditional marriage in Southeast Asia often occurs in phases, with a young couple living with the bride's parents for a period and then establishing a home of their own. The 1994 Young Adult Fertility and Sexuality Study (YAFS-II) shows how these traditions are evolving in the Philippines. YAFS-II found that young couples tend to pass through a continuum of increasing commitment, starting with dating and usually leading to some form of traditional or formally sanctioned marriage. Among women who described themselves as married, 73 per cent were married in a church or civil ceremony. More than half of these women mentioned that they had passed through other stages in their relationship with their husbands before formal marriage.

The other 27 per cent of women who described themselves as married reported that they were currently living with a partner (in Tagalog, *kasalukuyang may kinakasama*). Although not sanctioned by a formal ceremony, "living with a partner" usually describes a traditional Filipino marriage form in which commitment is public and life-long, rather than delimited or conceived as a trial arrangement. Elopement (*tanan*) is another widely recognized marriage institution in the Philippines, most common among low-income families but recognized and practiced across all social classes. A couple typically elopes because their parents are opposed to their marriage. They disappear for a short time, perhaps a few days, and then return to seek their parents' approval.

Under the threat of public embarrassment, the parents are likely to accept the situation. After a couple elopes, they may live together for a period of time or indefinitely. In some cases the elopement is followed immediately by formal marriage in a church or civil ceremony. Survey questions on dating and sex show a pattern of sexual activity beginning at some point on this continuum of commitment leading to marriage. Most of the sexual activity reported by young men and virtually all of the activity reported by young women occur within such a committed relationship. "Casual" sex in the Philippines is rare among women, and far from universal among men. Ethnographic studies have shown similar patterns in Indonesia and Thailand.

Policy issues

When marriage occurs more as a process than as a specific event, "marital status" becomes a rather poor basis for deciding whether to provide or withhold family planning and reproductive health services. Today, governments in many Asian countries are increasingly questioning policies that restrict services to clients who are married. The Philippine government's current family planning strategy, for example, promises reproductive health information and services for all, regardless of marital status.

By reducing the likelihood of accidental pregnancy, broadening access to reproductive health services will allow young people to move through the process toward formal marriage more thoughtfully and with greater volition. The resulting increase in personal control will be especially important for young women. The risk of HIV/AIDS and other sexually transmitted infections (STIs) raises another policy concern. By making condoms and counseling on disease risk available without restriction, government programs will provide life-saving benefits to young people who are sexually active and to their current and future partners.

SOUTH ASIA: PERSISTENCE OF TRADITIONAL MARRIAGE PATTERNS

In South Asia, even today, nearly every woman marries. Surveys conducted in the 1990s found that 99 per cent of women marry in India and Bangladesh, and 98 per cent marry in Pakistan. Men tend to marry at somewhat older ages than women, but marriage is also virtually universal for men. Although the average age at marriage is rising, many women in South Asia still marry while in their teens. In India, the average age at marriage for women rose from 16 years in 1961 to 19 years in 1991.

In Bangladesh, the rise was from 14 to 18 years over the same 30-year period. In Nepal, the average age at marriage rose from 15 to 18 years, and in Pakistan, it rose from 18 to 22 years. Most women in South Asia have their first child shortly after marriage. In India, among women age 25 to 49, the median age at first birth is 19 years. This means that half of all women have their first child at age 19 or earlier. In rural Nepal, 41 per cent of women have a child by age 20, and 17 per cent have a child by age 18.

Early childbirth is a serious health concern. In Nepal, infant mortality is 50 per cent higher for children whose mothers are in their teens than for children of mothers in their 20s. In India, it is 60 per cent higher. Research on family decision-making in South Asia's strongly patriarchal societies has also revealed patterns that are seriously detrimental to women's and children's health. One study in two communities of rural Bangladesh found that women were extremely restricted in terms of decision-making on health issues and associated physical mobility. Three-fourths of married women had little or no say in deciding whether to see a doctor when they became ill or whether to buy medicine for a sick child.

Nearly two-thirds could take a sick child to a hospital outside their village "only in an emergency" or "almost never." Women in these communities who were educated had greater decision-making authority within their families than uneducated women but less freedom to move outside the household. Wealthy women had both less authority and less freedom than poor women. Clearly, in a patriarchal society, wealthy households can afford to keep women in seclusion, while poverty forces women into contact with the outside world. Thus an individual woman's education and economic status may not necessarily improve her position in a male-dominated society—such factors may even diminish a woman's position if social expectations remain unchanged.

Patterns of household decision-making that are detrimental to women's health and well-being are not confined to rural Bangladesh. Only 28 per cent of married women in India report that they decide on their own whether to seek healthcare for themselves. Another 23 per cent participate in such decisions, but nearly half have no say at all in whether they should seek healthcare. Even among women with high school education or above, 39 per cent have no say in decisions concerning their own healthcare. A comparative study of women's roles in family economic decision-making further highlights restrictions on women's independence and authority in the patriarchal families of South Asia.

Among five Asian countries, women in Pakistan report the lowest levels of economic power, with Indian women a close second. Women in Thailand and the Philippines report the highest levels, and Malaysian women are in an intermediate position. Women who are educated, who own land, or who participate in paid work outside the family tend to have more authority within the home, but community and national- level differences—reflecting traditional attitudes and expectations—are also extremely important.

Policy issues

Several governments in South Asia have raised the minimum legal marriage age for women, but experience suggests that it is difficult for lawmakers to influence age at marriage and childbearing directly. In Nepal, the legal age at marriage for women is 16, but one in four rural women marries below this age. What types of policies and programs might be effective? Survey results from South Asia show women's education is the only factor consistently associated with an increase in the age of marriage and childbearing. Although the effects of primary education are small, early marriage and childbearing drop steeply among women with junior high or higher education.

Clearly, providing all women with education at this level is a long-term goal for most South Asian governments, but one benefit of such a strategy would be to reduce the number of women marrying and giving birth while still in their teens. Information programs that emphasize the health advantages of delayed marriage and childbirth could also be beneficial. The special challenge is to reach young women with low levels of education and little access to mass media. Community-level programs might usefully target the parents, husbands, and parents-in-law of such young women as well as the women themselves. School curricula might also place more emphasis on reproductive-health topics, including the benefits of postponing marriage and childbearing.

Reproductive-health education needs to be introduced in the last years of primary school because—for now—few women go on to higher education, particularly in rural areas. Finally, service-delivery programs could place greater emphasis on the needs of young married women. In India and Nepal, where family planning services emphasize sterilization, programs that offer temporary contraceptive methods could help young women delay and space births.

For women who still go on to give birth in their teens, targeted maternal and child health programs could help address the special risks to mothers and their children.

Research showing that wealth and education may not necessarily improve the position of women within the family also has practical policy implications. The importance of community attitudes suggests that policies targeting village-level institutions and influential community members might be an effective avenue for improving the status of women in patriarchal societies. Recent legislation in India, for example, requires that one-third of the positions on local councils (*panchayat*) be filled by women. Programs aimed only at individual women—such as providing schooling or jobs—are likely to fall short of their goals in the absence of efforts to change broader institutions and attitudes.

11

Thailand

Equality between the Sexes

This chapter examines the impact of gender awareness - or its lack - on social, educational, political and economic policy formulation, implementation and evaluation in Thailand. It argues that although Thai women's social, educational, political, and economic, opportunities have improved in recent decades, they still face significant gender bias in virtually all spheres of activity. At least partially, this is because despite Thai women's higher levels of education and consequent social and political involvement in recent years as compared with the past, they continue to be hindered by deep seated traditional gender biased values and thus have not participated in significant numbers in politics at the highest levels where they would have direct influence upon national policies related to gender equity in all fields.

In Thailand, discrimination against women is historically deep rooted and is caused by the traditional thinking of both sexes. Such thinking will not inevitably disappear merely through wishful thinking nor government officials uttering high sounding but ultimately empty platitudes. Although the total Thai population is roughly divided 50/50 male and female, women in Thailand lag behind men in employment opportunities and income as well as in political participation and representation at the highest levels of the civil service.

The root of the problem - deeply conservative social attitudes towards women's rights held not only by men but by many women as well - must first be explicitly addressed through specific, targeted national policies, which are fully implemented and evaluated for effectiveness, in order to eliminate gender discrimination and cultivate equality between the sexes. The Thai government, with so few women at its highest levels, and with a lamentable of genuine gender sensitivity among actual policy makers, has so far failed to do this in any meaningful way.

This chapter will examine traditional views of women's roles in Thai society as well as their roles in the modern workplace, including both the formal and informal sectors. Then, Thai women's access to education as well as participation in politics will be discussed from the perspective that until women are both educationally and politically empowered at the highest national levels, it is unlikely that gender sensitive policies will be fully formulated and effectively implemented. The paper will conclude with recommendations toward increasing gender focus in national policies.

TRADITIONAL VIEWS OF WOMEN IN THAI SOCIETY

Although the current overall status of Thai women may be considerably better than that of women in some other countries, throughout history their social, educational, political, economic, indeed human, value has been undermined and distorted. They have not been treated in the same manner as their male counterparts in terms of educational and employment opportunities as well as opportunities for political participation and advancement. As the NGO Thai Women Watch has noted. "Although in general, a majority of Thai laws do not discriminate against women in the economic and social areas, the influence of opinions and beliefs which have been nurtured in the cultural context that reflects the existing structure of unequal power relation[s] is still prevalent."

In 2007, the Thai population was comprised of 32 million women and 31.1 million men, bringing to mind Mao Tse

Tung's comment that "Women hold up half the sky." However, as a traditional Thai proverb notes, "Women are Buffaloes. Men are humans." In Thailand, buffaloes represent stupid though hard working and generally, though not always, placid animals. The proverb summarizes the divergent treatment of women and men in Thai society and by Thai traditional law during the Ayuthaya period (1350-1767), elements of which linger to this day. Women have not only been considered as brute animals, but in another traditional Thai proverb they were also viewed as less productive than men. *Chai Kao-Pluenk Ying Kao-Sarn* means that men are rice paddy while women are rice.

The rice paddy can continue to grow more rice after each harvest but the rice itself is the final product, which cannot increase in value. This rather negative perception of women's value has long played a significant role in determining women's status in Thai society. In modern times, although women's status is improving, inequality between females and males still exists in several significant aspects. In the home, major decision-making is done by men, while women have control over general household issues. In the , for important issues, the major decision-makers are always men. The same holds true, as will be seen below, at the highest levels of -making.

In religious life, women have always played a supporting role. Women's status in Thai Buddhism is far inferior to that of men. They are considered of less value than men. Up to the present, women in Thailand have not been allowed to be ordained as monks. The status that the women can attain in Thai Buddhism is that of nun. Nuns do not have high status commensurate with that of the monks. A nun is supposed to be the monks' servant and has very low status in the temple. in Thailand, therefore, is deeply rooted in Thai history and culture. At home, especially in rural areas, parents have traditionally (and many continue to do so at present) treated their male and female children differently.

Most boys had plenty of freedom and no or few household responsibilities. Parents expected life-long service from girls while boys were expected only to enter the monkhood temporarily to show their gratitude by gaining merit for the parents. Moreover, since the parents felt that sons were born to a superior role, they tended to provide them with as good an education as possible. Girls were traditionally left illiterate or barely literate, because the parents believed their ultimate goal was to get married and become homemakers. Therefore, other knowledge beyond that necessary for family life was neglected with girls. This path is still followed today in many families, especially in rural areas. However, in general this situation has improved, especially in urban areas and in families where parents are more educated and thus committed to providing extended formal education to all of their children regardless of gender.

GENDER INEQUALITY IN THE WORK PLACE

The inferior situation of many Thai women is due to the fact that Thai society has traditionally offered more opportunities for men and this has been reflected in national policies. The traditional conservative attitude toward women as followers and not leaders has been reflected in government policies and has contributed to their disadvantageous position in the labor market. Employers considered female labor to be temporary, unproductive, less skilled, marginal, and therefore having less value. This attitude, which has yet to be genuinely and persuasively countered by concrete government policies that pay more than mere lip service to gender awareness and equality, has led to unequal treatment between female and male workers.

The latter tend to receive higher wages/salaries than the former for the same position. Moreover, work-related training programs are usually provided for males rather than females in such a way that training times and places are not suitable for women. This partly explains why females rise to higher positions in both the public and private sectors much more slowly than males. As well, women's homemade products have not been valued at market prices while their labor has had a lower value than men's in the labor market in spite of the fact that their productivity might be the same or even higher. This has caused marked economic inequality between the sexes.

The gradual change in economic structure from an agrarian to an industrial economy since the 1960s has brought about a measure of change in traditional attitudes toward women. However, such change is very slow. Income and opportunity inequality between the sexes continues to be a prominent feature of economic life in Thailand and has only been partially addressed by policies at the national level. During the "golden era" (from the 1960s to the early 1990s), the Thai growth rate was impressive. While the manufacturing sector expanded dramatically in that period, the agricultural sector's share of GDP steadily declined. The industrial development policy would not have been possible without the hard work and the sweat of Thai women.

At present, although manufactured products still dominate the export sector, the situation has changed such that labor-intensive industries employing large numbers of women have declined in importance. From the late 1980s to the mid-1990s, large numbers of Thai were laid off, the majority of them women. These blue-collar women did not have high status or receive effective training from the workplace or from government, while their male counterparts did. This was due to the conservative values of their employers. Therefore, attempting to find a new job was almost impossible for these older, low-skilled women.

Many of them turned to self-employment, utilizing traditional Thai knowledge such as Thai massage, to carry on their lives. This situation is recurring now in 2009 with the decline in Thai exports because of the current global economic downturn. Although Thai women can work as well and as effectively as men, they face the pervasive socially conservative attitude that they are not generally qualified for positions beyond the most menial, which is reflected in their salary brackets. Women are far behind men in scale of income. For example, in 2003, males earned an average monthly salary above 10,000 baht (35 baht:$1:00 U.S.).

The ratio of female to male at such an income level is 1:1.4. Moreover, there is a belief that women's effectiveness and productivity at work declines faster than that of men. This, in turn, widens the income gap between the sexes in the long run. This out-of-date but persistent attitude does not necessarily come only from males. Some women also share it. Although women contribute significantly to the development process, the benefits rarely trickle down fairly to them. This is mainly because there is inadequate gender sensitivity in the policy and planning processes for national development. Women's roles are stereotyped by traditional gender-biased social values. They do not have equal rights in several respects and their domestic work is neither evaluated nor very much appreciated by mainstream economists and often even by their own family members.

Modern Thai women have played a crucial role in most types of economic activity. At home, the smallest social unit, women are responsible for most essential activities, including childcare and financial support. Within the , both government and private, large numbers of women have contributed their time and energy to the development process. There are also millions of women who work in the informal sector as hawkers, or in small factories. Thai Labor Force Surveys conducted by the National Statistics Office from 1988 through 2000 indicated that the rate of female participation in the commerce and service sectors is greater than that of men.

This does not hold in the manufacturing and agricultural sectors, but, nonetheless, the role of women in these sectors remains highly significant as well. Women are under-represented in managerial and senior administrative levels in the private sector. For instance, in the banking sector, in 1995 there were 442 male executives but only 190 female executives. In the same year there were 329 male branch managers and only 34 females in this position. As Vichit-Vadakan et al. pointed out, despite having made some significant progress in the workplace, "women are [still] less likely to be in charge."

THAI WOMEN AND EDUCATION

Human capital theory suggests that human capital acquired through education improves the productivity of the individual. Therefore, giving opportunities for education to the population will improve their potential and will increase the country's overall productivity. Neglecting education for either sex, but especially, since it has in fact been the case, for women, will slow economic growth. "If female schooling raises human capital, productivity, and economic growth as much as male schooling does, then women's disadvantage in education is economically inefficient".

Equality of education for males and females is therefore a *sine qua non* for development. Kingdon has pointed out that providing education to women greatly benefits society. It not only improves economic benefits but also enhances social gain such as a reduced infant death rate, reduced malnutrition, and smaller family size. Giving equal opportunity of education to women consequently gives them a better chance to earn and hence provide a better quality of life for their children and therefore a better future for the society.

One reason is that the mother always has a close relationship with the children, especially when they are young, which is the time to build the firm foundation for them. Kingdon also pointed out that a great deal of research suggests that ". . . a greater proportion of women's income than men's is spent on child goods". However, in several countries, especially developing countries, the girls lag far behind the boys in education. In some countries, societal norms, such as early age of marriage, mitigates against girls' education. But, "most importantly, when people live on low incomes - as in the rural areas of all developing countries - it is the mismatch between the cost and benefits of girls' schooling that causes the gender gap in education to persist".

Historically, as in many societies, Thai women had little chance to have formal education. Traditionally, women were supposed to get married at a young age and hence had no need to be literate. Therefore, most women only received training in household chores. Literacy was considered unnecessary for girls. Therefore, only women in the royal or noble families received some education while most of the common women had none. As well, the education available for people was established in the temple where the teachers were monks. Therefore, the women had a very slim chance to get access because Buddhist monks traditionally are not allowed to be close to females.

In the past three decades, there have been marked improvements in educational opportunities for women as statistics show; however, some significant educational inequality between the sexes still exists. As Vichit-Vadakan et al. noted, "Although there are now fewer differences in school enrolment between boys and girls, it is clear that men's and women's educational paths diverge, since at the tertiary level they take quite different courses." Thai men are far more likely than women to study such technical fields as engineering, architecture, law, mathematics and computer sciences, whereas women tend to study the humanities, social sciences, and medical and health services, particularly nursing.

There is more than simple choice of major on the part of individuals involved here. Toward the end of the 1990s, discrimination on the grounds of gender was still practiced in prestigious Thai universities. They imposed a quota based on gender in their admissions procedures for specific professional fields of study. Among the 18 fields of study resistant to women's admissions were, for example, veterinary science, biotechnology, fisheries, agro-industry, forestry and physical education. The year 2000 marked the first time that not only the percentage of girls in public universities was higher than boys, but that the absolute number was also greater.

Moreover, medical science, which used to be dominated by males, is now taken by many more women. However, several areas such as veterinary science, engineering and law are still predominantly male. The overall improvement in female access to education may be partly due to the *World Declaration on Education for All* that was adopted at the World Conference which took place in Jomtien, Thailand, in 1990. That declaration, according to Angela Little, "express[ed] a worldwide consensus on the importance of universal access to education" (in Graham and Rawlings, 1998, and Internet version, 03/04/2008).

Another factor that may affect women's education is the fact that families' natural resources are gradually limited; hence, more parents are willing to give their children more education to substitute for other wealth such as land. This may lead to better educational opportunities for women. Recently, the awareness of gender stereotyping within the national education system has increased. The stereotyped roles of females and males presented in text books have been reviewed by the Curriculum and Instruction Development Department in the Ministry of Education. Providing the right image of the two sexes to society, to parents, to teachers and to students themselves may help to narrow the gender gap in education. Consequently, this will help to narrow the economic and social disparity between women and men.

Gender disparity in formal education in Thailand has significantly narrowed during the past decades; however, the social, economic, and political status of women remains marginal relative to that of men. This author agrees with Stromquist that definitely " . . . gender equality requires more than equity in the 'quantity' of schooling made available to women". Education may certainly help women to improve their economic life and standard of living for their families; however, education per se is not enough to change economic, political and social inequality if public attitudes toward women remain rooted in traditional stereotypes that marginalize and devalue women. Increasing the number of women at all education levels does not mean giving them equality if the context they face is still biased toward them.

Many studies conclude that schools, through curriculum and teacher attitudes, only reinforce and perpetuate the gender ideologies that are at the core of existing . For instance, Lopez and Pollack have argued that many existing educational programs serve to reinforce existing power structures and gender stereotypes rather than to challenge them. This is the case in Thailand today. Education alone will not eliminate the underlying gender ideologies and material inequalities between men and women. Rather, educational policy makers need to take account of these concerns in designing and implementing gender sensitive curricula.

As Stromquist argued, traditional attempts to increase female education have focused more on the material needs and contributions of women than on the ideological and sociological forces that operate against them. While the increased educational attainment of Thai women is a positive trend not to be gainsaid, the full benefits will not be realized until the underlying social and cultural attitudes towards women change and are reflected in educational policy and curriculum development and in society generally.

Although disparity in education between the sexes still exists, the improvement of opportunity in accessing education is welcomed by women. It helps to improve their status at home and in the . They also gain more confidence and freedom. It remains, however, that traditional classroom education is not enough to secure gender sensitivity and equality. Only when conservative values are erased from the curriculum will there be hope for a more gender equitable society.

THAI WOMEN IN POLITICS

Thai politics has been historically, and continues to be, dominated by men. As Son (2009) has pointed out, "Even though Thailand has a strong record of commitments to gender equality, at present, women are significantly underrepresented in decision-making especially in national politics." While Thai women have played a very important role in the economic sphere, they have been very inactive in politics. Although equal participation of males and females in political decision-making is essential to a genuinely gender balanced society, in traditional Thai norms, politics is, quite simply, men's business. Women continue to remain most definitely the hind legs of the Thai political elephant.

In 1932, Thailand was transformed from an absolute monarchy to a constitutional monarchy. Thai citizens, including women, were granted the right to vote and to run for elective office for the first time. However, it was not until 1949 that a Thai woman won an elective seat in parliament for the first time. Also, in the same year, two women were appointed senators. From 1932 up to October 1996, there were only 124 women elected to parliament compared to 4,151 male representatives during that period. In the civil service, few women reach the upper ranks where national policies are formulated.

In 1993, there were 345,553 civil servants, of whom 54.8% were female, but most of them comprised 60% of workers at the lowest level of C1 to C3 civil service rank (the Thai civil service bureaucracy has 11 ranks numbered C1 through C11). At that time there were no females at the highest level, C11. The trend was continued although it has gradually improved. In 2005, out of a total of 345,019 civil servants in ranks C1 through C7, 61.2% were women. Out of 14,700 civil servants at C8 rank, 40.4% were women. At rank C9, 24.4% were women, with 16.4% at C10 and 9.7% at the highest rank C11.

The relative lack of women at the highest levels of the civil service is matched by their relative absence in the top ranks of government institutions such as the National Audit Commission, the Ombudsman's Office, the National Counter-Corruption Commission, and the Constitutional Courts and the Administrative Courts. In 2009 this C system will be revamped with new functional classifications. It will be necessary to wait and see if the new system favors or hinders women's advancement in the civil service to levels where they can have a constructive influence upon national policies.

As Vichit-Vadakan et al., (2006) noted, women have difficulty rising to the top levels of the civil service for several reasons. Among these reasons is the fact that men at the upper levels are accustomed to the women they work with being assistants and are thus not used to working with women on the same level as themselves and perhaps have difficulty perceiving women as being even capable of working at their level. As well, the committees which oversee promotion within the ministries are almost entirely comprised of men.

Finally, since men tend to associate with other men outside the job, e.g., on the golf course and elsewhere, those responsible for promotion decisions in the civil service tend to know already those male candidates up for promotion far better than they know female candidates. From the 1940s until the present, women representatives have constituted a very small percentage in both the elected parliament and the senate. In 2005, women comprised only 10.6% of the members of parliament. This is not surprising given that women only accounted for 11.9% of the candidates who stood for election.

Clearly, Thai women have not been very successful in politics at the national level. On the local level there has been discrimination against women as well. The Local Administration Act of 1914 barred women from running for election at the local level. By 1982, the law prohibiting women from becoming village chiefs and sub-district chiefs was changed with the proviso that all Village Heads and Sub-district Heads elected before that year would retain their positions until the age of 60 (retirement age in Thailand). Although the rule was changed, it is not easy for women to obtain such positions due to the traditional belief that such posts deal with dangerous work and, hence, are not suitable for women.

Indeed, in 2000, out of a total of 208,104 members of local government councils, only 13,236 were women. In 2005, only 3.3% of village heads were women, 6.6% of municipality council members, and 4.8% of provincial council members. The percentage of female mayors throughout Thailand rose from .024 (3) in 1980 to just .53 (8) in 2000. Although women are gradually increasing their political participation in local elective office, the increase is painfully gradual. The reasons why so few women enter elective politics are tied to the prevailing conservative social attitudes discussed above.

Whereas in the past, women's low level of education may have been a barrier to political participation, this is largely no longer the case. However, "public attitudes continue to stereotype women as reflected in public attitudes towards women who in the media and elsewhere have often been stereotyped as weak, indecisive, emotional, dependent and somehow less productive than men. Thai women themselves are certainly not immune to these traditional attitudes which play such a determinative role in keeping them out of politics. Many women also accept the notion that their role is to take care of the family and to leave anything beyond the family to men.

The general lack of success of women in politics may not be caused only by men but also by women themselves. Women do not have confidence in female politicians, which may come from traditional beliefs about women's roles or from jealousy. It is stunning that in many elections where women voters outnumbered men, a minimal number of women were elected. Until more Thai women are present at the highest levels of policy formulation and implementation, the notion of gender sensitivity will be unlikely to garner the commitment required to seriously influence policy.

In a talk given in Bangkok in January, 2009 about a UN publication about the Millenium Development Goals (MDGs), Unifem's Dr. Jean D'Cunha pointed out that gender sensitive political, social and economic accountability in line with the MDGs has thus far attained mixed progress globally. D'Cunha noted that "While much progress has been made at the policy level, there is a big gap between policy on the one hand and implementation and accountability on the other hand." This statement applies as well to Thailand where the government is well aware of the need to promote gender equality through a variety of policies. However, as D'Cunha argued in referring to the UN's MDGs, the problem lies not with the will to formulate gender sensitive policy but rather with the will to see to its full implementation and accountability.

As the NGO Thai Women watch has argued (2008), specific policies to eliminate are necessary. All government ministries and departments must take into account gender in any policy formulation, implementation and evaluation. The Thai government must proactively encourage and promote gender sensitivity and equality among all its civil service officials, female and male. As well, politicians, again both female and male, at all levels, local and national, need to be educated in and demonstrate sensitivity toward gender issues in the social, educational, economic and political arenas. NGOs dedicated to advancing women's rights economically, socially and politically must be supported. The government must establish a "Women Development Fund" for use by government agencies and NGOs in combating discrimination against women.

However, it is essential to keep in mind that gender discrimination is the result of deeply traditional conservative attitudes which must be modified in the workplace, the classroom, and the polling booth. To change ingrained attitudes, however, takes time. Therefore, a short-term policy and long-term policy must go hand-in-hand to secure women's equity. The short-term strategies need the cooperation of various governmental and non-governmental organizations. The government must legislate and, most importantly in a context where enforcement is often lax or non-existent, enforce laws to secure equal rights for women in all aspects.

The government and employers must provide legal rights information and grievance mechanisms to women workers to ensure that they will not be exploited. A quota system may need to be applied in the workplace where opportunities for women are limited. Political parties must be encouraged to actively recruit women candidates for office on both the local and national levels. As well, the government must itself act as a model for the people. For example, it should provide equal opportunity for women in all types of government positions. The law and legal policy is another important measure in assuring equal rights for women. Job discrimination because of gender differentiation should be legally prohibited.

Family law that acts against women should be abolished. Moreover, since the mothers have perhaps the greatest influence upon their children, equitable social treatment of mothers is a crucial issue. The mass media is another key factor in the attitude reconstruction process. Through the mass media, successful women should be introduced and popularized and traditional negative gender stereotypes abolished. This will not only help to stimulate women's self-esteem and self-confidence but will as well influence men to accept women as full human beings equal to themselves on all levels.

Finally, Thai women themselves are the most important factor for change. They must learn to think more critically and creatively at home, in schools, and in the workplace. Thai women must develop the self-confidence to be successful in any circumstances. They must overcome the belief that they are always inferior to men, that they are always and forever the hind legs of the elephant, never to lead but always to follow. Thai women should be proud to be women and should no longer pray for rebirth as males. The past two decades have seen considerable efforts by the government, non-governmental organizations and the women's movement to strengthen the roles and advance the status of Thai women in order to reduce gender inequalities. As a result, in present day Thailand women play an integral role in all aspects of national development.

THAI WOMEN AND THEIR ECONOMIC AND SOCIAL STATUS

Thai women participate actively in the labour force constituting nearly half of the economically employed population. Job opportunities are now much more accessible to women whose potential and capabilities have been recognized. During the late 1980's and the early 1990's, women formed the majority of workers in the export and tourism industries which brought the highest foreign exchange earnings. However, the economic crisis of 1997 has taken its toll and women have been the hardest hit. Sustained national economic growth in the pre-crisis years has improved many aspects of social development in Thailand. Women's health has improved and the literacy rate for women has increased significantly to 91 per cent. However, while women's conditions have improved in some areas, inequality still persists in others.

The promulgation of the People's Constitution in 1997 is the most significant positive change which has moved and will move the Thai society closer to the goal of gender equality.

The Constitution explicitly guarantees equal rights between men and women and requires that the state promote gender equality. This is the context to the more intensified advocacy for gender mainstreaming in recent years to ensure that voices of women are better heard and needs responded for the equitable sustainable development of the country. The success of such goal involves multi-pronged strategies, two of which to be discussed here include empowerment of women and mainstreaming gender perspectives in the national policy and planning processes.

MAKING WOMEN MORE VISIBLE

In spite of the active roles played by Thai women in all spheres of national development, traditional values and customs have somewhat ascribed a subordinate position to them in social hierarchies. Empowerment of women through increased representation at all levels has thus become a means for women's voices to be heard. In politics and administration, women's representation is still negligible. At the national level, women senators and members of parliament form less than 10 per cent of the total. At the local administration level, propelled by the *Thai National Commission on Women's Affairs (TNCWA),* the national machinery for the advancement of women, and colleague NGOs, women form around 10 per cent, an increase from 6.4 per cent in 1997.

In the government service, about 85 per cent of top executive posts are occupied by men. Women are also underrepresented in *ad hoc* committees where the direction of development and national policies are decided. Past and current efforts to increase women's representation have been directed at both the women themselves and at the changes in institutional power structure.

Within the government service, a recent initiative is the circulated guidelines of the Office of the Civil Service Commission, the government central personnel agency. The initiative provides recommendations to all government departments to take into consideration the proportion of female and male officials in such personnel administration practices as promotion particularly to the executive level, and provision of conducive to career advancement opportunities including provision of scholarships for education and training or work assignments. Such guidelines principally advocate for having one sex at not exceeding two thirds in number. Setting quota of female representation in the political arena has also been advocated by women's movements. One of the few achievements is the constitutional requirement of having females forming one third of members of any special parliamentary committee set up to deliberate on legislature related to women's affairs.

The most significant achievement is the recent imposition of having an equal participation of men and women in the Village Fund Committee. Through persistent advocacy and solidarity of governmental and non-governmental organizations working for women, the proposal won approval of the Prime Minister, recognizing the significance in the involvement of women for the effective implementation of the Fund. The One Million Baht Fund is one of the policies of the current government to bridge the gap between the rich and the poor by enlarging the economic opportunities at the grassroots level through the Village Fund allocated to all 80,000 villages and urban communities in the country.

MAINSTREAMING GENDER PERSPECTIVES IN NATIONAL DEVELOPMENT

To ensure a sustainable and equitable development, another important strategy is to mainstream gender perspectives in the national policy and planning processes. Within the government service, the *TNCWA* has launched a two-year gender-mainstreaming project with the support from the World Bank. The project has one very important component of laying the groundwork for gender capacity building in the government sector to ensure that gender perspectives are reflected in development policy and planning processes. The project thus initially aims at establishing a team of 5 gender trainers in 9 core government departments. Lessons learned from this pilot project after completion in the first half of 2002 will facilitate the planning for further government-wide gender mainstreaming activities, gender capacity building and institutionalization in particular.

Another related development is an initiative involving the planned appointment of a *"Chief Gender Equality Officer"* at the executive level in each government department as initiated by the TNCWA. The Chief Gender Equality Officer, to serve as the gender focal point in government departments, will have the main task of overseeing gender integration in policy and planning processes including delivery of services to the public in his/her respective government departments. Heading and being supported by a team of trained gender trainers/advocates, the Chief of Gender Equality Officer can be expected to be instrumental to effective gender mainstreaming in the government service.

Extending beyond the boundary of the bureaucracy to a larger context of the society as a whole, one finds that many non-government organizations have made a meaningful contribution to gender mainstreaming effort in the Thai society, either single-handedly or through NGO networks or in partnership with the national machinery. The *Women Constitution Network, Women in Politics Institute, Gender and Development Research Institute and Female Labour Union Movements* are some of the prominent ones, noted for their effective advocacy strategies for empowerment of women and equal participation of women and men.

In fact, in the context of gender mainstreaming approach, different institutional mechanisms have been installed and many gender-sensitive activities launched by NGO advocates. These have resulted in many gains for women and in the better integration of gender perspectives in the development mainstream. Among those include the emergence of government's clear policies for women, legislative changes, heightened public awareness on the contribution and changing roles of women by annually rewarding outstanding women, and a larger pool of trained women leaders through training to reshape the development agenda at the national and local levels.

12

A Woman of Vietnam in a Changing World

In an era of universal polemics and political unrest - with no thought of glory, with no fanfare or public notice - 265,000 women volunteered to go where they were needed, to do what was needed. The era was known as Vietnam, and these young women, most in their 20s, risked their lives to care for our country's wounded and dying. Their humanity and compassion equalled their lifesaving and comforting skills. For the first time in America's history, a memorial that honors women's patriotic service was dedicated in the nation's capital, placed beside their brother soldiers on the hallowed grounds of the Vietnam Veterans Memorial in Washington, DC.

It was the first tangible symbol of honor for American women. The multi-figure bronze monument is designed by New Mexico sculptor, Glenna Goodacre. It is a sculpture in the round portraying three Vietnam-era women, one of whom is caring for a wounded male soldier, stands 6'8" tall and weighs one ton. The Vietnam Women's Memorial Project was incorporated in 1984, and is a non-profit organization located in Washington, DC. The mission of the Vietnam Women's Memorial Foundation (formerly the Vietnam Women's Memorial Project) is to promote the healing of Vietnam women veterans through the placement of the Vietnam Women's Memorial on the grounds of the Vietnam Veterans Memorial in Washington, D.C.; to identify the military and civilian women who served during the Vietnam war; to educate the public about their role; and to facilitate research on the physiological, psychological, and sociological issues correlated to their service.

The Foundation has the support of every major veterans group in the country including the Vietnam Veterans Memorial Fund and more than 40 other diverse organizations. Diane Carlson Evans, a former Army nurse who served in Vietnam, is the founder and chair of the Vietnam Women's Memorial Foundation. She became the first woman in American history to spearhead a campaign to place a national monument in Washington, DC which recognizes the contributions of military women to their country, as well as civilian women's patriotic service. Vietnam Veterans were not welcomed home as the country desperately tried to put the war behind it. Before founding of the Vietnam Women's Memorial Project, little was known of the heroism of American women.

Yet over 265,000 military women served beside their brother soldiers - all of them volunteers. Approximately 11,000 American military women were stationed in Vietnam during the war. Ninety per cent were nurses. Others served as physicians, physical therapists and personnel in the medical field, air traffic control, military intelligence, administration and in many other capacities. An unknown number of civilian women also served in Vietnam as news correspondents and workers for the Red Cross, the USO, Special Services, the American Friends Service Committee, Catholic Relief Services and other humanitarian organizations. Many of these women were wounded or killed in the crossfire.

The Vietnam Women's Memorial Project has given women veterans a voice. It has helped to tell their story through the mass print and electronic media as well as in schoolrooms and universities and at conferences, seminars and conventions. As more and more Vietnam women read and hear of their sister's service, they come forward with their own experiences. Many of these women had never before shared their personal experiences with others - the pain was too deep. Now, through their poems, songs and stories, the healing of women veterans has begun. Silent no more, women veterans have a special role in discussions surrounding a call to arms, the role of women in the military and veterans benefits. Their insights into war make their contributions in peacetime as invaluable as their heroism in Vietnam.

A three-day Celebration of Patriotism and Courage, November 10-12, 1993, in Washington, D.C. highlighted the dedication of the Vietnam Women's Memorial on November 11, 1993 near the Wall of names and the statue of the three serviceman at the site of the Vietnam Veterans Memorial. Thousands of Vietnam veterans, their families and friends joined the nation in honoring these brave and compassionate women. The Vietnam Women's Memorial Foundation would like your help to support its mission. So far approximately 12,000 women veterans who served during the Vietnam era have been located by the Vietnam Women's Memorial Foundation. The stories and experiences we learn from the women who contact the Foundation are invaluable contributions to the history of this era.

Vietnam women veterans are encouraged to send in their service information and current address to the Foundation by using the Vietnam Women's Memorial Foundation's Sister Search form. The long awaited Dedication of the Memorial was made possible with a loan for its construction, design, and landscaping. The loan was substantial, but friends and supporters of the Vietnam Women's Memorial Foundation did what some may have thought was impossible...they managed to pay the construction debt in full! The Vietnam Women's Memorial Foundation continues to be faced with other obligations while fulfilling its program objectives. Please visit the "Your Support" page for information on how you can continue to help support the Vietnam Women's Memorial Foundation.

The good news is the constitutional and legal framework for gender equality has existed in Vietnam since 1945. The law provides the opportunity for equal participation in politics by women. However, in practice they are underrepresented. Most of the top leaders are men. There is only one woman in the Politburo. Fortunately, women are better represented in the National Assembly, where more than one-fourth of the 450 members are women. Other Vietnamese women hold some important positions in the government. For instance, the Vice President is a woman as are several ministers and vice ministers. More recently however, limited resources combined with economic reforms emphasizing economic growth and infrastructure, have had detrimental effects on social programs, including gender equity.

Meanwhile, there is growing awareness in Vietnam that neglect of women's role in the economy will place constraints on economic success. In response the government upgraded the National Committee for the Advancement of Women and is now chaired by a Vice-Minister, with participants from key central ministries. Vietnam's Plan of Action following the United Nations Women's Conference in Beijing recognizes a continuing need for policies and programs that will maintain and increase women's role in economic and social development. As a result of these actions and the renovation process that is transforming Vietnam's economy from central planning to market principles, women have strong representation in the economy.

They are significant contributors - making up 65% of the agricultural, 43% of the industrial and 70% of the informal labor force. In urban areas many women have shown great entrepreneurship and become the main income earners for their families, running thousands of home-based businesses generated by the market. Other women have not been so fortunate, the victims of public sector retrenchment under economic reform, which has had a disproportionate impact on women in lower-paid jobs. In rural areas the shift in control of agricultural production from cooperatives to households has placed new emphasis on the labor power of each family member.

As men migrate to the towns and cities for work, much of the increased burden for farm production is falling on women, many of whom must also sell products in nearby markets to meet daily needs. Reductions in the social services previously subsidized by the state further increase the workload for women. In addition, women often have less access to productive resources such as credit, tools, labor-saving technologies, technical services and training. The status and position of women in Vietnam have undergone significant improvements in the last fifty years.

Social indicators show a high degree of literacy (84% for women and 93% for men in 1992) and life expectancy (67.5 for females and 63 for men). But fundamental and widespread economic and social changes occurring since 1986 are presenting critical choices and challenges for Vietnamese men and women alike. There have been opportunities for women to add to the gains they have made in the last five decades, but on the other hand, there is a danger that they may be marginalized and even lose ground on their past achievements. While there is no legal discrimination, women face deeply ingrained societal discrimination.

Despite extensive provisions in the Constitution, in legislation, and in regulations that mandate equal treatment, and although some women occupy high government posts, few women compete effectively for higher status positions. The Government has ratified ILO conventions on Equal Remuneration and Discrimination in Employment. The Constitution provides that women and men must receive equal pay for equal work; however, the Government does not enforce this provision. Very poor women, especially in rural areas but also in cities, perform menial work in construction, waste removal, and other jobs for extremely low wages.

Despite the large body of legislation and regulations devoted to the protection of women's rights in marriage as well as in the workplace, and Labor Law provisions that call for preferential treatment of women, women do not always receive equal treatment. International NGO workers and many women reported that domestic violence against women was common. The law addresses the problem of domestic violence, and officials increasingly acknowledge the problem; however, authorities do not enforce the law effectively. Many divorces reportedly are due to domestic violence, but many women likely remain in abusive marriages rather than confront the stigma and economic uncertainty of divorce.

Prostitution, although officially illegal, appears to be tolerated widely. Some women are forced to work as prostitutes. The Ho Chi Minh City people's committee recently has acknowledged that more than 10,000 women in the city engaged in prostitution. Hanoi, the port cities of Danang and Haiphong, and smaller cities such as Can Tho and Nha Trang also have large numbers of women engaged in prostitution. There are reports that some exploiters in Ho Chi Minh City addicted young girls to heroin and forced them to work as prostitutes to earn money for drugs. Many more women are compelled to work as prostitutes because of poverty, a lack of other employment opportunities, or because they are victimized by false promises of lucrative work.

The Vietnam Women's Union and Youth Union, as well as international and domestic NGO's, are engaged actively in education and rehabilitation programs to combat these abuses. Trafficking in women for the purpose of forced prostitution, both domestically and internationally, is a serious problem. Women and girls are trafficked from southern delta and highland provinces to Cambodia, and from Northern provinces into China. There are reports that some women from Ho Chi Minh City and the Mekong Delta who married men from Taiwan were forced into prostitution after their arrival in Taiwan.

Women and girls frequently are misled by promises of well-paying jobs in those places. The party-controlled Women's Union has a broad agenda to promote women's rights, including political, economic, and legal equality, and protection from spousal abuse. The Women's Union operates micro-credit consumer finance programs and other programs to promote the advancement of women. International NGO's and other international organizations regard the union as effective, but they and Women's Union representatives believe that much time is required to overcome societal attitudes that relegate women to lower status than men.

The Government also has a committee for the advancement of women, which coordinates intra-ministerial programs that affect women. At present, 90% of adult males and 79% of adult females are literate. Of children aged more than 5 years old, 12% of girls and 7.5% of boys have never attended school, and these proportions have remained remarkably constant over the past 20 years. Gender gaps are prominent among the poor and ethnic minorities and in rural areas of the Northern Uplands, the Mekong Delta, the Central Coast and Central Highlands, due to school fees and the opportunity cost of child labor.

While the gender gap is closing for higher education, it persists in vocational and technical education (VTE), and signs of sex segregation in upper secondary and university education are becoming more obvious, with females clustering in pedagogy, social sciences, and linguistics, while males dominate technical and scientific courses. This segregation potentially disadvantages women from fully participating in new industries, such as information technology, biotechnology, and application of new materials.

Great advances have been made in access to health facilities, which benefits women directly because they need health services more than do men. However, pockets of disadvantage exist in remote areas and for the poor who cannot afford the fees introduced during economic reform (*doi moi*). Women's greater demand for health services because of their reproductive role and their susceptibility to reproductive tract infections means that the lack of health care services has a greater impact on women. Fee for service, ineffective implementation of the fee exemption program, and inequitable budget allocation mechanisms have resulted in unequal access to quality health care.

The fees and charges for these services are often out of the reach of the poorest families; they may forego accessing services and self-treat themselves and their children. Common health problems for ethnic minority women and their families include malaria, malnutrition, and respiratory and gynecological infections. These result in high levels of maternal mortality, obstetric complications, and maternal and child malnutrition. In resource- constrained households, women's share of food is lower than that of men.

Although more than 50% of families now use modern contraception methods, one of the major health risks to women is the dominance of intrusive forms of contraception (intra-uterine devices) and family planning (abortion). It is estimated that 40% of pregnancies are terminated, the highest rate in the world (2.5 per woman). New issues for women's health are emerging with increasing awareness of promiscuity and domestic violence. In an environment where the use of condoms is not common and intravenous drug use is a significant problem, the risks of contracting HIV/AIDS have also grown.

The fight against HIV/AIDS is intrinsically linked with women's empowerment. In 2000, 14% of HIV cases in the country were women, and the prevalence of HIV in female sex workers was 4%. Domestic violence is clearly a health issue for women. In recent years, official reports of domestic violence have increased and are more likely to be heard in court. There is no formal barrier to women's participation in the electoral process. Although representation of women elected to positions at the local level has increased, it is still low relative to their presence in the National Assembly. Women are poorly represented in strategic decision- making bodies such as party committees. There are no women in the Politburo and the proportion of women in the Central Committee has declined. Overall, the political decision-making role of women has deteriorated.

PARTICIPATION IN THE ECONOMY AND LEGAL RIGHTS

Women's labor force participation rates have been high since the war. However, since *doi moi* and improved economic conditions, their participation in the formal economy has declined. Economically active women are concentrated in agriculture where they contribute more hours of labor than do men to cultivation, livestock breeding, agriculture processing, and marketing of agriculture produce. Yet, they have only limited access to extension services. Since 1993, male farm employment has declined and the number of female farmers has increased.

It is clear that as nonfarm enterprises are becoming more economically attractive, women are being left behind in the less dynamic agriculture sector. Wage employment opportunities in rural areas are limited for women. Women are also less successful in establishing small and medium enterprises in the formal sector because of lack of resources including labor time, management skills, knowledge of the market, access to credit, and land. Less than one tenth of economically active women are now employed by the State. During the initial years of *doi moi,* it is estimated that female labor accounted for 70% of the loss from the state sector, and by 1999 only 42% of state employees were women.

Women work about the same time in income-earning activities but earn 14% less than men per month. These differentials decreased during the 1990s, although differences persist in the latter years of the working life cycle. According to the 1996 Constitution and relevant laws, women and men are granted equal rights with respect to economic opportunities, marriage and family matters, political participation, public administration, and ownership of property including land.

The 2000 Law on Marriage and Family stipulates that land-use certificates for household common land must list the names of both spouses, indicating shared possession. However, the 1993 Land Law, which predates it, does not mention co-ownership, and in 80% of cases, land-use certificates in rural areas are registered in the name of the male household head. This can make it more difficult for women to access credit and pursue business opportunities. Although women have equal property rights, they are often disadvantaged due to social factors, which cut across and often contradict the legislation, whose enforcement is often left to the discretion of local officials.

GOVERNMENT POLICY AND PROGRAM ON WOMEN

The Government has adopted a Gender Strategy and National Plan of Action for the Advancement of Women 2001–2005 (POA2), which is the most important gender-specific planning document. The Plan outlines 6 objectives and activities in the areas of employment and economic status for women, education and training, health, leadership and decision making, women's rights, and strengthening the national machinery. Each ministry has a Committee for the Advancement of Women, responsible for drafting ministry-based gender strategies and action plans to promote and facilitate gender mainstreaming. The Vietnam Women Union (VWU), a mass organization with more than 11 million members, operates at the commune, district, provincial, and national level. In addition to its mandate of raising awareness and advocacy at the grassroots level, the VWU has become more involved in implementing programs and projects.

ADB'S GENDER STRATEGY

The areas of more relevant gender gap in Vietnam include

1. Limited access to extension, credit, and land in the agriculture sector, where the female labor force is more prevalent, and difficulties in pursuing nonfarm employment prospects;
2. Lower enrollment in secondary and vocational/technical education, which in turn limits the potential for female employment and their voice in fertility choices; and
3. Creeping under-representation in state employment and in government decision-making positions.

ADB's country strategy and program, which focuses on economic growth through rural and private sector development, equalization in human capital endowments through universal lower secondary education, and improved with special emphasis on public administration reform, is well suited to addressing these gaps by mainstreaming these concerns in ADB operations, as in the following recommendations:

1. In its operations in support of agriculture and rural development, ADB will strive to create a level playing field for men and women in the diversification of agriculture production and the development of rural enterprises, through a focus on equal access to agriculture inputs, extension services, skills training, and productive resources such as land and credit.
2. In its operations in the social sector, ADB will ensure that gender equity and empowerment are promoted through equal access to secondary education and VTE. The choice of subjects will not be sex segregated. Achievement in secondary education is expected to lead to improved labor force participation, better control of contraception and fertility, and greater ability to overcome poverty. By promoting accessible health care and its equitable financing, ADB will also be benefiting women directly, given their greater dependence on health services during their reproductive years.
3. In the area of governance, ADB will contribute to gender mainstreaming in all government policies and programs, through gender-capacity building support to relevant government agencies and ensuring that all ADB assistance is gender inclusive. The focus will be on ensuring that civil service and public administration reform does not adversely affect women and that the reforms undertaken support the Government's gender mainstreaming goals.

IMPLEMENTING THE STRATEGY

The three areas of focus above—agriculture and rural development, socially inclusive development, and —are targeted to create benefits for women, greater equity for women in access to resources and services, and the empowerment of women both within the public and private domain. The aims of the strategy can be achieved by incorporating gender concerns into ongoing and proposed projects, which lend themselves to these strategic priorities.

The proposed approach will be implemented mostly by mainstreaming gender considerations into ADB projects, with particular attention to those in agriculture and rural development, small and medium enterprises, secondary education, health services and financing, and public administration reform. The routine conduct of gender analysis will be actively promoted in the design stage to ensure that women's needs are met and more effectively integrated. Collection of sex-disaggregated data at the design and benefit monitoring and evaluation stages will be required. Special components will be designed and resources allocated, where women are identified as a clear target group. Following are more specific recommendations.

AGRICULTURE AND RURAL DEVELOPMENT

Given women's significant role in the agriculture sector, ADB assistance will be designed to be responsive to women's roles, priorities and needs, and to ensure equal access to resources such as seeds, fertilizers, information, new technology, and extension services. Women's distinct role and responsibi-lities in the sustainable use of natural resources, as key resource users and managers, will be supported. For example, community awareness programs will be developed with women as a specific target group; women will be actively encouraged to participate in land-use planning, social forestry, and other income-earning opportunities; and provision will be made for women's access to and control over natural resources.

Poverty reduction initiatives will include a focus on reducing female poverty. Possible approaches include development of strategies to increase and enhance women's employment prospects in the informal sector, promoting rural nonfarm employment and income-generating opportunities, and providing greater access to credit. Community-based livelihood projects to address food security, crop and livestock diversification, and microfinance will be developed with poor women as a target group.

SOCIALLY INCLUSIVE DEVELOPMENT

The focus will be on improving access to and retention rates in secondary schooling and VTE for girls, especially poor and ethnic minority girls and women. To achieve these aims, ADB projects will explore mechanisms such as fellowships, application of affirmative actions principles, stipends, and targets. Girls' entry into nontraditional fields such as science, technology, and vocational and technical courses will be supported, through priority for female access to VTE and design of appropriate curricula to provide girls with realistic marketable skills.

GOVERNANCE

Improvements in and participation in decision making to become gender inclusive will be supported. The POA2 goals of gender mainstreaming in sectoral ministries through the review of skills mix and requirements and policy and planning procedures will also be supported directly or indirectly. The success in improving the well-being of women and reducing gender disparities in Vietnam has been impressive. According to national indicators on life expectancy, maternal mortality, basic education, and primary health care, the position of women compares favorably with that of neighboring countries and countries with a similar gross domestic product (GDP) per capita.

Vietnam ranked 108 out of 174 according to the United Nations Development Programme (UNDP) gender-related development index, with a 5-point better ranking than for the Human Development Index. However, these national indicators say little about the pockets of across the country—especially significant within poor households—and the challenges to female empowerment in the market economy and formal political system. The apparent lack of gender disparity at the national level compared to the profound gaps between rural and urban populations, rich and poor, and Kinh and ethnic minorities is often used as a justification for dismissing gender-and-development (GAD) issues in Vietnam. However, such judgments should be made cautiously.

The Asian Development Bank (ADB) 1995 country briefing paper on women in Vietnam pointed to the erosion of women's status as the market economy evolves. More recent GAD literature in Vietnam affirms that analysis and points to increasing differentials between men's and women's participation at the national level in strategically important areas, such as access to upper secondary education, technical and vocational education, state employment, access to credit and land, time worked, political representation, agriculture production, and family planning.

Of growing concern in Vietnam is the revelation of entrenched gender-based violence both within and outside the home, and health risks associated with excessively high rates of abortion. More importantly, the limited data available indicate that the gender gap is greatest and growing within poor and disadvantaged households. Much progress has been made through the policies of the Vietnamese Communist Party (VCP) and the Government since the 1950s. Gender equality was institutionalized in the 1946 Constitution and has been enhanced in each constitutional reform and through legislation and regulations. Challenging the legacies of Confucian and French rule, Vietnam reduced gender disparities in education, health, rights to property, access to income and resources, and participation in formal decision-making bodies.

Under the VCP, women became major contributors to economic growth through high levels of participation in agriculture, handicraft production, trading, and labor force participation, supported by a degree of socialized childcare and household responsibilities. Economic transition, which began in the 1980s, brought the unraveling of the cooperative agriculture system, which had the positive results of increased productivity and lower levels of poverty, especially in rural areas. However, with *doi moi* (policy of economic renovation), came economic competition and the user-pays principle. As a consequence, women's equitable position has been challenged.

Reproductive responsibilities, such as childcare and household duties, were no longer met by the community but by the household; consequently, the length of women's working day increased. Women in the state sector are required to retire 5 years earlier than men, which disadvantage them in achieving seniority. Women lost their jobs at a faster rate than men with rationalization of the state sector and they were not compensated by increased access to productive resources relative to that of men in the growing nonfarm and private sector. For example, as cooperative land was divided among the community, men were issued land-use certificates.

Credit was more easily obtained by men and men's greater mobility allowed them to search for employment opportunities further from home. The user-pays principle for such services as health and education also disadvantaged women because of their reproductive role, resulting in higher demand than men for health services; and because the opportunity costs for education of females are higher than for males. The gender gap appears when these costs increase at the upper secondary level. Furthermore, with greater decision-making power allocated to the political machinery (including the National Assembly and the provincial, district, and commune levels), women's representation began to decline.

Although national statistics indicate an improvement in general well-being of men and women, improvement for women has lagged behind that of men in certain areas and social groups. Pockets of gender disparity are apparent particularly within the poorer communities where there is competition for scarce resources. Statistical indicators of gender disparity either at the national or household level say little about changes in gender beliefs and practices and empowerment of women. In fact, social attitudes of inequality remain and are reflected both within the public space of the paid workforce and, especially, within the private space of the family. In the workforce, men expect to be senior to women.

Similarly, wives and daughters must defer to senior men especially in public. The gender impact of *doi moi* is indeed complex and the situation is still in a state of flux. Data from different sources including the 1989 and 1999 censuses, the Vietnam Living Standards Survey in 1993 (VLSS93) and 1998 (VLSS98), other surveys, and case studies are often contradictory.

Nevertheless, it is clear that economic reform will continue in Vietnam and agriculture will become a less significant economic activity. Nonfarm employment within both rural and urban areas will provide new opportunities for both women and men. As the economic transition continues, it is critical that women and men have equal chances to participate and that short-term as well as the more persistent gender disparities are redressed.

This will come through equal access to all forms of education, especially business skills and information technology, and equal access to productive resources, such as credit and political decision making. The overall situation is changing rapidly and statistically significant data are limited. Therefore, not surprisingly, analysis is still controversial. What is less controversial is the disadvantage suffered by the poor, many of whom are ethnic minorities. Women within these households are the most disadvantaged in Vietnam. The situation for many poor ethnic minority women has changed little as a consequence of *doi moi* and their position relative to men has deteriorated. Undeniably, Vietnam is still the leader in the subregion with respect to institutionalizing gender equity.

For Vietnam to maintain this position, at least three challenges arise for the Government:

1. Maintenance of gender equity priorities as the State progressively withdraws from intervention in the daily lives of people with the implementation of economic reforms (e.g., labor allocation and childcare)—policies on gender equity imposed from above may be difficult to sustain as a culture of patriarchy reemerges;
2. Transparency in monitoring gender gaps in access to services, especially in the flagship sectors of health and education of the previous command economy; and
3. Development of new and innovative policies and programs to deal with the problems outlined at the 1995 Beijing World Conference on Women, including domestic violence, choice of contraception, and women trafficking—a daunting task for any government.

In summary, although national indicators present a positive picture, areas of gender disparity exist, most clearly within the ethnic poor but also at the national level in vocational and technical education (VTE), upper secondary education, university, senior positions in bureaucracy, political representation, income levels, and hours worked. The sole focus on disparity and levels of participation of women—the methodology characteristic of the traditional women-in-development (WID) approach—reveals little about the effectiveness of women's participation and empowerment either in the public or private domain. It is argued here that more can be achieved in Vietnam with respect to the effectiveness of women's participation and empowerment.

SOCIAL STATUS OF WOMEN

In 1999, it was estimated that Vietnam had a population of 76.3 million. This represents a modest annual population growth rate of 1.54%, reflecting the relative success of Vietnam's family planning policy. Women comprise 50.8% of the population and are markedly overrepresented in the age cohorts higher than 50 years due to the dramatic loss of life, particularly of men, during the Vietnam War. This overrepresentation contributes to a high number of female-headed households (45% of those with heads more than 50 years old). Vietnam also has a young population, with about 44% of the population aged less than 20 years.

The youthfulness of the population creates excessive demand for job creation but also propels the rapid pace of economic, social, and cultural change that is evident today. The sex ratio indicates a male bias among those aged less than 15 years, which suggests male preference in children. Typically, if a couple produces two daughters, they will try for a son. If they have two sons, they are less inclined to try for a daughter. Female infanticide may also occur in some areas where ancestor worship and the need for a male heir are strong. National demographic statistics have improved for women and children during the last decade but the improvement has been geographically uneven.

The under-5 mortality rate fell from 55 to 48 per 1,000 live births from 1989 to 1999, the infant mortality rate declined to 37 per 1,000 live births by 1999 and life expectancy is 11 years higher than that of other countries of similar GDP per capita. During 1989–1999, delivery complications fell by 52%, maternal mortality halved from 2 to 1 per 1,000 births and the fertility rate declined from 3.8 in 1989 to 2.3. The crude birth rate fell from 30.1 per 1,000 women in 1989 to 19.9 in 1999. It was kept low among the Kinh through vigorous family planning campaigns and the two-child policy, which has been rescinded only recently.

The family planning policy made exceptions for ethnic minorities, who were allowed to have more than two children, particularly the smaller population groups. However, these statistics vary markedly by ethnic group, economic quintile, and region. Major gaps are evident between rural and urban communities. For example, in 1999 the infant mortality rate was 41.0 in the rural areas compared to only 18.3 in the urban areas, the crude birth rate was 21.2 compared to 15.9, and the total fertility rate was 2.6 compared to 1.7. Regional differences also exist, especially between the Southeast (Ho Chi Minh City) and Red River Delta (Hanoi) with the best records, and the poorer Central Highlands and Northern Uplands with the worst.

According to the 1999 Population and Housing Census Sample results, female-headed households comprised 21.6% of households and the proportion of female-headed households was higher (more than 30%) in both the poorest areas (northern mountains, the midlands, and the Central Highlands) and the most prosperous areas (Southeast). These differences were because of the higher loss of life in the mountainous areas than elsewhere during the war, which gave rise to a higher proportion of widowed female-headed households; and migration by men from both the poor and prosperous areas to take advantage of nonfarm opportunities offering higher income. The population of Vietnam is surprisingly mobile for an agriculturally based economy. About one third of the population aged more than 10 years has moved at least once and this increases to more than 50% in the Southeast.

The Southeast and the Central Highlands are net receivers of migrants. People move for economic reasons, government resettlement, to join other family members, in response to disasters such as floods and fire, and in the past because of war. Although 1999 census data on migration are not yet disaggregated by sex, case study research indicates that not only young men but also young single women are leaving the countryside to secure urban employment. In the longer term this will create pressure on urban resources.

MARRIAGE AND FAMILY

The extended family is the main social and economic unit within Vietnam. Although 71% of families reside as nuclear families, these families often live adjacent to their parents and households of siblings, and still function as an extended family. The expectation is that all people marry. In 1999, only 3.3% of those aged more than 50 years claimed never to have married. The mean age for first marriage is higher in urban than in rural areas but is rising slightly for both men and women in general: for men, 25.5 years in 1999 compared to 24.5 in 1989; and for women, 24 years compared to 23.2, respectively.

After a temporary rush toward early marriages in the early 1990s when housing land within the commune was being distributed to households, the age of rural marriage is also rising, with the exception of some ethnic minority groups in which underage marriage is still common. The divorce rate is still low in Vietnam, although it is increasing, especially in urban areas. According to the 1999 census, 13% of women aged over 15 years are widowed, separated, or divorced. However, this is probably under-enumerated due to the social stigma. Most Kinh communities are patrilocal, which means that after marriage the couple lives in the husband's village and often with his family if he is the first son.

Both sons and daughters may inherit land. However, if a woman marries into another village, it may be difficult for her to take up her land rights. In the case of divorce, the wife has rights over any land that she has brought to the marriage and theoretically over a proportion of land used by the couple. Patriarchy underpins the functioning of the family. Throughout their lives, Vietnamese women must defer firstly to their fathers, then their husbands, and finally their eldest son. Wives should be compliant; they should not be seen to be the major decision maker or income earner; they should be sexually available to their husbands and take responsibility for contraception. Husbands are responsible for the behavior of their wives and have the right to discipline them where necessary.

Because the role of wife is that of a peacemaker, acts of domestic violence perpetrated by men rarely attract community criticism and are instead interpreted as the failure of the wife. Reconciliation is the preferred outcome of any domestic dispute. Consequently, separated and divorced women often carry blame within the community. Unmarried women should be chaste. Evidence to the contrary brings shame even in cases of sexual harassment, rape, incest, and forced prostitution.

These social attitudes that diminish the standing of women in the community have indirectly sanctioned domestic violence, lack of choice of contraception, male irresponsibility with respect to the transmission of sexual transmitted diseases (e.g., HIV/AIDS), trafficking of women, and female infanticide. Although reliable comparative data are not available, there is no evidence to suggest that Vietnam is more advanced than its neighbors in the area of gender-based violence. Although patriarchy is strong, women have substantial decision-making power within the family and it is perceived that this power has increased. However, some areas of decision making appear to remain in the province of men.

Women complain that they have little control over male expenditure on alcohol, tobacco, and gambling. They also note their lack of input into reproductive decisions; pressure exists for women to produce male progeny and the husband often insists on more children until a son is born, even though high birth rates have detrimental effects on women's health.

HEALTH AND NUTRITION

Since the implementation of *doi moi,* Vietnam has achieved great advances in health care. Many facilities have been upgraded and access to community health care has improved. Almost all communes have a health center, and of these 30% have a doctor and 82% have a midwife or obstetrics-pediatric assistant. Although access has improved nationally, some communities, mainly in poor and remote areas, are underserved.

Women have a greater demand for health services than men because of their reproductive roles and women's susceptibility to reproductive tract infections. Therefore, the lack of access to health care services has a greater impact on women. Fee for service, ineffective implementation of the fee exemption program, and inequitable budget allocation mechanisms have resulted in unequal access to quality health care. The fees and charges for these services are often out of the reach of the poorest households. The burden of taking care of sick children and the elderly is passed on to women in the family.

Poor health among ethnic minority households is due to isolation, lack of clean water, lack of infrastructure and equipment, high fertility rates, poor quality soil, shortage of food supply, and limited access to community health stations. Common health problems for ethnic minority women and their families include malaria, malnutrition, and respiratory and gynecological infections. These result in high levels of maternal mortality, obstetric complications, and maternal and child malnutrition. The gender gap in adult nutritional status is greater in rural areas, in poorer households, and among ethnic minorities; in resource-constrained households, women's share of food is lower than that of men.

New issues for women's health are becoming evident with improved awareness of the impact on women's health of male promiscuity and domestic violence. Although awareness of male promiscuity and female prostitution is increasing it is not clear whether the incidence itself is also increasing. In an environment where the use of condoms is not common and intravenous drug use is a significant problem, the risks of HIV/AIDS have grown. Although the number of reported cases of HIV/AIDS in Vietnam is still low compared to that in Thailand, it is increasing.

By December 2000, the number of reported HIV infections reached 32,000. However, it is estimated that 107,000 people are living with HIV/AIDS (0.2% of the adult population), of which 65% of cases are related to intravenous drug use. The prevalence of HIV in female sex workers in 2000 was 4.3% and 14% of all HIV cases in the country were women. Without improvement in the status of women both economically and socially, the fight against HIV/AIDS is a lost cause. Women's empowerment and the decrease in the spread of HIV/AIDS are intrinsically linked. Social attitudes restrict sexual empowerment for women. Women are responsible for contraception and the use of condoms is low. Although more than 50% of families now use modern contraception methods, the choice of contraception in isolated areas is limited to intra-uterine devices (38.5%).

The use of oral contraceptives is increasing but the present rate is only 4–6% of couples. Oral contraceptives are expensive because they are imported. Supply is unreliable in remote areas and rural lifestyles are not conducive to the rigor of the daily regime. Abortion is still the most common form of family planning in Vietnam. It is estimated that 40% of pregnancies are terminated, the highest rate in the world (2.5 per woman). Such high incidence of intrusive procedures has negative implications for women's health. Domestic violence is clearly a health issue for women. In the past, domestic violence often went unreported and was dealt with by the family or sometimes the Vietnam Women's Union and neighbors rather than the law. Social attitudes, which sanction a husband's right to discipline his wife, meant that domestic violence was not seen as problematic.

Rather than address either the causes or consequences of domestic violence, the Vietnamese family's response was to preserve the marriage. In recent years, official reports of domestic violence have increased and a greater number of cases are being heard in court. This reflects a cultural shift with respect to the rights of women encouraged by international pressure for the Government to recognize such violence as a problem.

EDUCATION AND TRAINING

Progress in male and female education has been impressive in Vietnam and the official rate of female literacy is high compared to that in neighboring countries. The policy of the VCP since the 1946 Constitution has been to provide equal access to education for boys and girls to enable them to participate fully in achieving national goals. The correlation between education for women and reduced birth rates, improved nutrition, and health is now well known and Vietnam's success in these areas is in part due to the focus on education for girls. Fertility rates are 53% lower and child mortality is 75% less for girls who have attended at least lower secondary education than for girls without schooling.

Enrollment and attainment rates in primary school have increased across the country and enrollment is nearly universal at the primary level. However, these national statistics mask the disadvantage experienced by people in remote areas, especially ethnic minorities and the poor. Disadvantage includes not only lack of access to education but also the poor quality of education and low levels of attainment in many rural areas. At the national level, no difference is reported between boys and girls in enrollment rate in primary school. However, gender gaps appear in the poorest households, in the Central Highlands, and among the Chinese and the ethnic minorities.

Nationally, the gender gap appears in secondary schooling, at 6% in lower secondary and 11% in upper secondary.

However, these gaps are narrow, especially in comparison to the initial high drop-out rate of girls following *doi moi* from 1990/91 to 1993/94. The gap is most pronounced within the poorest households, the rural areas, the Northern Uplands, the Mekong Delta, the Central Coast, and among ethnic minorities. Of those aged more than five-years old, 12% of girls and 7.5% of boys have never attended school, and these proportions have remained remarkably constant over the past 20 years. Of those aged between 6-14 years who have never attended school, 50% are from ethnic minority groups. The gap is closing for higher education but not for vocational and technical education.

Of some concern is the appearance of a gender gap in the levels of schooling completed by men and women in the age cohorts below 22 years. In the adult population, although the national level of literacy is high, two out of every three illiterate people are women. At present, 90% of adult males and 79% of adult females are literate according to the conventional definitions of literacy. Mean years of schooling are a better measure of education than enrollments, which do not reflect completion. On average, females have only 5.6 years of schooling compared to 6.8 for males but the largest gender gap occurs between Kinh and ethnic minorities.

The real disparities in education are not around the issues of gender but in the different levels of achievement and performance of students in rural and urban areas, ethnic minorities and Kinh groups, and the rich and the poor. Within the rural poor and ethnic minority students, gender disparity is exacerbated, making women in this group doubly disadvantaged. The gap between girls and boys for the lowest income quintile is larger than for the top quintile. In the poorest quintile, the gap between girls and boys in primary school enrollments is pronounced at 5%, and reaches 12% in lower secondary.

The working hours of primary pupils from the poorest quintile are double those of pupils from the richest one. The working hours of female pupils are 20– 50% longer than those of males from all quintiles and this rate is 100% more for female Hmong children. For ethnic minorities, other obstacles to education are limited access to neighborhood schools, poor quality teachers, and the perceived irrelevance of the Kinh curriculum taught in Vietnamese language. Attendance at high schools for ethnic minority pupils usually involves boarding school, which is considered more dangerous for girls.

Although girls perform better in both Vietnamese language and mathematics in primary school, social expectation supports sex segregation in high school and university courses. Sex segregation extends into employment and it appears that gender stereotyping is becoming more pronounced. Before *doi moi,* women as well as men were encouraged to engage in technical areas. It was expected that girls would do well in mathematics at school and later become engineers and doctors. Now, females tend to cluster in pedagogy, social sciences, and linguistics while males dominate technical and scientific courses. Current sex segregation, especially in technology, potentially disadvantages women from fully participating in new industries fostered by the Government, such as information technology, biotechnology, and new materials.

LEGAL RIGHTS

The legal rights of women were first institutionalized in Vietnam in the 1946 Constitution. Since then women's rights have been a central tenet of and are reflected in Vietnamese legislation. Men and women have equal civil rights with respect to economic opportunities, person and property, marriage and family matters, political participation, and public administration. The courts and institutions protect these rights. The penal code and the penal proceedings code also protect women against violence. Vietnam's participation in the World Conferences on Women and signing the Convention on the Elimination of All Forms of Discrimination Against Women (CEDAW) have exposed the Government to international expectations on women's rights.

Tension exists between the law and international conventions. A criticism sometimes made on women's rights legislation in Vietnam is the tendency for it to be protective rather than equalizing opportunities and burdens. For example, the Labor Code promulgated in 1995 is generous but effectively restricts the choices of women workers and encourages the employment of men over women. It is stated in the code that women workers can take a day off per month during menstruation. The labor code reinforces gender stereotypes with its requirement for a compulsory crèche only when women are employed rather than for all parent workers, maternity leave rather than parental leave, and compulsory early retirement for women.

Tensions also exist between the State and tradition on gender equity, and as the role of the State diminishes, gender gains are more easily eroded. Since 1946, gender equity initiatives in legislation and the associated social support were imposed from the top. The VCP adopted strong gender equity measures, which were implemented through its central planning function. However, with the progressive implementation of *doi moi*, state support for gender initiatives is diminishing. Reproductive functions, such as childcare and household work, have been withdrawn. Clear articulation of gender concerns in such documents as the socioeconomic plan for the next 10 years has also diminished. As the State withdraws from gender concerns, the lack of synergy with culture gives rise to a lack of compliance with these laws at the local level.

Even now, the implementation of existing legislation seems to vary according to personal commitment within local institutions. According to the 1996 Constitution, women and men are granted equal rights regarding property. Relevant laws, such as the Civil Code (1995), the Law on Marriage and Family (1986, 2000), and the Land Law (1993), govern the ownership of property and the regulations regarding land. According to law, family members must be consulted before the household head can make decisions about the transfer, sale, rent, inheritance, mortgage, and contribution of land as equity for a business. Land-use certificates in rural areas are registered in the name of the male household head in 80% of cases.

In urban areas, the tendency has been to register the

names of husband and wife and usually the family members as well. Registration of land title is very complicated because land is the most valuable asset and in some circumstances may be registered in the name of a friend in order to disguise assets from the State. The 2000 Law on Marriage and Family stipulates that land-use certificates for household common land must list the names of both spouses indicating shared possession. However, in the earlier Land Law, there is no mention of co-ownership. Questions now arise as to whether the certificates will be reissued under joint names. There is little ground swell to force these changes and staff of the General Department of Land Administration has little training in gender issues; most discussion of land at the commune level still excludes women.

Traditions of patriarchy challenge gender equity legislation and militate against compliance. International pressure groups argue that legislated equal rights to land are pivotal in the empowerment of women. Some international lobby groups argue that traditional values concerning the rights and roles of women have prevented women from enjoying equal access to land use. In practice, when women divorce, it is possible that they lose access to land, because the disposal of land is an extended family matter rather than a matter for the individual. When two people from the same village marry, they acquire land from both sides of the family. Upon divorce, the woman retains rights to her portion. Because Vietnam is largely patrilocal and women move to the village of the husband, women's access to land after divorce is unpredictable.

Distance from her birth village to the couple's land and uncomfortable proximity to in-laws militates against maintaining use rights to the land. Under these circumstances, women may receive compensation in rice and livestock, but success often depends on personal connection. Widowed women do not necessarily take over the land-use certificate which may remain in the name of the deceased husband, be transferred to the eldest son, or revert back to the husband's family, but they are less disadvantaged than divorced/separated women.

Gender-based violence is not a Vietnamese problem but a global problem. It takes the form of trafficking of women, exploitation of women as sex workers, rape, and domestic violence. Data on gender-based violence in Vietnam are scant and anecdotal and the problem has only recently received public attention. Available data suggest that since 1990, about 10,000 women and children have been sold, mainly as sex workers. According to MOLISA and UNICEF, there are currently 200,000 women involved in the sex industry of whom 10% are children and the number of domestic violence cases that have reached the courts has increased. Although the legal framework to punish domestic violence is enshrined in the Constitution, the Law on Marriage and Family, and the criminal code, the incidence is widespread.

The Lao Cai Participatory Poverty Assessment found that 40% of women in a lowland village and 70% in a highland village were regularly subjected to physical violence. Social attitudes toward the appropriate role of women within the family mean that the victim is often blamed for gender-based violence, even for victims of rape, incest, entrapment, and domestic violence. Case studies suggest that domestic violence is usually linked to poverty, alcohol and/or gambling, jealousy, or mental illness. In the case study research, it was found that men often cite women "talking too much" as the main misdemeanor that prompts domestic violence.

In a society where the extended family is the dominant unit, it is not uncommon for other members of the husband's family—both male and female—to engage in domestic violence against the wife. Victims experience a deep sense of shame and usually consider it a private matter although the demand for counseling centers, which focus on marriage and family issues, has reportedly increased. High-quality counseling and health services as well as a change in men's attitude to women are required in order to improve women's health and safety.

ECONOMIC PARTICIPATION

The population of Vietnam in 1999 was 76.4 million, of which more than 50% were in the labor force, most of which is engaged in agriculture and household production in rural areas. Women's economic participation rate declined slightly from 52% to 49% from 1989 to 1999. The participation rate (proportion in the labor force of those aged 15–55 years) of women in 1999 was high at 67% but has also has declined from 71% in 1989. The reasons are complex and may include later entry into the labor force because more girls are students after the age of 15 years; earlier departure from the labor force because women retire earlier (retirement for female wageworkers is compulsory at 55 years of age, 5 years earlier than for men); the impact of increased competition in the labor market; discrimination against women; increased well-being; and the social pressure for women to withdraw from the workforce and engage in domestic duties.

The return of women to domestic duties, and the "glass ceiling," discriminates against women reaching leadership positions and earning high salaries. In the past, the advantage of working until 60 years was insignificant because the salary for senior positions was little more than for a junior position. However, this has changed in recent years. Women form a greater proportion of the labor force in rural areas (49%) than in urban areas (46%). Income-generating opportunities for women in rural areas are greater than in urban areas due to access to household agriculture production and activities associated with agriculture, such as small-scale food processing (e.g., production of noodles, drying fish), handicraft production, trading, and limited seasonal labor.

The VLSS98 found that one quarter of urban women were not engaged in income-generating activities. Data from the VLSS93 and VLSS98 show that the proportion of women involved in domestic duties declined, but the censuses of 1989 and 1999 show the opposite. Urban household incomes are on average higher than rural household incomes, so the necessity for women to work may be perceived as less critical in urban areas. This is especially so in a changing social context in which patriarchal tendencies are reemerging and a male's status is elevated if he can support a nonworking wife. The

1999 Population and Housing Census shows that 39% of the labor force are involved in wage labor and of these 42% are women.

According to the VLSS98, which is a smaller sample, 38% of wage employees were women. Furthermore, between 1993 and 1998, male wage employment in rural areas increased at a faster rate for men (9%) than for women (4%), indicating an increase in seasonal farm laboring. In urban areas, wage employment showed no increase for women during this period, but an increase of 5% for men. In recent years, the State has become a less significant employer, especially for women.

Only 7.3% of economically active women are employed by the State. Women lost jobs in the state sector faster than men and by 1999 only 42% of state employees were women. During the early period of *doi moi*, it is estimated that female labor accounted for about 70% of the loss from the state sector. However, with continued reform of the state sector, it is expected that labor redundancy will be a male problem because most of the remaining overstaffing is of males in transportation and mining. In 2000, the Government announced a decision to reduce the public service by 15%. If this decision is implemented, past experience shows that there may be a more detrimental impact on women than on men.

Women total about 51% of nonstate sector employment. However, the women who lost their jobs in the state sector are not the same as those who have joined the nonstate sector. Increased competition in the state sector meant that employees with low skill and low productivity, including many older women, were made redundant or given early retirement, whereas those engaged in the nonstate sector tend to be young and relatively more skilled. Retrenchments from the state sector also resulted in the movement of women to household duties or self-employment in the informal sector.

For some, the informal sector is preferred because the flexibility is more compatible with family responsibilities in spite of the disadvantage of increased insecurity and fewer fringe benefits than in the state sector. But in the private sector income opportunities are greater with higher salaries and availability of overtime work, particularly in foreign-invested enterprises. The nonstate sector includes private domestic enterprises, the collective sector, joint ventures, and 100% foreign-invested enterprises. Foreign and domestic capital has created employment opportunities for women both in administration and light manufacturing, such as in textiles, clothing and footwear, and food processing. Women employees dominate in the foreign-investment sector (72%), the collective sector (54%), and joint ventures (52%).

Although gender divisions in wage labor exist, they are not as rigid as in many other countries. As a consequence, competition exists between male and female workers. The national pattern is that women are overrepresented in education, sales, food processing, accounting, and textile and garment manufacturing, and underrepresented in administration, management, services, skilled manual labor, and unskilled labor. Rural women wageworkers concentrate in agriculture, skilled manual labor, unskilled labor, and as educational professionals. Women's labor in rural areas is also used as a tool to overcome hardship.

Women are brought into a family through marriage to ease labor shortage. Young girls who leave the rural areas to seek employment in urban areas find unskilled jobs as street vendors, garbage collectors, maids, laborers and in cafes, restaurants, and beer stands. Women in Ho Chi Minh City have been sold to foreigners to ease poverty; children are adopted out for money. Economic participation does not guarantee empowerment. In urban areas, both men and women are engaged in skilled manual work. Women are concentrated in occupations of skilled manual workers (e.g., textile and garment workers and construction), professionals in some fields including education, and unskilled workers.

Urban men's occupations are more diverse, with a greater concentration of skilled workers in mining, metal works, woodworking, manufacturing, and handicrafts. Even in sectors dominated by women such as education, men hold most senior management positions. Although the seniority of women in both the public sector and state-owned enterprises was notable in 1989, women have become less prominent because of increased competition for senior positions. Women work about the same number of hours in income-earning activities but earn 14% less than men. Nevertheless, during the 1990s the wage gap between men and women decreased—from 33% in 1993 to 22% in 1998.

The gap between fringe income of men and women also decreased in this period, from 85% to only 23%. However, the wage differential varies over the working life cycle. Wage incomes for female heads of household start to decline once they reach 50 years old, whereas for men it continues to increase during working life. Wage rates are about 31% higher for both women and men in urban than in rural areas, but the wage gap in both areas is remarkably similar. It is clear that the gender disparity in income stems from levels of qualification, ability to hold several positions simultaneously, and overtime. Employees may have a substantive position as well as a position in a special "project," which also contributes income. It is easier for single childless women than for mothers to take advantage of such opportunities. Furthermore, wages in the foreign direct-investment sector tend to be higher than in the domestic sector. Women with children and/or who care for the aged, and older women with few skills or qualifications are the first to leave the wage labor force.

Bibliography

Adburgham, Alison. *Women in Print. Writing Women and Women's Magazines from Restoration to the Accession of Victoria.* London: Allen & Unwin, 1972.

Arnold, Ethel M. *Literature for Ladies, 1830-1930.* Manhattan: K.S.A.C. Press, 1930.

Barrell, Joan. *The Business of Women's Magazines.* 2nd ed. London: Kogan Page, 1988.

Beetham, Margaret. *Victorian Women's Magazines : An Anthology.* Manchester: Manchester University Press, 2001.

Boston Women's Health Book Collective. *Our Bodies Ourselves.* New York: Simon & Schuster, 1976.

Braithwaite, Brian. *The Business of Women's Magazines: The Agonies and the Ecstasies.* London: Associated Business Press, 1979.

Braithwaite, Brian. *Women's Magazines: The First 300 Years.* London: Peter Owen, 1995.

Brody, Michal, ed. *Are We There Yet? A Continuing History of Lavender Woman.* Iowa City; Aunt Lute Company, 1985.

Burman, Barbara, ed. *The Culture of Sewing: Gender, Consumption and Homedressmaking (Dress, Body, Culture).* Oxford: Berg, 1999.

Coakley, Mary Lewis. *1907-Sex, Sisterhood, and Self-Delusion: What Happened to Women's Magazines?* New Rochelle: Arlington House, c. 1979.

Dancyger, Irene. *A World of Women. An Illustrated History of Women's Magazines.* Dublin: Gill and Macmillian, 1978.

Danky, James P., ed. *Women's Periodicals and Newspapers from the 18th Century to 1981: A Union List of the Holdings of Madison, Wisconsin Libraries.* Boston: GK Hall, 1982.

Doughan, David, and Denise Sanchez. *Feminist Periodicals, 1855-1984: An Annotated Critical Bibliography of British, Irish, Commonwealth and International Titles.* Brighton: Harvester, 1987.

Eskridge, Melissa J. *How the Psychology of Women Is Presented in Women's Magazines,* 1986.

Ferguson, Marjorie. *Forever Feminine: Women's Magazines and the Cult of Femininity.* London: Heinemann, 1983.

Friedan, Betty. *The Feminine Mystique.* New York: Dell Publishing Co., Inc., 1963.

Gough-Yates, Ann. *Understanding Women's Magazines: Publishing, Markets and Readership.* London: Routledge, 2003.

Grimstad, Kirsten and Susan Rennie, eds. *The New Woman's Survival Catalog.* New York: Berkley Publishing Corporation, 1973.

Hermes, Joke. *Reading Women's Magazines: An Analysis of Everyday Media Use.* Cambridge: Polity Press, 1995.

Hoffmann, Phyllis P. *Women's Magazines.* 1983.

Incantalupo, Patricia. *The Portrayal of Women in Sport Advertising in Two Women's Fitness Magazines,* 1992.

Johnson, Judy M, ed. *Spot Illustrations from Women's Magazines of the Teens and Twenties: 828 Cuts of Women, Family, Home, Garden, Etc.* New York: Dover Publications, 1989.

Mann, Robert S. "Women and the Newspaper." *The University of Missouri Bulletin,* no. 2640.

Millum, Trevor. *Images of Woman: Advertising in Women's Magazines.* London: Chatto & Windus, 1975.

Ramet, Adèle. *Creating a Twist in the Tale: How to Write Winning Short Stories for Women's Magazines.* Plymouth: How To Books, 1996.

Shevelow, Kathryn. *Women and Print Culture: The Construction of Femininity in the Early Periodical.* London: Routledge, 1989.

Sievers, Sharon L. *Flowers in Salt: The Beginnings of Feminist Consciousness in Modern Japan.* Stanford: Stanford University Press, 1983.

Waller, Jane, and Michael Vaughan-Rees. *Women in Wartime; the Role of Women's Magazines 1939-1945.* London: Macdonald Optima, 1987.

White, Cynthia L. "Growth between the Wars: 1920-1938." In *Women's Magazines 1693-1968.* London: Michael Joseph Ltd, 1970.

White, Cynthia L. *Women's Magazines 1693-1968.* London: Michael Joseph Ltd, 1970.

Winship, Janice. *Advertising in Women's Magazines, 1956-74.* Birmingham: Centre for Contemporary Cultural Studies, University of Birmingham, 1980.

Winship, Janice. *Inside Women's Magazines.* New York: Pandora, 1987.

Yackey, Lena Millicent. *Contributions of Women's Magazines to Homemaking Problems on Food.* New York, 1930.

Index

U

V

W